Where the Old Roads Go

WHERE THE
OLD ROADS GO

*Driving the First Federal Highways
of Arizona, California, Colorado,
New Mexico, Nevada, and Utah*

George Cantor

Harper Perennial
A Division of HarperCollins Publishers

HarperCollins books may be purchased for educational, business, or sales promotional use. For information, please call or write: Special Markets Department, HarperCollins Publishers, Inc., 10 East 53rd Street, New York, NY 10022. Telephone (212) 207-7258; Fax (212) 207-7222.

FIRST EDITION

Library of Congress Cataloging-in-Publication Data

Cantor, George, 1941–
    Where the old roads go : driving the first federal highways of Arizona,
  California, Colorado, New Mexico, Nevada, and Utah / George Cantor. —1st ed.
      p. cm.
    Includes index
    ISBN 0-06-273075-4 (pbk.)
    1. Southwest, New—Description and travel—1981– 2. Roads—
  Southwest, New—History. 3. Southwest, New—History, Local.
  4. Cantor, George, 1941–   —Journeys—Southwest, New. I. Title.
  F787.C36   1992
  979—dc20   91-55385

92 93 94 95 96 ◆/MB 10 9 8 7 6 5 4 3 2 1

For Sherry,
beside me on the passenger side.

Contents

Introduction

On the second day of travel for this book, I left Alamogordo, New Mexico at dawn on a sparkling winter morning and headed north on U.S. 54. As I watched the rising sun turn the snowcap of Sierra Blanca into a crown of gold, I became convinced that I hadn't made a wrong turn when I decided to follow the old roads into the Southwest.

It had seemed altogether logical to write the first volume of *Where the Old Roads Go* about New England. The winding lanes that run among its green hills and white steeples are the very essence of the sort of travel experience that old roads can provide. Places with a history, people linked to the land, roads that tell a story. Moonlight in Vermont. Old Cape Cod.

In New England and New York, the old roads preserve their identities, too. They seem to maintain their sense of individuality with a certain scrupulousness. Even when their routes have been taken over by an Interstate, the old roads are usually kept up at a slight remove, bearing their shield-shaped highway numbers and going about their business.

This isn't true in the six states that make up America's southwestern corner. Looking at the highway maps, I could see that many of the old roads had simply been cut off or cut up by the

Interstates. Roads that once had spanned the country from the Atlantic to the Pacific now stopped in Arizona or Utah, with the remainder of their routes usurped by newer superhighways. Distances appeared greater here, the roots shallower, and the history paler.

However, what I found as I traveled were roads that had been in use before the Plymouth Colony was settled, villages that were ancient when Boston was still a circle of huts, and churches whose bells tolled before those on Connecticut's greens were even cast.

Along the way, I wandered into the old mission at Zuni Pueblo and spent a magical morning with an Indian artist, who explained the symbolism of the religious wall paintings he and his father had worked on for the last 20 years; I shivered in the predawn stillness while waiting for the sun's first rays to strike the Grand Canyon; and I walked through the eerie quiet of the former Japanese–American detention camp at Manzanar.

There was the restaurant on U.S. 89, in Kanab, Utah, owned by a family that specializes in catering mobile kitchens for forest firefighters; and the guide at the Sharlot Hall Museum, in Prescott, Arizona, who told me the story of the remarkable woman for whom the place was named with all the pride of place of any Yankee.

Yes, the Interstates do chop up many of the old roads here. Route 66 is just a memory now in the region of the country that it once unlocked. But a tiny segment of that road does survive…and I followed it to recapture a sense of what the early automotive travelers saw and felt as they drove west. I also have outlined 22 other drives in which the history and beauty of the Old Southwest still come shining through. This is Old Road country, too.

Where the Old Roads Go

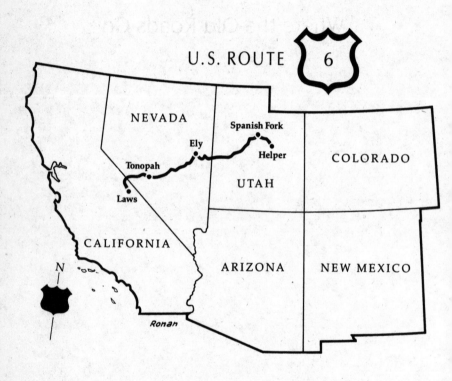

U.S. ROUTE 6

NEVADA

Spanish Fork

Ely

Tonopah

Helper

UTAH

COLORADO

Laws

CALIFORNIA

ARIZONA

NEW MEXICO

N

Ronan

Across the Great Basin

◯

U.S. 6

Helper, Utah to Bishop, Calif.
583 miles

This is the final segment of what used to be America's longest road. Now it's only number two, behind U.S. 20, because California took away its last few hundred miles and gave them a state highway number instead. Nasty business that. So while U.S. 6 once ran all the way from Provincetown, Massachusetts on the tip of Cape Cod, to Long Beach, California, its official end is now in Bishop, just over the state line from Nevada.

The Interstate system also chops up this road's identity throughout Colorado and eastern Utah. We won't pick it up until it breaks away from U.S. 191 in central Utah and starts a journey that takes it through the Wasatch Mountains, some of the most barren desert in the country, America's newest national park, and storied Nevada mining camps, to the base of the Sierra Nevada.

MILEPOSTS

The road diverges from U.S. 191 just north of Helper and quickly heads into the Price River Canyon. There's a Bureau of Land Management campground just off the road, with hiking trails to scenic overlooks above the gorge. The road follows a natural gap between the mountain ranges of the state's central area, one of the first avenues of Utah's exploration. Spanish parties sent out from Santa Fe to try and find an overland route to Monterey, on the Pacific coast, came this way in 1776.

At Soldier Summit, the highest point on the route at 7,454 feet, you're at the meeting point of three national forests. Ashley is to the east, Uinta to the north, and Manti La Sal to the west. This is also the divide between the Colorado River and Great Salt Lake, a geographical pivot for the entire state. The Soldier in the name supposedly came from a military man buried here; but how long ago, and whether he was Spanish or American have been obscured by time.

The area to the south was once the site of a number of ozocerite mines. Ozocerite is a mineral wax substance used in expensive candles because of its higher boiling point. Only one other deposit of the stuff, in The Ukraine, was ever located.

As the road descends, it enters Spanish Fork Canyon, an area noted for its spectacular fall colors. The river was named for those early gadabouts from Santa Fe, Frs. Silvestre Velez de Escalante and Francisco Atanasio Dominguez. Road and river lead into the Utah Valley, acclaimed by the peripatetic priests as the fairest in all of New Spain. It is still a lush and glowing vista, coming after the stark desert and mountain country behind us. While the Spanish were the first to visit the site, the town itself was settled by a Mormon group from Iceland in 1850.

The highway turns abruptly south here, away from the heavily populated heart of the state and along the western slope of the Uintah Range. About midway between Spanish Fork and Salem is the site of the Dream Mine. The image of huge lodes of ore came to a local Mormon bishop in his sleep in 1900 and he sank tunnels into the mountain here for the next 40 years trying to find them. He didn't. All of which indicates that if you follow your dreams there is always the chance of getting shafted.

Salem is built around a pond and was, in fact, originally called Pond Town. Payson is built along Peteetneet Creek but its founders had the good sense to simply name it Payson. It is regarded as Utah's onion capital and its Annual Onion Days draws large crowds over Labor Day Weekend. Mt. Nebo, at 11,528 feet, looms high on the southern horizon. The peak is named for the mountain from which Moses was given his one brief look at the Promised Land.

Santaquin was named for a Ute chief, although his father had been an equally prominent tribal leader. But his name was Squashhead. Now which one would you name your town for? This is sour-cherry country, but just a few miles to the west the main cash crop is peaches. The town of Elberta is named for that variety of the fruit.

In between is Goshen, another town with Biblical associations. It is named for the part of Egypt inhabited by the Israelites. Among America's Bible-reading pioneers Goshen was an ever popular name for agricultural settlements, because the Good Book described it as a land of plenty. This site was personally selected by Brigham Young, but it is not quite as plentiful as it used to be. When first settled it was situated on the southern shore of Utah Lake, but the vast irrigation projects in the surrounding farmlands have caused the water to recede four miles from Goshen.

Now the highway crosses the Tintic Range and enters the valley of the same name. The area is studded with old mining towns that sprang up after George Rust struck gold here in 1869. Over the next half-century, $363 million in gold, silver, copper, lead, and zinc was taken from this valley. **Eureka** is the best preserved of the mining towns in the vicinity and a museum of the Tintic district's mineral fortunes is contained in City Hall. The nearby towns of Mammoth and Silver City contain vestiges of former mining prosperity.

Little Sahara Recreation Area preserves a region of shifting sand dunes, the northern edge of the Sevier Desert, belonging to the Bureau of Land Management. There are two campgrounds on the site and a visitor center. This is sheep country here on the desert's rim—Jericho Campground was named after a former shearing depot for the Pahvant Valley herds. (By the way, Jericho makes the third reference in the last 50 miles to places associated with the wanderings of the Israelites on the way to Canaan. It isn't hard to figure out how the Mormon settlers viewed their own entrance into the Promised Land of Utah.)

The highway crosses the Sevier River and enters **Delta**, leading town of an area that was once a marshy wasteland. But water diversion projects turned it into farms and at one point it produced one-quarter of all the alfalfa seed in the United States. West of Delta is the start of the Great Basin. This vast region lying between the high ranges of the Rockies and the Sierra, containing no natural outlet to the sea, was named by explorer John C. Fremont. A Great Basin Museum in Delta serves as an introduction to the history and ecology of the area. The national park of the same name still lies ahead of us in Nevada.

Just past Delta is the turnoff to the town of Deseret. Although the name seems to refer to the stark surrounding country, Deseret is actually a word that turns up frequently in Mormon chronicles. It means "honey bee." The bee was a symbol of industry and fruitfulness to the Latter Day Saints, and the name was originally applied to the entire territory settled by the Mormons. It's still seen in the names of many Utah businesses, including one of Salt Lake City's daily newspapers. This town was named for Fort Deseret, established nearby in 1866 during the Ute Black Hawk War, which really wasn't as much a war as it was a series of guerilla raids directed against settlers in the remote southwestern part of the territory. The raids lasted three years and about 50 settlers were killed before peace was made. The ruins of the old fort are now part of a state park, with a picnic area set up around it. (The Ute leader Black Hawk had no connection with the Sac chief of the same name for whom an earlier war in Illinois was named.)

Just west of the old stock-raising town of Hinckley was the site of the Topaz Relocation Center, where 10,000 Japanese-Americans were interned during the wartime hysteria that followed Pearl Harbor. (The center in Manzanar California, is described in the chapter on U.S. 395.)

The road enters the wild, barren country of the Sevier Desert. Again, the name is misleading. Sevier comes from the Spanish word *severo*, which early chroniclers took as a reference to the severity of the land. But historians now feel it was probably named for San Severo, a Spanish saint, and then altered by American settlers in honor of frontier statesman John Sevier. The original road ran to the north of the current route, through even more rugged country in the Confusion Mountains, named for the crisscrossing arroyos on their slopes. The new route, cut through in the 1940s, simply skirts the edge of Confusion. It also runs along the northern shore of dry Sevier Lake.

After this long, desolate run, things perk up considerably across the state line in Nevada. Wheeler Peak, second highest in the state at 13,061 feet, dominates the skyline. It is also the centerpiece of **Great Basin National Park**, established in 1986. This was formerly Lehman Caves National Monument. The caves, largest limestone caverns in the west, are still an integral part of the park, but its scope was expanded to embrace features that define the distinct geology, animal life, and scenery of the Great Basin. There are mountain meadows and a glacial field along the drive, which runs up to the 10,000-foot level of Wheeler Peak. A hiking trail from the end of that road leads to the Bristlecone Pine forest. These trees are among the oldest living things on Earth, with one stand estimated to be 4,000 years old. Wildlife in the park ranges from animals found on the desert floor to subarctic species on Wheeler's slopes. The Lehman Caves are noted for the rich colors of the limestone formations. The entrance was discovered in 1885 by Absolom Lehman. He was hauling logs down the mountain when he broke through the snow's crust and suddenly found himself amid stalagmites. Non-strenuous tours run for 90 minutes and the temperature is a constant 50 degrees. The entrance to the National Park is south from the highway on Nevada 487 through the town of Baker.

U.S. 6 continues on its scenic way as it heads west. It climbs to Sacramento Pass, at 7,154 feet, drops into Spring Valley, then ascends once more to Conners Pass, at 7,723 feet. This is an outstanding mountain drive along the southern edge of Humboldt National Forest. There are turnouts and scenic overlooks at the crest of both passes. As the road drops once again into Ely, there is a turnoff to the south on an unnumbered county road, which leads to a unique bit of pioneer history. The Ward Charcoal Ovens were built in the 1870s during a silver mining boom in Ely. Charcoal was needed to fire the smelters that reduced ore from the mines. Whole forests in White Pine County were denuded for the ovens in this fuel-scarce area before the boom ran its course. This group of six beehive-shaped ovens on the slopes of Ward Mountain are among the best preserved in the state and are designated a state historic monument.

The highway skirts the edge of the copper-mining town of Ely, which is described more fully in the chapters on U.S. 50 and U.S. 93. It bends around 7,316-foot-high Murray Summit and strikes off across open country, with Ward Mountain towering to the east.

Angling southwest, the highway clips a corner of Humboldt National Forest, crossing over at 6,999-foot-high Currant Summit. The flat formations of the Pancake Range rise to the north as the road enters an area of dark volcanic rock. Just beyond Black Rock Summit is the turnoff to Lunar Crater. This 400-foot-deep pit was created by violent volcanic upheavals about 1,000 years ago. Cinder cones and piles of frozen lava were tossed about in wild disorder, creating a landscape that looks as wild and untouched as the surface of the moon. The crater is six miles south of the highway on a dirt road.

The crossroads of Warm Springs is all that remains of a stage-coach stop on the Ely–Tonopah line. The road passes grazing lands on the edge of Toiyabe National Forest, with 9,327-foot Pinon Peak on the north and the 9,404-foot bulk of Kawich Peak on the south.

There is a terrible beauty about this empty land. Isolated peaks, each fold of their crenellated surfaces clearly outlined against the sky, rise in the distance. The desert floor stretches off to an endless horizon. A man-made structure is an event, every shack a land-mark. Nevada is one of the fastest growing states, but almost all the population is clustered in the metropolitan areas of Las Vegas and Reno. Out here in the center, fears about overpopulation and crowding and gridlocked roads seem like impulses from distant galaxies. There is nothing here but open space.

Tonopah is a town of about 2,000 people but it seems like a metropolis in this area. To be fair, it once almost was. Around the turn of the century, it was Nevada's liveliest mining camp. That's a long time ago, but still it remains the seat of Nye County, mostly because there aren't any other towns in Nye County. The county was even emptier than that back in May 1900, when Jim Butler wandered into the area looking for some runaway burros. With not much else to do, the part-time prospector chipped some rock from a nearby shelf. It looked a little like silver ore, but Butler was too broke to have it assayed. A friend sent it up to the school superintendent in Austin, who dabbled in chemistry. He ran some tests and hurriedly sent a message by stagecoach that Butler better get back to where he found it and stake out a claim. A reluctant fortune hunter, Butler still believed the find was a fluke. His wife persuaded him to return three months after his first find. She named his claim Mizpah, another one of the Biblical references in which this road abounds. In Genesis, Mizpah was the name of a stone tower built by Jacob and his father-in-law, Laban, as an emblem of the Lord's care. The word means "watchtower" in Hebrew.

The name was well-suited, because the first return from the smelter came in at $800 a ton. Since then, the Mizpah and surrounding mines have brought in $125 million. The Austin superintendent quit his job and came down to stake a claim and lay out a new town. The assayer who had turned down Butler's original request for a free evaluation came running to get in on the strike, too. Mrs. Butler named the new community, as well as the mine, choosing two Shoshone words that mean "greasewood spring."

The great Klondike gold rush was coming to an end, and prospectors flocked to Tonopah. Even Wyatt Earp showed up to open a bar. But Tonopah was an unusually orderly place for a mining town. Violence was kept to a minimum and well-run city services developed. The gracious Mizpah Hotel opened in 1907 and six years later silver production was clicking along at $9.5 million annually. But that was the peak. The mines began to decline soon after and by 1930 the town had shrunk to its present size. The Central Nevada Museum, just south of Tonopah's center, features displays from all the old mining towns in the vicinity, of which Tonopah is the only one that can still be called a town. There is antique mining equipment, the central telephone switchboard from nearby Goldfield, a restored miner's cabin, and a wide variety of other local historical exhibits, both inside and outside the museum building. The Mizpah Hotel has also been handsomely restored and houses a restaurant and casino. A few small mines still operate in the area and some locations permit access to rock hounds. Check the Chamber of Commerce for a list. Old Jim Butler is recalled each Memorial Day weekend, with dancing, parades and burro races, to salute the beasts that brought him here.

The pink peaks of the Monte Cristo Range rise to the north as U.S. 6 heads out of town. After the publication of Alexander Dumas's romantic adventure, "The Count of Monte Cristo," in the mid-19th century, the name became synonymous with great wealth. Early miners in this area, admirers of French literature, named the mountains in anticipation. They did find some turquoise near Coaldale, but the most lucrative mines in the area are indicated in the town's name.

Soon the towering summits of the Sierra become visible on the western horizon. We cross Montgomery Pass, and directly to the south is Boundary Peak, the highest point in Nevada at an elevation of 13,140 feet. As soon as we cross into California, peaks a good 1,000 feet higher that are part of the White Mountain range rise on the east. The highway turns south into the Chalfant Valley and with the Inyo National Forest along the heights at either side of the road, we pull into the old railroad town of **Laws**.

FOCUS

On April 1, 1883, the first train on the Carson and Colorado Railroad arrived in Laws. The line had only been incorporated three years before to serve the mining communities of west central Nevada and the growing agricultural settlements of California's Owens Valley. Its southern terminus was extended four months later to Keeler, California, a supply base for silver mines near the north shore of Owens Lake.

The *Slim Princess* was a nice, tidy little narrow gauge line that for the next 77 years was a familiar part of the daily routine of this area. Before the roads were built, this line was the area's only connection to the rest of California; hooking up with Pullman service to Los Angeles at its southern terminus, and with the main line of the Southern Pacific, heading for San Francisco Bay, on the north.

The Slim Princess was the lifeline of the eastern Sierra. The line carried farm products to the mining camps and urban markets on the Pacific Coast, and ores designated for outside smelters. It brought back manufactured goods. Then on April 30, 1960, they shut the railroad down.

Use of the line was "declining and unpredictable," said the Southern Pacific in its application to discontinue service to the Interstate Commerce Commission. Moreover, the time lost in transferring shipments between the standard-sized cars and this narrow-gauge anachronism, the last of its kind west of the Rockies, was economically disastrous.

The original Carson and Colorado Line had gone out of business long before, swallowed up by the Southern Pacific in 1900; although executive R. J. Laws, for whom this town was named, was retained as superintendent. The name itself was discontinued in 1912. Twenty years later, passenger service through Laws ended, and in 1943 they tore up the track to the north, between here and Mina, Nevada. Service continued between Laws and Keeler but it was just a matter of time before that too came to an end, and 17 years later time ran out.

But the Southern Pacific was not without a sense of history. On the last day of the line's operation, the railroad deeded the Laws station, an assortment of rolling stock, Locomotive Number 9 (a Baldwin built in 1909), and the surrounding land to the city of Bishop and Inyo County. And on April 1, 1966, exactly 83 years to the day that the railroad came to Laws, the station was reborn as a railroad museum.

Laws is now a wonderful evocation of an old railroad town, the sort that has just about disappeared from America. The original depot is still in place, looking as it did when the Slim Princess was in its prime. The Post Office, which closed when the trains stopped coming, is open again. A variety of historic buildings from the Owens Valley have been brought here and assembled in a small-town setting. The station agent's home may be visited, as well as a Wells Fargo office, a country store, and other businesses that would have flourished in such a community.

The biggest attraction is still the rail apparatus, including the hand-operated turntable that was used for the entire life of the

Laws terminal. There is an original water tower, pumphouse, and loading bunkers. Railroad buffs will want to linger for hours. Even those whose nostalgia for railroads is limited to whistling a few bars of "Chattanooga Choo Choo" will find it fascinating.

* * *

The road runs on another five miles to Bishop, market center of the Owens Valley, where it comes to an end at the junction with U.S. 395. Its final 314 miles, which once made U.S. 6 the longest old road in the country, are now as much a memory as those antique railroad mementoes back in Laws.

VISITING HOURS

UTAH

Delta: Great Basin Museum, (801) 864-5013. At 328 W. 100 North. Tuesday–Sunday, 1–4. Donation.

Eureka: Tintic Mining Museum, (801) 433-6842. Top floor of City Hall. Call during weekday business hours. Free.

NEVADA

Great Basin National Park: (702) 234-7331. Lehman Caves are open daily, 8–5, Memorial Day–Labor Day, tours at 9, 11, 2, and 4 at other times. Admission.

Tonopah: Central Nevada Museum, (702) 482-9676. South of downtown, on Logan Field Road. Daily, 11–5, May–September; Tuesday–Saturday, noon–5 at other times. Free.

CALIFORNIA

Laws: Railroad Museum, (619) 873-5950. On U.S. 6. Daily, 10–4; some exhibits closed, mid-November–February. Donation.

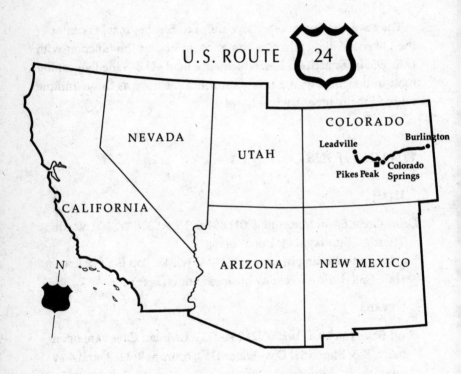

U.S. ROUTE 24

COLORADO

NEVADA

UTAH

Leadville

Burlington

Pikes Peak

Colorado
Springs

CALIFORNIA

N

ARIZONA

NEW MEXICO

Pikes Peak or Bust

⬡

U.S. 24

Burlington, Colo. to Minturn, Colo.
319 miles

This was one of the roads intended to fill in the open spaces between major midwestern routes. It begins in the northern outskirts of Detroit, then stays beyond the fringe of most urban areas on its way, with the exceptions of Toledo and Kansas City. Its path across Indiana, Illinois, Missouri, and Kansas is predominantly rural, but by the time it reaches the Colorado border it has hooked up with Interstate 70.

The partnership only lasts another 86 miles, then U.S. 24 darts towards **Colorado Springs** and a run into the Rockies and the magnificent South Park area, under the shadow of legendary Pikes Peak.

MILEPOSTS

Where does the West begin? Well, you can make a good case for Colorado. While some of its old cow towns and Santa Fe Trail landmarks make Kansas a credible candidate, the state still looks to the agricultural Midwest to get its bearings. Once you cross the Colorado line, though, there is no doubt what part of the country you are in.

Burlington drives the lesson home. It has turned an area just off its business district into Old Town, a main street out of the mythical West. Authentically restored buildings from surrounding Kit Carson County fill the functions they might have served at the time of the great cattle drives. There is melodrama in the theater, dancing in the saloon, gunfights in the streets and, for the more studious, a museum recapping a history of the state's eastern plains. A railroad town, Burlington prospered briefly as a grain-shipping point early in the 20th century, when the price of wheat steadily climbed and farmers moved onto the plains. But the agricultural depression of the 1920s and the Dust Bowl of the following decade ended all that. Now it's a cow town again and each June Burlington puts on a Longhorn Cattle Drive, to give everyone an idea of what a cowboy's life was like in the last century.

An easier way to go horseback historically is to mount up on the Kit Carson County Carousel. A National Historic Landmark, this merry-go-round was built in 1905 and is one of the largest wooden carousels remaining in the country. The throbbing sounds of the Wurlitzer Military Organ send the brightly colored animals circling around a centerpiece of oil paintings. It operates throughout the summer and during the Christmas season.

The highway is locked in with the Interstate here, paralleling the old Burlington and Northern rail route, which is now operated by Mid-States Railroad. Bethune is another onetime grain town which has reverted to a ranching economy. The World War I years brought in the peak prices for corn raised here, and in a burst of enthusiasm its residents named it for the French town on the western front. V.S. King, less of a romantic, simply named the town he founded after his niece, Vona.

Most of the places named for railroad magnate Henry Flagler are in Florida, the state he practically developed single-handedly. But here on the Plains is a rail town that bears his name, too. Just north of town is Flagler Reservoir, an unexpected speck of blue amid the surrounding brown landscape, which is a treasured recreation grounds and wildlife preserve.

In **Arriba**, the Tarado Mansion was originally built as the Adams Hotel. Reopened as a museum in 1973, this six-columned structure, which looks like a cotton plantation that took a wrong turn somewhere in Arkansas, has acquired an eclectic assortment of historic items from the region. These include the harp of Mrs. George Custer and the tea coat of the Unsinkable Molly Brown.

The plains roll on, climbing in elevation as they head for their meeting with the Front Range of the Rockies. Genoa perches on the crest that divides the Arkansas and South Platte River watersheds. A wooden tower west of town gives travelers their first panoramic view of the mountains, which are now about 70 miles ahead.

Limon grew up as a rail division point along the old Smoky Hill Trail from Kansas, which is now the route of U.S. 40 (see that chapter for a further description). This is where the Rock Island Line came through from the east. Rides are given along its old right-of-way on the Twilight Limited, a restored 1924 passenger coach drawn by an engine that once hauled logging trains in the Michigan north woods.

The town is a switching point for the highways, too, as U.S. 24 drops south and follows the Rock Island route from this point on. Many Colorado towns bear names of Indian origin, but this route has two communities with names drawn from the Asian India. According to the story, the wife of a Rock Island official was so caught up in a Rudyard Kipling novel that she named Simla and Ramah after locations in the book.

Now the mountains loom ahead as a constant presence and the road angles southwest into the booming city of Colorado Springs. Established as a health resort, the place is now the second biggest community in the state, with a population of more than 250,000.

The highway enters the east side of town as Platte Avenue. Just a few blocks to the north, across Union Boulevard, is the U.S. Olympic Complex, training site for the country's Olympic teams and headquarters for the governing organization. The same factors that made the Springs attractive to its first promoters as a resort—a mountain-edge setting and mild year-round climate, were the decisive factors in its being selected for this facility. It has an ongoing program of training for international competitions, with facilities for 14,000 athletes on the 36-acre site. There are six gymnasiums, an indoor shooting range, a velodrome, a sports medicine center, and the offices of fifteen different sports organizations. Walking tours are given daily.

The highway skirts the center of town and then heads west onto the broad shoulder of **Pikes Peak**.

FOCUS

Nowhere else in America did the West change so quickly. In just 12 years, the wagon trains bearing the motto "Pikes Peak or Bust" had disappeared, to be replaced by sanitariums and picture-postcard stands. The crude mining camps and hell-for-leather roughnecks were gone, and in their place came publicists who dabbled in romantic images and liveried servants at the front doors of mansions.

At the beginning of the 19th century, Pikes Peak was first glimpsed from afar by an exploring party, who were awestruck at its isolated grandeur and doubted that it could ever be climbed. By the end of the 19th century, excursion trains carried tourists to its summit and a woman would stand at the crest and compose a song that became a hymn to the country's natural beauty.

Most people are amazed to learn that Pikes Peak, at 14,110 feet, only ranks as the 28th-highest mountain in Colorado. Its name is so well known, so much a symbol of the westward movement, that they simply assume it is the top of the Rockies. It was really the mountain's position, standing apart from any other peak of a similar height, that led to its singular identification.

The first published description of the mountain was written in 1806 by Lieutenant Zebulon Pike. Lewis and Clark were on their way home from the Northwest when this U.S. Army officer started off on his expedition up the Arkansas River, the first organized exploration of the southwestern lands on the Spanish frontier. Pike was in the vicinity of Las Animas (see U.S. 50) when he first saw the peak and estimated its height at 18,000 feet. Pike's book about his adventures was published in 1810, before Lewis and Clark managed to break into print, and his descriptions raised huge excitement about these lands. Even when the first recorded ascent of the mountain was made in 1820 by Dr. Edwin James, and his expedition decided to officially name the peak in his honor, no one paid any attention. It was so imprinted on the popular consciousness as the peak that Pike had found, that no name change was possible. It was officially recorded as Pikes Peak in a map published in 1835 and the case was closed.

The route through Ute Pass to the great trapping grounds of South Park, now followed by U.S. 24, made Pikes Peak a familiar landmark to the earliest western travelers. When gold was discovered here in 1859, such travel increased enormously. This was the era of "Pikes Peak or Bust," when this one mountain became the catch phrase for heading West. The mines busted quickly and the Civil War soon stopped the rush altogether, but its power as a symbol of the West had been established forever.

That's when William J. Palmer arrived to cash in on the symbol. An executive with the Denver and Rio Grande Railroad, Palmer was also a born promoter. He felt that the aura of adventure associated with Pikes Peak could be transferred to a resort at its base.

He envisioned a western rival to Newport, Rhode Island, a place for the wealthy to enjoy the salubrious air in civilized comfort, and, not so incidentally, ride his railroad to get there. A settlement already existed at the place Palmer chose, a scrungy mining town called Colorado City. Rather than traffic with the yahoos of that community, Palmer plotted an entirely new town just down the hill to the east, on the old wagon road to Raton Pass.

By the mid-1870s, Colorado Springs was established as a fashionable resort, and, to a more serious purpose, as a center for treating tubercular cases. The clear mountain air was regarded as helpful and the presence of natural springs, in an age convinced of the benefits of thermopathy for every ailment, clinched it.

Palmer was masterful at manipulating imagery. An area of red sandstone rock formations on the western edge of his new town was familiar to the first settlers. The rowdy bunch in Colorado City had suggested turning it into a beer garden. But attorney R. E. Cable, who owned the property, indignantly refused, saying instead that it was a garden of the gods. Palmer seized on that and formalized Cable's description. Garden of the Gods became the essence of western romance, the most famous of the region's natural wonders. It was illustrated in countless chromo reproductions and hung in living rooms throughout the East. Naturally, anyone who traveled west wanted to see it, and they would take Palmer's railroad to get there.

By 1891, a cog railroad had been built from another of Palmer's communities, **Manitou Springs**, to the summit of Pikes Peak. Two years later, Katherine Lee Bates made the trip. Moved by the unencumbered view across the plains, she wrote the poem that became known as "America, the Beautiful." The poem's images of natural wonder and benevolent progress perfectly reflected the late 19th-century concept of harmony between man and nature that evidenced God's grace upon America. The song is also much easier to sing than "The Star Spangled Banner." For those put off by the martial theme of Francis Scott Key's verse, "America, the Beautiful" has come to be regarded as the "Alternate Anthem."

Another woman who shaped the image of the West also came to this area. Helen Hunt Jackson was one of the first popular writers to portray Indians with sympathy. Her most famous novel, *Ramona*, was written after she had moved to California. But her 1881 book, *A Century of Dishonor*, which chronicled the broken promises and harsh treatment of Native Americans, was written during her residence in Colorado Springs. Three reconstructed rooms of her home are exhibited in the city's Pioneer Museum, a few blocks off U.S. 24, on South Tejon Street.

In the 1890s, the gold strike at Cripple Creek came in, and Colorado Springs became the commercial center for the mines. Newly enriched prospectors built their mansions along Cascade Avenue. Between 1900 and 1910, it was the richest city per capita in the nation. The McAllister House Museum, in one of the oldest Victorian residences in the city, displays material relating to that era.

Colorado City was long ago absorbed by its more respectable neighbor, but part of the old mining camp has been restored as an Historic District. Old Colorado City is now an entertainment and shopping area. Watch for the turnoff, near 21st Street, as you leave The Springs heading west.

The drive through the Garden of the Gods also leaves U.S. 24, just west of The Springs. Now a city park, this is still a landmark of the West, and the fancifully titled formations are a mandatory stop on any trip through the area. Best times to visit are morning or late afternoon, when the sun is low and reflects off the red rocks. Also take in the White House Ranch, at the far entrance to the park. This is a fine re-creation of a working Colorado ranch at the time when the western myths were being created.

Manitou Springs is the terminal of the cog rail line that climbs to the top of Pikes Peak. The automobile road to the summit begins a few miles ahead in **Cascade**. But in the middle of Manitou Springs is a museum displaying the cars that have entered the Pikes Peak Hill Climb since its inception in 1923. The Race to the Clouds is held every Fourth of July weekend. The train ride from town climbs 7,500 feet in 80 minutes to the top of the mountain Zebulon Pike thought could never be conquered. On clear days, you can see Denver and most of the route you have just driven across eastern Colorado. It is still the fruited plain and purple mountain majesty Katherine Lee Bates saw a century ago. From the summit, little seems to have changed.

* * *

The springs here were known to French trappers as early as the 1730s and John C. Fremont visited them on his 1843 trip. They were neutral ground among the Indian tribes, a fact that led Palmer to name them for Manitou, the Great Spirit. Since this word is part of the Algonquian language, spoken by peoples 1,000 miles or so to the east, the name is a bit of a stretch. The town's Victorian district is now a National Historic District, with Fountain Creek splashing through the center. There is a sizable arts and crafts presence in the shops, making it a fine place for strolling. Miramont Castle, a 46-room Victorian mish-mash of romantic architecture, built in 1895, is preserved as a museum of the period.

Now backtrack to the eastern entrance of town and take the U.S. 24 bypass. This leads to the turnoff for Cave of the Winds. Known for its enormous rooms and richly adorned formations, the cave is still being explored and expanded, with new passageways opened to the Temple of Silence area in the late 1980s. But the cave is only part of the attraction. Access is by a narrow, one-way road, which on the return trip passes through Williams Canyon, a splendid scenic drive.

Back on Highway 24, the road immediately enters Pike National

Forest and start its climb to Ute Pass. In Cascade is the turnoff to the Pikes Peak Highway, a 19-mile toll road that twists its way 7,300 feet up the mountain. The road is usually open from May through October, but the season can be shortened emphatically by weather. This is mountain driving at its most challenging, with hairpin turns and narrow shoulders. It is recommended that those who get nervous on this sort of road take the bus tour and that those who do make the drive pay careful attention. It is also a good idea to switch off the air conditioner, unless you enjoy watching that little pointer on the temperature gauge wiggle up into the red area. The road, opened in 1915, is not the highest in the state (the ascent of Mt. Evans, to the north, goes 154 feet higher). But it's high enough to reach the top.

Back on the ground, U.S. 24 runs through the community of Woodland Park, at the base of the Front Range. At Divide is the turnoff to Cripple Creek, opened in 1918 as a toll road over the grade of the Colorado Midland Railroad. The trains had stopped running a few years before when major mine operations shut down.

We ascend to 9,165-foot high Ute Pass, which commanded the entrance to the territory of the Ute tribe and which they vigorously defended in several battles with Plains peoples, especially the Arapahoe. It was Colorado's Thermopylae, a strategic passage running through such a narrow defile that it could be defended by vastly outnumbered forces. The same consideration also made it a preferred hangout for highwaymen. The "Bloody Espinozas," a clan of cutthroats, were credited with killing a dozen men, travelers heading to the gold fields. There are two dozen stories told of gold shipments that vanished and stagecoaches that disappeared on this road.

The gold and stagecoaches may never be found, but in 1874 an even greater marvel turned up just south of **Florissant**, at the western end of the pass. Fossil beds buried by volcanic ash and lava 35 million years ago were discovered, with intact specimens of insects, leaves, and giant tree stumps—a museum of a prehistoric world buried alive. The Florissant Fossil Beds are now designated a national monument. Many of the specimens taken from their place of burial are on display, and there is a nature walk to a fossilized sequoia forest as well as a tour of the homestead that was inhabited here when the beds were uncovered.

The South Platte River is crossed at Lake George and just to the south of town is Eleven Mile Canyon Reservoir, a part of the Denver water system noted for its brown and rainbow trout.

The road climbs once more to cross Wilkerson Pass, at 9,507 feet, and enter South Park. This valley within the mountains, about 40 by 30 miles across, was the hunting ground of the Ute for generations. Among the mountain men of the 1830s, it was legendary; not only for the abundance of pelts to be had here but for its mild climate and hospitable surroundings. "It was a paradise," wrote Bernard De Voto, in his history of that era, *Across the Wide Missouri.* "It was the last place in the mountains where the old life could be lived to the full." You can still sense that wonder today as you cross South Park, hemmed in by its towering ranges. Just past Hartsel is another of the South Platte system reservoirs, Antero.

The highway crosses Trout Creek Pass and enters the Arkansas River Valley. Some of America's mightiest rivers—the Arkansas, Rio Grande, and Colorado—rise within a few miles of each other on the Continental Divide of central Colorado. The Denver and Rio Grande Railroad parallels the Arkansas through this area.

Across the narrow valley are the peaks of the Collegiate Range. Watch for the turnoff, marked Midland Scenic Drive, for a spectacular view of the area. These mountains were named for Ivy League schools by an exploring party in 1869. The highest of them, at 14,420 feet, was called Mt. Harvard, because that's the school most of the party had attended. Appropriately enough in such distinguished company, the farms in the area are known for growing lots of lettuce.

The area around Buena Vista abounds in whitewater rafting outfits, with the Browns Canyon stretch of the Arkansas, south of town, the destination of most of them. It is ranked as one of the top whitewater trips in the country.

This area has the greatest concentration of peaks exceeding 14,000 feet in the Rockies. They line up one after the other to the west in San Isabel National Forest. This avenue of the giants makes Highway 24 an unmatched scenic drive. The skyline culminates in Mt. Elbert, highest in the state at 14,333 feet. It rises just past Granite, north of the Colorado 82 turnoff. They had run out of colleges by the time they got around to this one, so it was named for a 19th-century state politician.

Malta was the smelting center for the fabulous riches taken from the mines of the next city on the route, the legendary **Leadville**. This is the highest city in America, perched at an elevation of 10,200 feet—almost twice the altitude of the mile-high city, Denver. At one point in its history, Denver was the only city in Colorado that could look down on Leadville in terms of population and wealth. In the 1880 Census, Leadville's population was registered at 30,000 and many of the legendary fortunes in America were made here. The Guggenheims, who became great philanthropists and leading supporters of the arts in New York, began here in the smelters. Horace Tabor, whose life became the stuff of tragic opera, made his fortune in Leadville. So did Johnny Brown, whose wife, Molly, proved "Unsinkable" and became the stuff of musical comedy. Two billion dollars were taken from the ground here. Most of the wealth was in gold and silver, but fortunes were also made in lead, zinc, copper, iron—it was as if all of the earth's treasures were somehow thrown together under the rocky ground of Leadville.

The gold strikes were first made in California Gulch, which you pass through near the southern entrance into town. The mines had been abandoned when early prospectors found the ore too difficult to extract. But Tabor, who was the postmaster, and a few others were persistent, and in 1875 it was found that the mud in which the gold was buried was actually lead carbonate, with an extraordinarily high concentration of silver. Down to a $17 grubstake, Tabor hit the Little Pittsburg mine and parlayed this claim into ever larger ones. His luck was fabled. Some of Leadville's less reputable citizens conspired to sell him a salted mine, a worthless property in which ore had been deliberately planted. Tabor deepened the shaft and hit the Chrysolite, another bonanza. He eventually acquired control of the Matchless, the richest silver mine ever found in the state. When Leadville was incorporated as a city in 1878, Tabor was its first mayor. He later moved to Denver and became a political leader and one of the most free-spending sports in American history. He eventually divorced his wife, Augusta, and married teen-aged Elizabeth McCourt Doe in a Washington, D.C. ceremony in 1883, with President Chester Arthur in attendance at the reception.

In ten years, however, the bottom fell out for both Tabor and Leadville. Rumors of manipulation and insider trading knocked the floor out of the stock prices in area mines. Production began declining and several of the wealthier residents moved to Denver. Damaging fires destroyed much of the business district. Finally, the price of silver collapsed in the Depression of 1893 and Tabor's holdings became worthless. His political connections managed to get him a job in Denver at his former position, postmaster, but he died broke in 1899. His deathbed advice to his wife, "Hold on to the Matchless," was taken literally, and the impoverished "Baby Doe" Tabor lived another 36 years in a cabin on the property, refusing all offers to sell. The story was the basis of the Gian-Carlo Menotti work, "The Ballad of Baby Doe."

Leadville's gold mines did enjoy a brief revival, and the Little Johnny supplied the fortune that Molly Brown used to crash Denver society and survive the Titanic. But Leadville never recovered its former prosperity and the town today is about one-tenth of its peak size. But it is filled with reminders. Never a ghost town, Leadville has always been a functioning community that carries its past proudly.

The Tabor Home has been restored to reflect the period during which Horace and Augusta lived here, from 1877 to 1881. The opera house Tabor built in 1879, in which mining magnates showered visiting beauties with gold coins as they performed, has been preserved just as it was when the last show was put on, complete to dressing room and sets. The Matchless Mine, two miles east of town, displays the cabin in which Baby Doe was found frozen to death in 1935. Take in the Healy House, an excellent evocation of an authentic boarding house for miners. Costumed guides help you recapture the texture of what life was like in Leadville during its boom years. The Dexter Cabin, on an adjacent lot, was built by another mining millionaire and furnished sumptuously, despite its bare exterior. Pay a visit, as well, to St. George's Episcopal Church. Built in 1880, it's a great example of Victorian church architecture and furnishings.

U.S. 24 crosses the Continental Divide at Tennessee Pass and enters White River National Forest, running along the Eagle River. To the west is the Mount of the Holy Cross, named by explorers in 1869 because snow formations on its slopes seemed to resemble the shape of a cross. It impressed Henry Wadsworth Longfellow enough that he wrote a poem that popularized the sight.

The highway passes through a succession of old smelting towns before ending at the junction with Interstate 70, just a few miles west of the bustling ski resort of Vail.

VISITING HOURS

COLORADO

Arriba: Tarado Mansion, (719) 768-3468. On U.S. 24. Monday–Saturday, 10–5; Sunday, 11–5. Admission.

Burlington: Kit Carson County Carousel, (719) 768-3468. North, on 15th St. Daily, noon–6, Memorial Day–September. Admission.

Cascade: Pikes Peak Highway, (719) 684-9383. 7–6:30, June–August; 9–3, May, September, October. Toll.

Colorado Springs: McAllister House, (719) 635-7925. North of downtown, at 423 N. Cascade Ave. Wednesday–Saturday, 10–4 and Sunday, noon–4, May–August; Thursday–Saturday, 10–4 at other times. Admission.

Pioneers Museum, (719) 578-6650. West of U.S. 24, downtown, at 215 S. Tejon St. Monday–Saturday, 10–5; Sunday, 1–5. Free.

U.S. Olympic Training Complex, (719) 578-4618. North of U.S. 24 at eastern edge of city, at 1750 E. Boulder St. Monday–Saturday, 9–5 and Sunday, 10–4, Memorial Day–Labor Day; opens at noon on Sunday at other times. Free.

Florissant: Florissant Fossil Beds National Monument, (719) 748-3253. South of the town on county road. Daily, 8–7, Memorial Day–Labor Day; 8–4:30 at other times. Admission.

Genoa: Tower, (719) 763-2309. West of town on I-70 Frontage Rd. Daily, 8–8, Memorial Day–Labor Day. Admission.

Leadville: Healy House, (719) 486-0487. On U.S. 24, at 912 Harrison St. Daily, 10–4:30, Memorial Day–Labor Day. Admission.

Matchless Mine Cabin, (719) 486-0371. East on E. 7th St. Daily, 9–5, June–Labor Day. Admission.

Tabor Opera House, (719) 486-1147. U.S. 24 at 4th St. Monday–Friday and Sunday, 9–5:30, Memorial Day–September. Admission.

Limon: Twilight Limited train rides; Reservations, (719) 775-2373.

Depot is located at E and 1st. Monday–Saturday, 7:30–9:30, June–September. Fare.

Manitou Springs: Cave of the Winds, (719) 685-5444. West, from U.S. 24 Bypass. Daily, 9–9, summer months; 10–5 at other times. Admission.

Miramont Castle, (719) 685-1011. Off U.S. 24, at 9 Capitol Hill Rd. Daily, 10–5, Memorial Day–Labor Day; 11–3, September. Admission.

Pikes Peak: Pikes Peak Cog Railway, (719) 685-5401. Town center, off U.S. 24. Daily, 8–5:20, mid-June to mid-August; 9:20–2:40, through September; 9:20 and 1:20, May, early June, October. Fare.

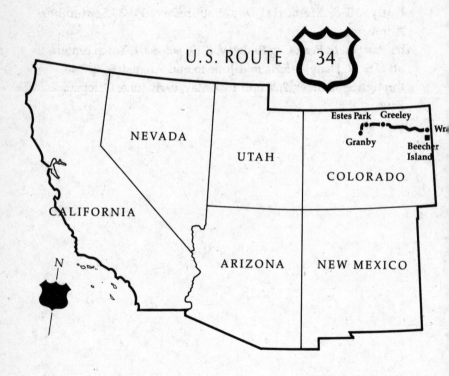

U.S. ROUTE 34

Estes Park Greeley
Granby Wra
Beecher
Island

NEVADA

UTAH

COLORADO

CALIFORNIA

N

ARIZONA NEW MEXICO

Roof of the Rockies

$\bigcirc$

U.S. 34

Wray, Colo. to Granby, Colo.
227 miles

For most of its run across the country, U.S. 34 follows the route of the old Burlington Zephyr. It comes out of Chicago, across the southern tier of Iowa, and through the center of Nebraska before entering Colorado.

In its relatively brief appearance in these pages, the road completes its crossing of the Great Plains through several outposts of frontier lore. Then it turns into a splendidly scenic drive, through Big Thompson Canyon to the resort of **Estes Park**. Finally, it weaves across the roof of the continent, as Trail Ridge Road, through Rocky Mountain National Park.

MILEPOSTS

The highway comes into Colorado following the Republican River's north fork. **Wray** is a ranching town hemmed in by riverside cliffs and canyons along the Burlington Northern tracks.

FOCUS

The Battle of Beecher Island sounds like a rough version of the big scene in hundreds of Western movies: Surrounded by overwhelming forces, the gallant troopers hold on until the last possible moment, when the U.S. Cavalry comes galloping to the rescue. Nonetheless, that is exactly what happened here. It was the fight that inspired a great Western cliché.

At the end of the Civil War, it was generally assumed that the Indian Wars would also be over soon. The great engines of commerce were making their way west and the goal of the government was to pave the way for them. The plan was to pacify the Plains tribes, change them from hunters to farmers, and win permission for the railroads to cross their lands. The fact that some of these goals were impossible, or even contradictory, didn't enter into the calculations. So when Congress created the largest standing peacetime army in 1866, most of the manpower was sent to enforce Reconstruction in the defeated South. The West got what was left over to accomplish this ambitious policy.

Four new cavalry regiments were created specifically for the Western campaigns. Among them were the Seventh, with George Custer as its lieutenant colonel, and the Ninth and Tenth, which were all-black units. The army had been faced with the problem of what to do with the black troops who had fought with the Union in the Civil War. There was no sentiment for integrating them into the general command structure, so separate black units of cavalry and infantry were formed and remained as segregated forces well into the 20th century.

The Ninth and Tenth Cavalries would find themselves in the thick of the action during the Indian wars for the next 25 years. Posted from Montana to Arizona, they were called in wherever the threat was greatest from the Sioux, Cheyenne, or Apache. They came to be known as Buffalo Soldiers, or Brunets, and were regarded as the most formidable of opponents by the tribes they fought. Fourteen of these men would win the Congressional Medal of Honor for acts of heroism during the Indian campaigns. Because of the bigotry that came to permeate the armed forces, it would be

80 years before that many black soldiers would have the chance to win the honor again.

In 1867, the focus of the Indian campaigns shifted to western Kansas. Ominously, war parties drawn from the Kiowa and Comanche were linking up with the more northern tribes—Sioux, Cheyenne, and Arapahoe—to conduct raids. The advance of the railroads and white settlements aroused Indians across the entire frontier and several of the more able tribal leaders tried to unify their forces to stop the encroachments. General Philip Sheridan, hero of the Shenandoah Valley campaigns, assumed command of the military department in 1868 and organized a company of 50 scouts to act as a mobile response force. When a wagon train was attacked near the Colorado line late that summer, the scouts were sent out from Fort Wallace. Under Colonel George A. Forsyth, they tracked the attackers along the Arikaree River.

On the morning of September 17, they were surprised themselves by an overwhelming force of warriors from the northern tribes. "The ground seemed to grow them," Forsyth wrote later. Outnumbered almost 20 to 1, the scouts retreated to an island in the river. They called it Beecher Island in honor of a lieutenant killed in the initial attack.

The scouts were able to dig out a barrier in the sand as the Indians prepared for a frontal assault. This was a highly unusual tactic, but the Indians did not usually get to fight with such a numerical advantage. Roman Nose, one of the most capable of the Cheyenne, led the charge. What he didn't realize was that the scouts had recently been supplied with repeating rifles, carrying seven charges. The volleys went crashing into the oncoming Indians, killing Roman Nose and forcing the others to retreat to the far bank. With the most respected leader dead, the three tribal units were never again able to mount a coordinated assault.

That removed the immediate danger, but the trapped scouts were still faced with the prospect of a siege and eventual starvation unless help arrived. Two of them managed to slip past the Indian lines that night and traveling by dark through hostile country got back to Fort Wallace.

Nine days after the attack began, the Tenth Cavalry reached Beecher Island. By that time, Forsyth was critically wounded and almost half his forces were either dead or severely injured. They were on the verge of making a hopeless break for freedom when the Tenth routed the besieging forces.

Beecher Island was a disheartening defeat for the tribal alliance, which was never again able to muster such numbers in Colorado. Relics of the battle are preserved in the Wray Museum, across the street from the courthouse. The battle site is south of town by way of U.S. 385 and an unnumbered county road. A flood washed away the island in the Arikaree in 1935, but historical markers indicate the outline of the battle. The Beecher Island Reunion is held each year on the anniversary of the battle, with black powder shoots and games on the site.

* * *

The road heads west across the Plains from Wray, passing the Sandsage State Wildlife Area, which has observation points that command views of the protected animals within its boundaries. Yuma, the center of a dryland farming area, celebrates Ole Threshers Day each September, with demonstrations of antique agricultural equipment and a 19th-century-style harvest festival.

West of Platner, however, you can see the farming of the Plains advancing into the future. The Central Great Plains Research Station, run by the U.S. Department of Agriculture, showcases test plots on which experimental farming techniques are tested. They are visible from the highway.

Akron was the only town that already existed when the railroad came through in 1882. The word is Greek for "Summit" and this town perches on a crest of the rolling high Plains. (The city back in Ohio, incidentally, is located in Summit County and got its name because it also sits high on a divide between two watersheds.) Just west of town are Fremont Buttes, with their natural chair formation. A road leads to the top and a view of the surrounding South Platte River Valley.

U.S. 34 reaches that river at **Brush**. The Platte provided an important trail to the West, through Nebraska and eastern Colorado. "A mile wide and an inch deep," snorted the pioneers, because its flow in summer was usually just a trickle. The name itself means "flat" and was usually applied to streams with little discernible current. While boaters never went very far on the Platte, towns and military posts grew up along its banks and developed as links for western-bound travelers from Omaha.

The town of Brush was named for a pioneer rancher in what is now sugar beet country. Many early settlers were of Danish descent; they built the Eben Ezer All Saints Church in 1918. This Gothic edifice is meant to resemble a church in medieval Denmark, something that Hamlet might have found comfortable in his more lucid moments. There is a Danish pioneer museum on the grounds.

Fort Morgan grew up as a military post in 1866 to protect travelers on the South Platte Trail and was named for its first commander, Colonel C.A. Morgan. A monument marks the fort's location on Riverview Avenue. The town has also designed a walking tour of a nine-block stretch of Main Street, showing off its unusually well-preserved turn-of-the-century business district. Pamphlets are available at the Fort Morgan Museum, which has several exhibits on the history of the area and the role the town played on the Overland Trail. You can still see the tracks made by wagons along that trail, on the north side of Interstate 76, to the west of the Fort Morgan exit. As you go, take a look at Rainbow Bridge across the Platte, on Colorado 52. Built in 1923, the bridge is now on the

National Register of Historic Places and makes a compelling sight, surrounded by these barren Plains.

U.S. 34 joins the Interstate west of Fort Morgan but soon breaks away to the northwest. A few miles past that point is the turnoff to Orchard, where many of the exteriors were shot for the television mini-series "Centennial," based on the 1976 James Michener novel about Colorado. Michener did much of his research in this area and his fictional town was meant to be a composite of several communities in the Fort Morgan-**Greeley** area.

The road follows the South Platte and passes Empire Reservoir—a popular place for boating and fishing and part of the state's first major irrigation project—before entering Greeley.

When newspaper publisher Horace Greeley exhorted young men to "Go West," this is the place he had in mind. Greeley was the most influential journalist of his day. He founded the *New York Tribune* in 1841 as a mass circulation daily, but instead of imitating the scandal sheets of the time he used it as a forum to support temperance, the antislavery movement, and the opening of the West. He made it a mouthpiece of the emerging Republican Party and its weekly edition became the first nationally circulated publication, reaching 200,000 homes and turning Greeley into a formidable shaper of opinion and an unsuccesful presidential candidate in 1872. Greeley was so taken with economic opportunities in the West that he sent his agricultural editor, Nathan Meeker, to found a colony in Colorado. He arranged the purchase of 72,000 acres near the junction of the South Platte and Cache le Poudre Rivers. After 1870 he sold the land off in 160-acre parcels for $150 each. Expansively boosted by the *Tribune* throughout the East, the Union Colony prospered as a co-operative community and was responsible for the earliest irrigation projects in the area, such as the ones seen on the way into town. After Meeker left to accept an appointment as an Indian Agent, the place developed along more conventional lines. Meeker eventually was killed at the agency in the Ute uprising of 1879, one of the few media casualties of the Indian Wars.

The adobe house in which Meeker lived is now a museum, displaying many of his possessions and family heirlooms. A more elaborate memorial is Centennial Village, built in 1976 to celebrate 100 years of Colorado statehood. Historic buildings from all over the county were gathered here in a park-like setting to show the evolution of the area from 1860 to 1920. At the University of Northern Colorado, established here in 1889, a study used by Michener while researching *Centennial* is preserved in the library building. The primary crop planted by the Union Colony was potatoes and they were acclaimed with an annual Spud Rodeo. That has grown into the Greeley Independence Stampede, the largest Fourth of July rodeo in the country and a major fireworks show.

West of Greeley, we advance steadily into the foothills of The Rockies. Longs Peak, highest point in Rocky Mountain National Park, at 14,255 feet, rises to the southwest.

Loveland was the name of a Colorado Central Railroad executive and the town was named for him in 1877. But hundreds of thousands of Americans regard the place as Cupid's hometown. Each February they inundate the post office here with valentines to be remailed with its postmark. Loveland has decided to play along with the gag and even adds a specially designed Cupid cachet to each letter. The town tops it all off with a February 14 Sweetheart Sculpture Show and Sweetheart Balloon Rally. The town also has become known as something of an arts center, and Benson Park, just north of the highway on 29th Street, is filled with pieces of sculpture done by local residents. Loveland is the center of a prosperous orchard area. Many of these fruit farms were started by prospectors who came down busted from the hills and decided to make their fortune from the land in another way.

West of Loveland, the road plunges into Roosevelt National

Forest and Big Thompson Canyon. Of all the entrances to the heartland of the Rockies, this may be the most beautiful. The gorge cut by the Big Thompson River is regarded as one of Colorado's finest canyon drives and it is a magnificent entryway to the state's busiest summer resort, **Estes Park**.

Once out of the canyon you are at the very base of the mountains, and travelers have come to this spot to gaze at them since 1865. With the Union secured and the railroad edging its way west, Americans seemed to undergo a change in how they felt about this region. The pioneers would continue heading west for another generation, but already the sense of an era passing away was developing. Just 30 years before, only the mountain men, cut off from civilized comforts for years at a time, penetrated these mountains. But in the 1860s, travelers came to the Rockies to admire them, even to paint them. No longer a heart-stopping barrier in the wilderness, they had become objects of admiration, almost veneration. Joel Estes had settled here in 1860, but when the tourists began arriving five years later he pulled up stakes and disgustedly retreated further into the mountains. The Earl of Dunraven paid a visit in 1871 and spread the word about the splendor of the setting throughout Ireland and Britain. Afterwards, Estes Park became a favored stop of Europeans doing the West. German-born Albert Bierstadt arrived and made the place even more renowned with his romantic landscapes of the Rockies. He claimed that from the perspective of an artist, the visual composition here was almost perfect.

The sights that so moved these early tourists are enveloped now by the national park, on the western boundary of Estes Park. It was created in 1915 to preserve such scenery from commercial exploitation. Consequently, Joel Estes's old homestead has become the major tourist base for the area, a development with which he would probably be appalled.

Amid the clatter of 20th-century tourism, there are still corners of charm in Estes Park. Although its shopping area is jammed during the peak summer months, it can be a delightful stroll if you catch it in the off-times. The MacGregor Ranch, just north of town, preserves the homestead of one of the valley's oldest settlers and displays what life was like in this area in the 1870s. The Stanley Hotel is the oldest of the traditional inns and has just come through a handsome refurbishing. Built in 1909 by the inventor of the Stanley Steamer automobile, the red-roofed resort is an attraction in itself and mounts a series of concerts and theatrical productions throughout the summer season. The town retains a strong Celtic flavor, perhaps a legacy of Dunraven, and each September it stages a Scottish–Irish Highland Festival, complete with bagpipes and games.

An aerial tramway runs to the top of Prospect Mountain for an overview of the area. But compared to where this road is heading, that ride is only a warm-up. As U.S. 34 enters the national park, it becomes Trail Ridge Road, ascending to 12,183 feet as it makes its way across the Continental Divide. This is surely among America's top mountain drives and among the top ten in the world. It follows the ridge of the Rockies for 45 miles, along an Indian trail above the timber line, through an unending panorama of superb high mountain scenery. It is the highest continuous paved road in America.

An alternate approach, however, is to leave Estes Park on U.S. 36 and enter the national park at Beaver Meadows. This will enable you to stop at the visitors center for a good introduction to the marvels ahead. Route 36 rejoins Highway 34 after just a few miles and you miss none of the most scenic portions of the drive. As a bonus, you get get an exceptional view of the park's entire eastern range from Many Parks Curve, just west of the visitors center. This is not an especially taxing drive, although it does draw heavy traffic during the summer. But you won't really want to go fast, anyhow. The road is well engineered and even flatlanders should feel reasonably comfortable making the crossing. The temptation is to pull out at every overlook and there is absolutely no reason not to. Although the distance between Estes Park and Granby, at the western end of the national park, is just sixty-two miles, you should allow a minimum of three hours to make this drive. A cafeteria near Fall River Pass makes a good lunch stop to break up the trip. The road usually opens around Memorial Day and is generally closed by snow in mid-October. Early September, right after the height of the summer season, is absolutely the best time to take this drive. But early June, when the wildflowers are at the peak of color, is not a bad alternative.

The western descent is an easier drive, far less steep and with more meadowlands. Rushing past on the west for part of the way are the headwaters of the Colorado River, which is born a few miles ahead in Grand Lake. This is the largest natural body of water in the state, measuring 12 miles in length and one mile in width. It is connected by channel with the larger Shadow Mountain Lake and Lake Granby, both reservoirs, to form a chain called the Great Lakes of Colorado.

The town of Grand Lake is a resort, but much less bustling than Estes Park. It does have the world's highest yacht club, however, and the regattas it hosts on summer weekends, with the towering peaks as a backdrop, are a dazzling sight. The lake was avoided by the Utes who lived in the area because they believed that its frequent mists were formed by the souls of fellow tribesmen drowned when their raft capsized as they tried to escape a hostile attack.

The highway skirts the western shore of all three Great Lakes, through the Arapahoe National Recreation Area. The waters of Granby Lake are part of a massive irrigation project, in which water is pumped across the mountains into the farms of arid northeastern Colorado. Tours of the pumping plant and a reasonably concise explanation of the mechanics involved in this

Colorado River project are given during the summer months. The road then weaves in and out with the Colorado for its last few miles, until it reaches the junction with U.S. 40 that marks its end.

VISITING HOURS

COLORADO

Brush: Danish Pioneer Museum, (303) 842-2861. Adjoining Eben Ezer All Saints Church, at 122 Hospital Rd. Monday–Friday, 8–5. Free.

Estes Park: MacGregor Ranch, (303) 586-3749. North of U.S. 34, on MacGregor Ave. Tuesday–Saturday, 11–5, Memorial Day–Labor Day. Donation.

Aerial Tramway, (303) 586-3675. Town center, at 420 E. Riverside. Daily, 9–6:30, mid-May–mid-September. Fare.

Fort Morgan: Museum, (303) 867-6331. At 414 Main St. Monday–Friday, 10–5 and Sunday, 1:30–4:30. Free.

Greeley: Centennial Village, (303) 350-9224. 14th at A St. Monday–Friday, 10–6 and weekends, 1–6, Memorial Day–Labor Day; Tuesday–Saturday, 10–3, mid April, May, September, mid October. Admission.

Meeker Home, (303) 350-9221. 1324 9th Ave. Same hours as Centennial Village. Admission.

Rocky Mountain National Park, (303) 586-2371. Trail Rodge Road open, late May–mid-October. Admission.

Wray: Museum, (303) 332-5063. Across from courthouse on U.S. 34. Friday, 2–4, June–August. Free.

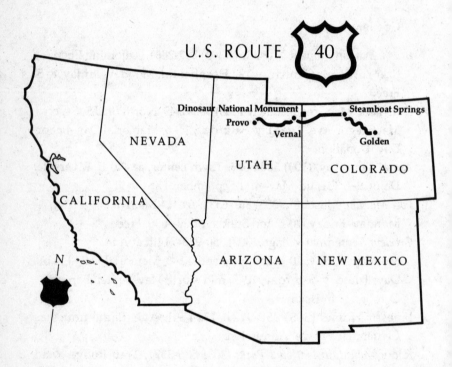

U.S. ROUTE 40

Dinosaur National Monument
Provo
Vernal
Steamboat Springs
Golden

NEVADA

UTAH

COLORADO

CALIFORNIA

N

ARIZONA

NEW MEXICO

Land of the Dinosaurs

⬡

U.S. 40

Denver, Colo. to Provo, Utah
477 miles

Built along the route of the first federal highway, the National Road, U.S. 40 no longer girdles the nation as it did until the 1960s. It begins in Atlantic City, New Jersey, and between Baltimore and St. Louis still traces the path of the oldest overland route to the West, along the present Interstate 70.

The highway finally breaks away from the Interstate in Kansas and enters Colorado as part of the old Smoky Hill Trail. It runs through Denver, where we'll pick it up, crosses the Rockies at Berthoud Pass, then swoops into the core of Dinosaur Country. But its former route to San Francisco is just as extinct as the dinosaurs, and the road now ends on the slopes of Utah's Wasatch Mountains.

MILEPOSTS

The Smoky Hill Trail was used as a middle way by those traveling from Missouri to the Colorado diggings. More direct than either the Platte River or Santa Fe Trails, it was also more barren. Travelers came to refer to it as the Starvation Trail. In later years, however, towns grew up along the Union Pacific right-of-way and developed as railheads for cattle drives from the big ranches in Texas and New Mexico.

U.S. 40 enters Colorado on the route of the old trail and follows it as far as Limon. There it joins up once more with Interstate 70 and follows this road as it loops around Denver. We'll start our trip just before it swings west, at the Golden Road exit. This will take us to one of the state's more interesting historic communities, the old territorial capital of **Golden**.

Although the precious yellow metal was its reason for being, the town was actually named after a local prospector, Tom Golden, whose occupation, apparently, was ordained at birth. Situated closer to the mining camps, Golden was a great rival of Denver for political influence and was actually the state capital from 1862 to 1867. But Denver's location on the new rail routes gave it an advantage its upland competitor could not match. The Astor House Hotel, built in 1867 and restored as a museum, and the row of structures along the nearby 12th Street Historic District, give some idea of Golden's appearance in those days. The DAR Pioneer Museum, in the Civic Center, on 10th Street, also contains first-rate displays on Golden's glittering past.

In recent years, the town has been associated more closely with beer and quakes. The Adolph Coors Co. has been making beer here since 1873 and its Golden brewery is the largest in the world. Coors beer is almost synonymous with the Rockies and grew from a semi-cultish regional brew into the third largest seller in the country, paralleling Colorado's success in attracting a younger, more affluent traveler. The quakes are a part of the Colorado School of Mines, the oldest and possibly largest college in the world dedicated to the study of mineral science and engineering. The U.S. Geological Survey set up its National Earthquake Center here in Golden, and whenever a quake occurs anywhere on the globe its reading on the Richter Scale of intensity is usually determined with instruments here. The Geology Museum, on campus, is regarded as among the best in the world.

Golden is also the final resting place of that old scout and showman, Buffalo Bill. "how do you like your blue-eyed boy, mr. death?" lower-case poet e.e. cummings asked upon the demise of William F. Cody, in 1917. The Iowa-born frontiersman was the John Ford of the pre-movie entertainment era, bringing the sights and sounds of the Old West to an international audience with many of its original characters. His Wild West shows began touring in 1883 and were an institution across America while the frontier was not yet a distant memory. In no small part, Cody created the images of the West that prevailed in popular culture for the best part of a century. His gravesite overlooks Denver and a panorama of the Plains. A small museum contains memorabilia of his long career, much of it totally fictitious but no less exciting for that. The grave on Lookout Mountain is reached by way of Lariat Loop Road from central Golden.

After returning to Golden, you can leave town on westbound U.S. 6, which rejoins Highway 40 and Interstate 70 after a few miles. The road enters Clear Creek Canyon and then arrives at **Idaho Springs**.

There is some dispute over the location of the first big gold strike in Colorado. Central City, a few miles to the north, maintains that its claim was the first to be worked, in 1859. But Idaho Springs, justifiably, states that the claim here was the first to be filed. Prospector George Jackson was working Clear Creek Canyon late in the fall of 1858 when he found traces of gold in the embers of his campfire. Knowing that it was too late in the season to do any further investigation, he quietly filed his claim in Denver and waited for spring. By summer the boom was on and the canyon filled with a new tent city.

The Argo Tunnel, which carried ore from the Central City lodes after 1913, emptied out here. Argo Mill, along Riverside Drive, now offers self-guided tours through the vast refining plant and an adjacent hand-dug mine, the Double Eagle. There are also historical displays on mining and a chance to pan the waters for gold yourself. There are still 200 active mines in the area, among them the Edgar, which is also an underground classroom for students at Colorado Mines. The radium hot springs, which were first opened in 1868, continue to refresh bathers as well.

U.S. 40 ducks off the Interstate at Empire and immediately enters Arapahoe National Forest to climb Berthoud Pass, crossing the Continental Divide at 11,314 feet. The pass is named for the engineer who ran the first survey through the area in 1861. **Winter Park** is the closest major ski area to Denver. The resort is served by special trains which make the run from the city through Moffat Tunnel in about two hours. Trains also operate during Winter Park's Music and Jazz festival each July. Moffat was the first rail tunnel through the Rockies, opening in 1927, and the new accessiblity created this ski area. The rail route it replaced, across Corona Pass, is now a scenic highway, but is not recommended for standard-drive vehicles. The Winter Park chair lift also operates during the summer months to give visitors a view across this area, just south of Rocky Mountain National Park.

The road now enters the Fraser River Valley. The town of Fraser has trademarked "Icebox of the Nation" as its official motto, although why anyone would want to boast about that is a bit baffling. The place regularly registers the coldest readings in the 48 contiguous states throughout the year. It is more comforting to dwell upon Fraser's World's Best Fourth of July Picnic, which features some of the snappiest old-time fiddlers in the West.

Tabernash is named for a Ute chief who was killed here in 1879. This is the gateway to Middle Park, one of three high mountain valleys, running from the Wyoming border to the Arkansas River, which are a feature of the Colorado Rockies. As with the others, Middle Park was a favored hunting ground of the Utes and they defended it vigorously, chasing out the odd French or Spanish trapper who ventured into it. As a result, it lay somewhere between the claims of those two nations in this area and was never formally acquired by the United States government. That oversight was taken care of in 1936, on Colorado's 60th anniversary of statehood, and Middle Park officially joined the Union.

Granby is an old rail center, on the Denver and Rio Grande, that developed as the western gateway to Rocky Mountain National Park. The junction of U.S. 40 with U.S. 34 is just west of Granby and the attractions nearby are described in that chapter.

The **Hot Sulphur Springs** that named the next town first emerged to heal a dying, abandoned chief. That's the legend, anyhow, and they are still in use here, the first settlement along the trickle that will swell into the mighty Colorado River. The Grand County Museum (the Colorado, by the way, was originally known as the Grand) has exhibits emphasizing the role of pioneer women and the growth of skiing in this area. But we'll hear much more of that just a few miles ahead.

Kremmling is the largest town in Middle Park and many rafting expeditions on the Colorado put in just west of here. The road swings north, following Big Muddy Creek, and enters Routt National Forest through Rabbit Ears Pass, at a height of 9,426 feet.

On the far side is Yampa Valley. Pioneers who entered the area in the 1870s were startled to hear a chugging noise that sounded for all the world like a steam riverboat. It came from one of the hot springs that speckled the area, and so they called the town that grew up nearby Steamboat Springs. The place first came to the attention of tourists as a spa, but that all changed when Carl Howelsen arrived in 1913 and started jumping off the local hillsides on skis. Most people associate skiing in Colorado with steep downhill runs, but it first appeared in the state as the Nordic version, ski jumping. This was introduced to America in Michigan's Upper Peninsula, where it was brought by Scandinavian iron miners in 1887. When the U.S. Ski Association was formed in 1904, at Ishpeming, Michigan, jumping was the form of the sport that dominated national competitions. It wasn't until the 1930s that the more glamorous downhill version was imported from Austria and Switzerland.

Steamboat made the switch to downhill skiing without missing a slalom gate, but nonetheless it has retained its Nordic roots. Howelsen Hill Ski Complex, just off U.S. 40 by way of the 5th St. bridge, is a ski jump training facility surrounded by a city park. The famed Steamboat downhill complex is just east of town on U.S. 40. Although eclipsed in recent years by the big money pouring into Aspen and Vail, Steamboat remains one of the top venues for those who place sport above sociability. The bath houses still soothe aching muscles resulting from both varieties of skiing with their 104-degree springs, although the one that so amused the pioneers with its chugging no longer exists.

Fish Creek Falls, three miles from town on a marked side road, is a lovely spot, complete with a wooden bridge at the foot of the 283-foot drop.

West of Steamboat, the road enters an extended basin along the Yampa River, through an area of coal and oil activity and sheep ranching. The Trapper is a working surface coal mine, just south of **Craig**, which offers weekday tours. A somewhat less gritty experience is a visit to "Marcia," the private Pullman car built for rail tycoon David Moffat in 1906. He was the builder of that rail tunnel through the Rockies near Winter Park, and this county is also named for him. It's a pretty enormous county, too, stretching all the way to the Utah line, 90 miles away. This is wide open rangeland, with ranches and rolling hills stretching off to the horizon, and no settlement bigger than a crossroads.

In Dinosaur, however, is a hint of big things to come. The surrounding area is the site of some of the greatest fossil finds in the country and Dinosaur National Monument is to the north of here.

There is a visitor center near the town, with audio-visual displays and orientation guides—but no fossils. The park is really a double-faceted facility. The fossil part is in Utah, while Colorado has the scenic section. A paved road heads 31 miles north from the visitor center to the overlook at Harpers Corner, where the Yampa meets the Green River at the base of Steamboat Rock. But that's a long side trip and the big deal at Dinosaur is really those bones ahead of us.

FOCUS

Dinosaurs have haunted the popular imagination of America for years. They are a staple of science fiction and movies; they turned up as one of the preliminary bouts for King Kong and in a long succession of other flicks; and they figured prominently in one of the more memorable sequences of Walt Disney's "Fantasia." Science museums around the country find that acquiring a dinosaur skeleton is one of the best fund-raising schemes available.

A television sitcom based on the domestic life of a dinosaur family debuted in 1991. A best-selling novel of the same year postulated the re-animation of the beasts in the lab from DNA molecules recovered from fossil fragments. Those who raised children from the 1970s on may have been amazed to learn that the extinct lizards were more popular than cowboys among the sub-teen set.

Here in northeastern Utah is dinosaur heaven. In a cliffside quarry, north of the town of **Jensen**, is the greatest concentration of dinosaur bones ever found on this continent. First discovered in 1908, the cliff has yielded tons of fossil-bearing rocks. Many of the bones were sent off to museums decades ago, but National Park Service policy in recent years has been to leave fossils in place so visitors can see exactly how they were situated.

About 145 million years ago, the present Uintah Basin was an enormous low plain fed by many rivers. Near the mouth of one of these prehistoric rivers was a sandbar, and the bodies of animals that died upstream came to rest there, buried deep in the protecting sand. Towards the end of this period, the area became a seabed, and over the eons, silica replaced the organic material in the bones of the dead animals.

When the Rockies were formed, this old sea bottom was uplifted, too, and became the face of a cliff. A few more million years flashed by and the forces of erosion slowly wore away the rock that covered the ancient sandbar, which now overlooked the Green River. The first boat expeditions to the Grand Canyon came this way, putting in along the Green a bit to the north in Wyoming. While it was understood that the area was rich in fossils, Major John Wesley Powell passed right by on his scientific expedition in 1869 without suspecting the trove that was practically above his head.

It wasn't until another 40 years had passed that paleontologist Dr. Earl Douglass was sent here by Pittsburgh's Carnegie Museum. By this time, the region had been carefully surveyed and it was almost certain that a major fossil find would be uncovered in the vicinity.

Local ranchers called his attention to this ledge, on which they had noticed rather peculiar-looking protruberances. Dr. Douglass took a look and found himself gazing at the partially exposed skeleton of a brontosaurus. Within seven years, the area was given National Monument status to protect the quarry, and the country's major museums mined it for fossils.

As many as 19 wagons loaded with bones would depart here at one time in the 1920s. Much of the country's intense interest in dinosaurs originated with the bones taken from this quarry. They supplied the first reconstructed skeletons exhibited in America's big city museums. But since that time, more than 2,300 bones have been excavated and left on the face of the ledge in extruded relief. This work continues each year and may be observed by summertime visitors to the quarry.

The quarry has yielded the remains of all sizes and shapes; from the camptosaurus, no larger than a human being, to the allosaurus, a nasty number who ate flesh and had teeth as sharp as razors. This is the dinosaur that haunts the pages of science fiction tales. Not many of them were found here, though. Even 145 million years or so later, that is oddly reassuring.

* * *

The dinosaur theme continues in **Vernal**, the commercial center of the Uintah Basin. The Utah Field House of Natural History adjoins Dinosaur Gardens, in which 14 of the beasts have been reconstructed in an area set up to resemble Utah of the Jurassic Period. The museum itself contains many of the fossils taken from the Jensen quarry and a diplodocus skeleton, the only fully articulated dinosaur in the area.

Vernal was named by its settlers in the 1870s because it was a green space in the surrounding arid landscape. They were a pretty canny lot. Spotting a loophole in the parcel post regulations, they built the local bank by having the bricks mailed to private homes here in lots of seven. The rates were cheaper than freight charges for the same load. The scheme forced a change in postal regulations after 1919. The Bank of Vernal still stands on Main Street.

The road continues west, south of the Uintahs, the only major mountain range running east-to-west in the country. Remnants of a 1970s oil boom in the area are recalled in the name of Gusher, a crossroads at the entrance to the Uintah and Ouray Reservation. The administrative center, Fort Duchesne, was established as a military post by President Lincoln in 1861, when the reservation covered almost the entire Uintah Basin. But when the state government ascertained that this land was not as worthless as it first looked, the Indians were restricted to a smaller area and the more fertile portion was opened to settlement. There are now about 1,600 Native Americans living on reservation land. A few military buildings from the 1880s survive on the site of the former post.

Teddy Roosevelt once camped nearby and that seemed a good enough reason to name the next town for him when the land was opened to homesteaders in 1905. Samuel Gilson, a former Pony Express rider, had come into this area about 20 years before and was told of a place to the south where a sort of glossy coal that did not burn could be found. He quickly spotted commercial possibilities for the product in electrical insulation and marketed it as Gilsonite. Immodest, but enriching.

The origin of the town of Duchesne's name is a bit clouded. Some sources say it was the name of a French trapper who came into the area in the 1840s, others say it belonged to a French nun. It doesn't seem likely that they were the same person.

Starvation Lake, just west of town, was formed by a dam on the Duchesne River. A state park is at its western end. Starvation was a name attached to many places throughout the west, where unfortunate immigrant parties ran out of food. Oddly enough, this one is just a few miles east of Fruitland. That appellation, though, came out of a developer's imagination. This is all grazing land and there has never been any sustained agricultural efforts.

The road now swings north into Deep Creek Canyon and the Strawberry Reservoir. Built in 1915, this was the first big federal reclamation project in the state, diverting water to the Utah Valley, on the far side of the Wasatch Mountains, through a 19,000-foot-long tunnel.

The road crosses a shoulder of the Uintahs, at the 8,000-foot level, and descends into the Heber Valley. The area is named for Heber C. Kimball, a leading advisor to Brigham Young. Sent out to settle the area in 1859, a group of pioneers found their way blocked by an avalanche in the mountains. No problem. They simply took apart their wagons, carried them around the impediment, reassembled them on the other side, and went about their business. **Heber City** is the marketing center of the valley, lying between the Wasatch and Uintas. A train known as "The Heber Creeper" leaves here for scenic runs through the Wasatch canyons to Provo. The ride takes about three and a half hours. Next to the depot is a Railroad Museum with the state's largest collection of steam equipment.

From Heber City, U.S. 40 continues north another 20 miles to its conclusion at the junction with Interstate 80. Let's turn south here instead to catch the final 30 miles of another old road, U.S. 189. This is a far more scenic conclusion to the trip. It passes Deer Creek reservoir, another reclamation project. The dam here impounds the Provo River before it enters Provo Canyon and transports more water to the Utah Valley for irrigation. The project was first envisioned by Brigham Young in 1856, but wasn't actually built until the 1930s.

The road now becomes a lovely excursion into Uinta National Forest and Provo Canyon. Bridal Veil Falls comes tumbling out of the canyon walls here in two cascades. An aerial tramway rises 1,753 feet from the canyon floor to an absolutely spectacular view of the falls far below. You can also look west to **Provo** and Utah Lake, as well as north to towering Mt. Timpanogos. It's an unforgettable sight and a perfect place to end this trip.

VISITING HOURS

COLORADO

Craig: Trapper Coal Mine, (303) 824-4401. South of town on
   Colorado 13. Monday–Friday, 8–4. By apppointment. Free.

Dinosaur National Monument Visitor Center, (303) 374-2216. On U.S. 40, east of Dinosaur. Daily, 8–4:30, June–August; Monday–Friday at other times. Free.

Golden: DAR Pioneer Museum, (303) 278-7151. In the Civic Center, at 911 Tenth St. Monday–Saturday, 11–4, June–August; noon–4, at other times. Free.

Coors Brewery Tours, (303) 277-BEER. 13th and Ford Sts. Monday–Saturday, 8:30–4:30, June–August; 10–4, at other times. Free.

National Earthquake Center, (303) 236-1500. On Colorado Mines campus, at 1711 Illinois. Call for appointment. Free.

Buffalo Bill's Grave and Museum, (303) 526-0747. On Lookout Mountain Road. Daily, 9–5, May–October; Tuesday–Sunday, 8–4, at other times. Admission.

Hot Sulphur Springs: Grand County Museum, (303) 725-3939. East of town on U.S. 40. Daily, 10–5, Memorial Day–Labor Day; Wednesday–Friday and the first and third weekends of the month at other times. Donation.

Idaho Springs: Argo Mill, (303) 567-2421. Off Interstate 70, at 2350 Riverside Dr. Daily, 9–7, mid-May–September. Admission.

Edgar Mine, (303) 567-2911. Colorado at 8th St. Tuesday–Saturday, 8:30–4, mid-June–mid-August. Admission.

Winter Park: Chair Lift. On U.S. 40. (303) 726-5514. Daily, late June–mid-September. Fare.

Utah

Heber City Heber Creeper Railroad and Museum, (801) 654-2900. Depot at 6th W. and Center Sts. Reservation required. Daily, Memorial Day–September; Saturday in April; weekends in May. Phone for schedule.

Jensen: Dinosaur National Monument Quarry, (801) 789-2115. North of town on park road. Daily, 8–7, Memorial Day–Labor Day; 8–4:30 at other times. Admission.

Provo: Bridal Veil Falls Tramway, (801) 225-4461. Northeast of city, on U.S. 189. Daily, 9–9, mid-May–mid-October. Fare.

Vernal Utah Field House of Natural History, (801) 789-3799. At 235 E. Main. Daily, 8 A.M.–9 P.M., June–August; 9–5, at other times. Admission.

U.S. ROUTE 50

COLORADO

Lake Tahoe   Austin
Placerville   Ely
        Carson City   UTAH   Grand Junction   Canon City
                                                    Montrose   Pueblo   La Junta
        NEVADA

CALIFORNIA

N

ARIZONA   NEW MEXICO

The Long Voyage West

U.S. 50

THE SANTA FE TRAIL

Holly, Colo. to Grand Junction, Colo.
438 miles

This is another of the erstwhile coast-to-coast highways. It still starts off in sight of the Atlantic, in Ocean City, Maryland, but the closest it gets to the Pacific is Sacramento, California, instead of its former terminus in San Francisco.

Because of Interstate interruptions, U.S. 50 divides rather neatly into two sections in this part of the country. The first section enters Colorado along the mountain branch of the Santa Fe Trail. It then follows the Arkansas River into the Rockies, crosses Monarch Pass and hooks up with the Gunnison River, which it follows to its junction with the Colorado at (where else?) **Grand Junction**. The highway then begins an intimate involvement with freeways and other roads through Utah and doesn't work its way loose again until Ely, Nevada, at the start of the second section we'll travel over.

MILEPOSTS

This is the oldest road from the east into Colorado, the route of explorers and hopeful traders along the Santa Fe Trail. The Zebulon Pike party came this way in 1806, following the Arkansas

River west, and it was from this road that Pike first glimpsed the peak that carries his name. A generation later, commerce bound for New Mexico followed in his path. After Mexico won its independence from Spain in 1821, the path became a pioneer highway. The Cimarron Cutoff, an alternate route to Santa Fe, struck off on a more direct southwesterly route from western Kansas. But its water supplies were less reliable and it also passed through the heart of Comanche country. Although significantly shorter, it was also more dangerous. So the bulk of traffic came this way as far as **La Junta**, then cut south on what is now U.S. 350 to Raton Pass and the link-up with the cutoff.

This is also the lowest part of the state. Holly, the first town across the Kansas line, sits at an elevation of 3,397 feet, a mere bump in the road for Colorado. The oldest irrigated farms in the state are here, and this section of the Arkansas Valley is one of Colorado's richest agricultural areas. The road is lined with produce stands between here and Rocky Ford from late summer through early fall.

The pioneers called it the Big Timber Country, for the stands of towering cottonwoods along the river. It was also a popular campground for Indians. The Bent brothers, proprietors of the Santa Fe Trail's largest trading post, which we'll encounter in a few more miles, set up a subsidiary branch in this area to catch travelers early on. The town of **Lamar**, named for Grover Cleveland's Secretary of the Interior, eventually grew up on the site when the Santa Fe Railroad tracks came through on the route of the old Trail. Big Timbers Museum, just north of town on U.S. 50, recalls Lamar's beginnings and also showcases the work of local artists.

The road crosses to the north bank of the Arkansas and just south of Hasty is the dam that forms the John Martin reservoir. The largest body of water formed in the area by Army Corps of Engineers projects, the reservoir is the main water-sports resource in southeastern Colorado. There is an excellent view over the lake and surrounding plains from the road across the dam.

The town of Fort Lyon is on the site of the military outpost that was Kit Carson's last stop. The legendary scout was the Indian agent here at the time of his death on May 23, 1868. He was taken to his former home, in Taos, New Mexico, for burial (see U.S. 64). A museum in the nearby town of **Las Animas** is dedicated to his memory and explains the development of the surrounding land.

Just short of the bridge across the Arkansas to Las Animas, however, is a turnoff west on Colorado 194. This is the road we want to take to Bent's Old Fort National Historic Site.

FOCUS

The first man known to have traveled the Santa Fe Trail was Pierre Vial, a wandering trader. But he was heading in the other direction, west to east. He showed up in St. Louis in 1792 with a load of goods from New Mexico and returned the following year. It took another 30 years, until Mexico won its independence from a Spain determined to keep it off limits to all outside trade, before large-scale commerce became attractive.

The summer of 1821, when Mexico proclaimed its freedom, William Becknell and four partners left Missouri with a caravan of pack animals carrying trade goods. Uncertain of the reception they would get, the men were undertaking a considerable risk. The feeling back in St. Louis was that they would be ruined, if not imprisoned—the fate of other traders under Spanish rule. But when Becknell came back five months later with profits in hard currency, the rush was on. In the spring of 1822, the first wagon trains to head west on the Santa Fe Trail left Franklin, Missouri and the history of the Southwest was changed.

Watching developments with interest were three residents of St. Louis, the brothers Charles and William Bent and their associate, Ceran St. Vrain. The three men were experienced in the Missouri

River fur trade of the north. They had learned how to deal with mountain men and Indians and also had acquired some capital. As the fur trade started petering out, they decided that the main chance lay in the Arkansas Valley.

Setting up shop at the southern turnoff of the Trail's mountain route, the three gradually came to monopolize the trade of the southern Cheyenne and Arapahoe tribes. According to historian Bernard de Voto, their methods were revolutionary on the Plains. They treated the Indians fairly, "maintaining an unheard of standard of honor in dealing with them." They kept a permanent truce in the vicinity of their post and by 1834 they had built the largest and most important trading depot on the entire trail and, perhaps, in the entire West.

This is where manufactured goods from the east were exchanged for products out of Mexico and the Navajo country to the west. The Plains Indians came to the post to barter buffalo robes and the mountain men came in from the South Park area with their pelts. Through the 1830s and 1840s, Bent's Old Fort was the hub of the Southwest. With its 15-foot-high adobe walls and corner watchtowers it resembled a medieval fortress and was called the Castle of the Plains. More than 100 employees worked within the 180- by 135-foot interior, with its open central area and rooms for trappers, laborers, soldiers, Indians, and visitors placed around the sides. It was almost completely self-sufficient, an island of comparative comfort in the midst of endless wilderness.

But the changes put in motion by the very success of the fort had doomed it. The riches of New Mexico reached the East and amplified the call of Manifest Destiny, the political doctrine that an American seizure of Mexico's land in the Southwest was divinely ordained. In 1846, military units began gathering at the fort as it became the advance base for General Stephen Kearney's invasion of New Mexico. When war with Mexico was declared, the fort became a full-fledged staging area and the military overwhelmed the area.

The war was a political and ecological disaster for the Bents. The resources around the fort were despoiled by the sheer number of men and animals that had to be supplied. The appearance of the military alarmed the local tribes and the long truce set up by the Bents was shattered. Open warfare broke out on the Plains. Within a year, Charles—the older of the two brothers and the guiding genius of the business operation—was murdered in his home during an uprising that followed the American takeover of Taos.

William Bent, who had brilliantly balanced the interests of the various groups who visited the fort, tried to carry on alone. But in 1849 a cholera epidemic swept the area. The trappers had gone from the mountains. Formerly friendly Indians were now hostile and avoided the area. Bitter and broken, Bent set fire to his fort that summer and left the area forever.

For 127 years, nothing remained. But in 1976, the National Park Service finished a meticulous recreation of Bent's Old Fort as it appeared at the peak of its influence. It is the summer of 1845 again and forever here. James Polk is President as trappers and Indians, St. Louis merchants and Santa Fe craftsmen, and pioneers and scouts meet to re-enact the life of this piece of Western history. A calendar of special events is planned throughout the year.

* * *

Continue along the fort road, along the north bank of the Arkansas, to the next bridge, at Colorado 109. This will take you back to U.S. 50, on the south side of the river and immediately into the town of **La Junta**. The name means "the junction" and it is where the Santa Fe Trail met the Navajo Trail, the confluence that brought Bent's Old Fort into being nearby. La Junta didn't develop until the railroad arrived, in 1875, and then it became a major shipping center for cattle and produce in the Arkansas Valley. Even today, all the roads in the area radiate from this town, which remains the valley's commercial hub. This is prime melon-growing land and farms here are also known for their sugar beet production. Here, on the campus of Otero Junior College, is the Koshare Indian Kiva, a museum of Southwestern Native cultures. It features exhibits from Plains tribes, Pueblo and Navajo, with basketry, quiltwork and jewelry. It is also home to the Koshare Dancers, Explorer Scouts who perform various dances from the area during the summer months.

The highway is four lanes wide as it shoots through Swink, named for the state senator who championed the irrigation projects that are the basis of the area's prosperity. Rocky Ford, named for a pioneer crossing of the Arkansas, is famed for its cantaloupe, a strain developed by the aforementioned Senator Swink. The produce stands around this town are the most eagerly patronized in the state during the early autumn harvest.

Jim Beckwourth was one of the legendary mountain men. A mulatto, he also claimed to be a Crow war chief. He was, in fact, famous for his fabrications and was one of the first of the early scouts to offer his story in autobiographical form. When some of his former associates heard that Beckwourth's book had been published, they sent a representative into the closest town to buy it. Not being terribly experienced with bookstores, the emissary returned, instead, with a Bible. Opening it at random, one of the men began to read about Samson fixing torches to the tails of foxes to burn the fields of the Philistines. "There's one of Beckwourth's lies," one of the men exclaimed. "I'd know them anywhere." Beckwourth did discover one of the most accessible passes across the Sierra to the California gold fields (see U.S. 395) and was also the founder of Pueblo.

The third biggest city in Colorado started off as a trading post established by Beckwourth in 1842 at the meeting of the Arkansas and Fountain Creek. The site had been visited by Spanish traders from Santa Fe and by Pike's expedition of 1806. An adobe fort sixty yards square, the place thrived. Although never a serious commercial rival to Bent's Old Fort, back up the road, it became the largest settlement in southern Colorado. But on Christmas Day, 1854, a sudden Ute attack almost wiped out the settlement. It had dwindled to a population of two before a party from St. Louis arrived four years later and, using much of the adobe from Beckwourth's fort, built a new community that they named Fountain City. It eventually absorbed the older town, although the name given to it by Beckwourth won out. When the railroads came through in the 1870s, Pueblo developed as the major industrial center for the output of the state's mines. Its smelters and mills turned it into a booming city of 25,000 by 1880, the biggest coal and steel producer in the West. It is still Colorado's top industrial city.

U.S. 50 divides several miles east of the city. Stick with the main road when it branches off from the business route. This will take you past the Pueblo Memorial Airport and the home of the International B-24 Memorial Museum. The airport was used as a training base for the men who flew this bomber during World War II and the museum carries exhibits of their combat experience. Adjacent to the B-24 memorial is the Fred E. Weisbrod Museum, where more than 20 original aircraft from the war are on display.

Continue on Highway 50 to westbound Colorado 96 and take that road through the Interstate 25 viaduct to Santa Fe Avenue. Now turn south and follow the signs for Union Avenue. This is where you'll find the city's greatest concentration of historic structures; it's a fine place for a stroll. The walk leads past the historic Vail Hotel, the huge Union Depot and about 40 buildings dating from before 1890, many of them converted into shops and restaurants.

Now head north on Grand Avenue to 14th Street. Just to the east is Rosemount, built in 1893 by one of Pueblo's most prominent families. What makes this 37-room mansion unique is its state of preservation, with most of the original furnishings still in place just as they were when it was occupied. This is an especially nice trip back to the city's Victorian past.

Grand Avenue will eventually lead you back to U.S. 50, a fast four-lane highway heading west. The road still follows the valley of the Arkansas River, as it has since it entered the state. This is orchard country and you'll see apple and cherry trees on both sides of the highway. The mountains, which have loomed in the distance ever since La Junta, are now a surrounding presence. In **Penrose** there is an enterprise that also deals in exalted heights: Estes Hi-Flier, manufacturer of model rocket kits and kites. The company offers tours of its facilities here, as well as demonstration launchings.

Canon City had a choice back in 1868: It could have picked either the state prison or the state university. Figuring that crime was probably a better long-term growth option than education, it took the prison. That turned out to be a fine investment which is still paying off. The Territorial Prison Museum contains exhibits of past incarcerations, as well as a shop selling handcrafted items made by the inmates. Another bonus was Skyline Drive, a scenic road west of town that runs along a ridge and opens out on views of Canon City. It was built by convict labor.

Before acquiring such stability, the town had a rough time of it. Starting off as a mining camp, Canon City very nearly ceased to exist in the early 1860s. The population had dwindled to a total of Anson Rudd and his family. Rudd's faith was rewarded when the town revived after the Civil War, and his one-room cabin is preserved on the grounds of the Municipal Museum. A more substantial stone residence, built by Rudd in 1881, is also there.

One of the town's mayors at this time was Joaquin Miller, who would move on to California and become famous as a poet and homespun mystic. His inspiring poem, "Columbus," was destined to be proclaimed heroically ("Sail on, sail on and on...") by generations of American schoolchildren. But when Miller suggested changing this town's name to Orodelphia, the residents of Canon City simply made little whirring motions next to their heads with their fingers and bade him Godspeed to the Sierras.

Royal Gorge, the great canyon of the Arkansas that gave Canon City its name, is about eight miles west of the city, by way of U.S. 50. This critical passage was the object of pitched battles between crews of the rival Santa Fe and Denver & Rio Grande railroads in 1875 when the two lines nearly went to war over the right of way. The Denver line won out, but the big advance in transportation didn't come until 1929, when the world's highest suspension bridge was completed across the canyon. Royal Gorge Bridge is 1,053 feet above the river and such a spectacular sight that an entire array of attractions has developed around it. Visitors enjoy exciting perspectives from an incline railway that drops to the foot of the gorge at a 45-degree angle and an aerial tramway that sways across the chasm. Passenger cars and minivans can also be driven across the bridge for the view from the top. And rafting companies in Canon City schedule trips into the canyon itself for the view from directly underneath.

If you aren't fully gorged after all that, there is a narrow-gauge rail trip that runs to the rim of the canyon below the bridge. It leaves from the access road to the bridge south of Highway 50. Also on this road is Buckskin Joe, which may look like just another roadside ersatz Wild West attraction. Well, it is, but it does have a history. It was built as a set for shooting silent Westerns back in the days of Tom Mix, and was later used for exterior shots in "Cat Ballou" and "True Grit."

The highway sticks close to the Arkansas as it winds past Cotopaxi, which somehow got itself named for a mountain in Ecuador by someone who spotted a resemblance. Zinc mines in the area were worked for years. In Coaldale, the prize was travertine and from its quarries was taken the stone used in many public buildings in Washington, D.C.

Salida is Spanish for "exit" and the town was built where the Arkansas emerges from canyon country, at the base of the Sangre de Cristo Range. The railroad developed the place when it came through in 1880 but it is an older mode of transportation that gives

Salida a boost today. Each June, kayakers crowd into town to partic-
ipate in the FibArk Boat Races, a 26-mile run that is the sport's most
important North American event. All sorts of other water-borne
entertainments have grown up with the race and Salida itself has
developed into one of Colorado's top whitewater rafting centers.
Several outfits run trips along the Arkansas and Dolores rivers. Its
entire downtown area is a National Historic District and not far
away is the state's largest indoor mineral bath, with hot springs
bubbling up at temperatures just below 100 degrees.

To the northwest is 14,229-foot Mt. Shavano, named for a Ute
chief. According to legend, while the chief was praying for a dying
friend, the outline of an angel appeared in the snows on the mountain's eastern face. The Angel of Shavano returns each year and is
visible from March to June and September to November.

After passing an area of more mineral baths at Poncha Springs,
the road begins its climb to **Monarch Pass** and embarks on a 125-
mile journey through some of Colorado's most varied and magnificent scenery. It crosses the Continental Divide here at 11,312
feet. There is a ski resort at the summit and during the summer
months tram cars ascend another 600 feet for a view across the
roof of the Rockies, extending all the way back to Pikes Peak, 72
miles away.

We left the Arkansas on the eastern approach to the Divide, but
as we descend the western side we pick up another watery companion. This is Tomichi Creek and it gurgles alongside the road all
the way into Gunnison. The town, the county and the river that
rises nearby are all named for Captain John Gunnison, who left his
mark on the land by surveying a rail line through the area. This
sort of thing happened a lot in the West. By the time the highway
surveyors for the old roads came through, though, all the best
places were named. It seems unfair somehow.

This is a pretty little place, one of those Colorado towns where
the elevation is higher than the population. It sits at 7,703 feet and
is surrounded by the Gunnison National Forest (there's that man

again.) It grew up as the commercial center for the mines at Crested Butte to the north. Now it centers on matters recreational. Fishermen know it for its trout streams and the Roaring Judy Fish Hatchery, where 200,000 pounds of rainbows are reared each year, is just north of town. Ranching is also a major part of the economy and on the third weekend in July Cattlemen's Days, with its rodeo, is held as it has been every summer since 1905.

Just west of town, the highway enters Curecanti National Recreation Area, a chain of three connected man-made lakes in the heart of canyon and mesa country. The easternmost lake, Blue Mesa, was formed in 1965. It is the largest body of water in the state and its 20-mile-long shoreline has become one of Colorado's top water recreation areas. Many of those trout from Roaring Judy eventually make their way here, along with ample kokanee salmon. The entire system is part of the Colorado River Storage Project and Highway 50 follows the shore of Blue Mesa Lake for its entire length.

At Elk Creek, 16 miles west of Gunnison, there is a visitor's center and a chance to get acquainted with the area's attractions and recreational facilities. Nature walks are scheduled in summer. This is also the departure point for boat tours of Blue Mesa and Morrow Point Lakes. Reservations for the 90-minute trip are required.

Look for the Dillon Pinnacles, towering rock formations above the reservoir, about seven miles beyond Elk Creek. They make for an outstanding scenic stop. Three miles further on is the overlook above Blue Mesa Dam. The road veers away from the water, but at Cimarron there is another visitor center. A museum shows off artifacts from the canyons that were flooded by the lakes, including an engine and cars from the railroad that once ran through them. Take the turnoff to Morrow Point Dam, just to the north. The double curvature, thin-arch construction, the first such dam built in the United States, is worth seeing in itself, and there are also self-guided tours to the underground power plant.

While many of the Gunnison's canyons are now lakes, the Black Canyon remains as it was, one of the West's narrowest and deepest gorges and a place of hauntingly dark beauty. The name comes both from the absence of color in the ancient rocks through which the river cuts, and from the absence of sunlight that penetrates its steep, 2,700-foot high walls. Protected as a National Monument, the Black Canyon's narrowest width at the top is 1,100 feet, but the river churns through only a 40-foot-wide opening at one point. Colorado 347 runs north from Highway 50 and turns into a scenic drive along the canyon's southern rim.

U.S. 50 now enters the fertile Uncompahgre Valley, irrigated by waters diverted from the Gunnison. The tunnel that carries this flow was built in 1909 and you can see it about seven miles east of **Montrose**. The town is the center of rich orchard and vegetable farms, much greener in appearance than most of the land in western Colorado. In fact, its settlers thought it looked a lot like Scotland and named the place after the hero of a Sir Walter Scott novel. The more practical side of the pioneers is displayed in the old Denver and Rio Grande depot, now a historical museum with an especially extensive collection of antique farm equipment. They didn't sit around reading Scott all the time back then.

The highway turns sharply north along the Uncompahgre, through the largest fruit-growing area in the state. The theme of this entire drive seems to be produce stands. That's because Highway 50 is rarely out of sight of a river on its entire journey. The road is really a fertile strip across Colorado. Besides the wide assortment of fruit in this area, you should also sample the sweet corn. The farms around Olathe have the reputation for growing the best in the state.

Delta is ground zero of the fruit belt, but it is also the start of dinosaur country. The western strip of Colorado, once part of a prehistoric sea, has some of the country's most fertile fossil grounds, too. Dinosaur Dig quarry, just outside of town, has yielded prize specimens. On the other end of the evolutionary scale are the butterflies in Delta's County Museum. Many of the specimens displayed here are as extinct as the dinosaurs and may be the only ones in existence. This lush area was also favored by the Utes, whose land it used to be. The Council Tree, where one of their greatest leaders, Ouray, would meet with his lieutenants, is just north of Delta.

The huge bulk of Grand Mesa is visible to the northeast as the highway leaves town. This is reputedly the largest flat-topped mountain in the world, although it's hard to imagine how anyone would go about measuring something like that. Everybody loves superlatives, though. Its average elevation is about 10,000 feet and the tableland is dotted with 300 lakes and reservoirs. Highway 50 stays to the west of the mesa, though, and picks up the Gunnison River once more. The road stays with it right into **Grand Junction**, where the Gunnison meets the Colorado.

This is the largest town between Denver and Salt Lake City, a marketing and transportation center for the surrounding farm country. It was once part of the Ute Reservation, but that arrangement ended in 1880 when the fertility of the nearby riverland was ascertained. The Utes were removed to more barren grounds to the south and a land rush held here the following year. The start of the orchard culture followed soon after. One of those old farms continues to present agricultural life the way it used to be. Cross Orchards is a living history farm, showing off the way rural life was a few decades after Grand Junction's founding. The town also has an outstanding regional museum, with some of the best displays of natural science and history in the state. The Museum of Western Colorado's biggest draw, however, is Dinosaur Valley. Many of those fossils uncovered back around Delta have been reassembled here into huge beasts. Some of them are animated and when they give out a loud roar....well, even though you know it's just show biz, you still keep an eye on the exit. There is also a working paleontology lab on the premises to show how scientists go about analyzing bone fragments and fitting them into the whole structure of creatures that died off even before humans walked the planet.

U.S. 50 rolls on through the orchards a little longer before combining with Interstate 70 and having its identity extinguished for a few hundred miles. To finish the drive, head west, instead, on Colorado 340 into Colorado National Monument. The road leads to Rim Rock Drive, a scenic spin above canyons and amid the eroded sandstone of the Uncompahgre Plateau. Huge monoliths, carved into balanced rocks and giant pipe organs, line the road, which also opens out on views across the farms of the Colorado Valley. The road makes a loop back to U.S. 50 and rejoins it near the town of Fruita, an aptly named place to end this drive through Colorado's most fertile acres.

VISITING HOURS

COLORADO

Canon City: Territorial Prison Museum, (719) 269-3015. First at Macon. Daily, 8:30–5, May–September; 1–5, Wednesday–Sunday at other times. Admission.

Municipal Museum, (719) 269-9018. Sixth at Royal Gorge Blvd. Daily, 9–5, mid-May–mid-September; daily, 1–5 at other times. Free.

Colorado National Monument Visitor Center: (303) 858-3617. Western entrance of park, on Colorado 340. Daily, 8–8, June–Labor Day; 8–4:30 at other times. Admission charge to park, visitor center is free.

Curecanti National Recreation Area: Elk Creek Visitor Center, (303) 641-0406. Eastern entrance, on U.S. 50. Daily, 8–4:30, Memorial Day–Labor Day. Free. Cruises leave from Elk Creek Marina, daily, memorial Day-Labor Day. Advance reservation required. (303) 641-0402 for schedule.

Cimarron Visitor Center, (303) 249-4073. Western entrance, on U.S. 50. Daily, 10–4:30, Memorial Day–Labor Day.

Delta: County Museum, (303) 874-3791. Fifth at Palmer. Monday–Friday, 1:30–4:30, June–August. Friday only at other times. Donation.

Grand Junction: Cross Orchards, (303) 434-9814. 3073 F Road. Wednesday–Saturday, 10–4, May–October. Admission.

Museum of Western Colorado, (303) 242-0971. Fourth and Ute Aves. Monday–Saturday, 10–4:45, Memorial Day–Labor Day; closed Monday at other times. Free.

La Junta: Bent's Old Fort, (719) 384-2596. East, on Colorado 194. Daily, 8–6, Memorial Day–Labor Day; 8–4:30 at other times. Admission.

Koshare Indian Kiva, (719) 384-4411. 115 W. 18th St. Daily, 9–5, June–August; 12:30–5 at other times. Admission.

Lamar: Big Timbers Museum, (719) 336-2472. North of town on U.S. 50. Daily, 1:30–4:30. Admission.

Las Animas: Kit Carson Museum, (719) 456-2005. Ninth and Bent Ave. Daily, 1–5, Memorial Day–Labor Day. Free.

Monarch Pass: Chair Lift, (719) 539-4789. On U.S. 50. Daily, 9–4, mid-May–mid-October. Fare.

Montrose: County Historical Museum, (303) 249-2085. At Main and Rio Grande, in the railroad depot. Daily, 1–5, May–October. Admission.

Penrose Estes Hi-Flier Kites, (719) 372-6565. On U.S. 50. Phone for reservation and schedule.

Pueblo: Weisbrod Museum and International B-24 Memorial Museum, (719) 948-9219 and 948-3355. At Pueblo Memorial Airport, off U.S. 50. Daily, 8:30–dusk. Free.

Rosemount, (719) 545-5290. At 419 W. 14th St. Monday–Saturday, 10–4, and Sunday, 2–4, June–August; Tuesday–Saturday, 1–4 and Sunday, 2–4 at other times. Admission.

Royal Gorge: Incline Railway, Tramway and Bridge, (719) 275-7507. Daily, daylight hours. Admission.

Buckskin Joe and Rail Trip, (719) 275-5149. Immediately north of Royal Gorge Bridge. Daily, daylight hours, Memorial Day–Labor Day. Admission.

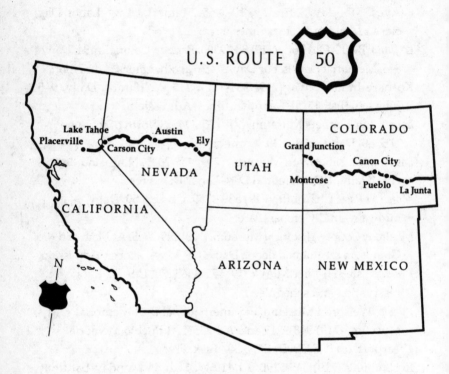

U.S. ROUTE 50

COLORADO

Lake Tahoe
Placerville
Carson City
Austin
Ely
Grand Junction
Canon City
Montrose
Pueblo
La Junta

NEVADA

UTAH

CALIFORNIA

N

ARIZONA

NEW MEXICO

The Loneliest Road

〇

U.S. 50

Ely, Nev. to Placerville, Calif.
407 miles

U.S. 50 takes off on its own once more at the old copper town of **Ely**, heading straight west across Nevada on what has been called The Loneliest Road in America. Between Ely and **Fallon**, a distance of 257 miles, only two settlements of any size break the expanse of wilderness, and both of them are relics of the mining era.

There are mementoes of Pony Express days on this route, memorable views of Lake Tahoe and the Sierra and a conclusion at the mother lode of all Western mines, the source of the California Gold Rush.

MILEPOSTS

The road shakes clear of U.S. 6 in East Ely and heads into Ely. This was a small gold mining camp until 1902 when investors associated with the Comstock Lode, on the far end of this road in Nevada, decided to take the plunge and put in the capital to exploit its copper. Everyone knew the copper was there. The trouble was getting it out to where it could do some good. Ely was far from any rail line and the costs of smelting the ore were beyond the means of any local group. They even had to borrow money in 1868 to get the town laid out. John Ely, a land speculator from

Pioche, came through with a $5,000 loan and got the place named for him. But when prospectors hit the Ruth mine in 1900, the really big money started pouring in. Nevada Consolidated acquired all the area holdings and by 1906 the Nevada Northern had been built up the Steptoe Valley to the Union Pacific main line. (See U.S. 93 for a description of that railroad and its former terminal, closed since 1983 and now a museum in East Ely.) It was a good investment. By the time the copper finally gave out in the 1970s, more than a half a billion dollars had been taken from the ground here, making Ely the richest copper town in the state's history. The basis of its economy is now ranching and recreation, but memories of the mining era are preserved in the White Pine Museum, which features several original locomotives used by the Nevada Northern.

The site of the Ruth Mine is just west of town along U.S. 50. You can turn off and take a peek at the pit, just to the south of the road. Nearby is Garnet Hill, a popular spot for rockhounds, where samples of its namesake stone are plentiful.

Between here and Eureka, the highway crosses four mountain ranges, all of them between 6,500 and 7,500 feet high. The original plan by Nevada Consolidated was to run the connecting rail spur to the Ely mines along this route from Eureka, but the mountainous terrain made that impractical. So our old road makes the run alone.

Across Robinson Summit is the White Sage Valley. Once the mountains to the south were denuded of their pines: all of them had gone into charcoal ovens for smelting down the copper at Ely. But the range is now part of Humboldt National Forest and the growths have been replenished. The area is dominated by 10,475-foot-high Mt. Hamilton. Moorman Ranch was named for a stagecoach stop that operated here from 1869 to 1885, serving the mining camp of Hamilton on the mountain's slopes. It had a population of 10,000 in its peak years but is deserted today.

As you traverse this area, you may begin to understand why this is known as the "loneliest road." As a promotion, several communities along the route pass out bumper stickers and t-shirts that read: "I survived Highway 50." The road won the tag in a *Life* magazine article, which indicated the highway had no services (which is pretty much true) and no attractions (a shocking falsehood.)

Take Eureka. This is one of the most photogenic of the state's old mining towns, with an opera house, a courthouse and all sorts of vintage tumbledown buildings. The name was apt, too. As you'll recall from your Greek history, Archimedes was given the task of trying to figure out if the golden crown of King Hieron II was actually made of baser metal. While the king was suspicious, he was also possessive, and melting down the crown to get the answer was disallowed. Now we cut to the famous bathtub scene, in which Archimedes figures out how to measure an object's composition by the water it displaces and leaps out unclad to race through the streets shouting "Eureka," or "I have found it." Things like this apparently happened all the time in ancient Greece.

The moment of truth was less dramatic here. They found lead-silver deposits but no one could figure out how to extract the ores. Finally, Albert Arentz developed the siphon tap to discharge bullion from the smelter and it was Eureka time in Nevada. Once they began to get the lead out in 1870, the town developed into a major mining camp and a spur was brought down from the Central Pacific. By 1891, the smelters had closed but $40 million in silver and 250,000 pounds of lead had been taken. The Eureka Sentinel Museum, housed in former newspaper offices, has exhibits of those days and the wealth of Victorian buildings makes Eureka a delightful place in which to amble.

To the west, the road runs arrow-straight without a turn across a broad valley for 23 miles. Toiyabe National Forest is to the south, on the heights of 10,220-foot Antelope Peak. Near Hickison

Summit is a state recreation area that shows off petroglyphs drawn by native people between 1000 A.D. and 1500 A.D. The site commands a view of flatlands in all directions, and is also just a few miles north of Nevada's geographic center.

The highway now enters the national forest, climbs across Austin Summit, and comes to another of the state's mining town gems.

FOCUS

"There it is, boys," said the old prospector, turning his pouch upside down on the bar and allowing its contents to tumble out. "Lander County turquoise, best in the world. I got me a mine of it out there. Don't even have to hide it. Nobody will ever find it."

He's right about that. The city of Indianapolis could be out there and nobody will ever find it. For about one hour's drive in any direction, Austin is the only place there is. Just a few miles from the heart of Nevada geographically, this old mining town is very near the heart of its spirit, as well. It is a place that treasures its past and counts its treasures not only in its turquoise but in its solitude. Suggest that it's a ghost town, though, and you'll get a long stare of resentment from practically all of its 400 residents.

"Back in the hippie days, a bunch of young teachers from the San Francisco area came here to work in the school," one longtime resident recalled. "One Fourth of July they hung out a banner that said: 'Free America.' We all thought they were crazy. What could be freer than this?"

Free spirits are sort of an Austin tradition. The town grew from a wide spot in Toiyabe Canyon to a settlement of 10,000 within the space of a few months in 1863. This was the first significant silver strike in central Nevada and Lander County was simply carved out of the middle third of the state, since no one was doing anything else with it at the time. As other mining camps developed, though, other counties were formed and the boundaries shrank. The first order of business was relocating the town from the foot of the canyon to a more secure location on higher ground. Since there was no road, this was difficult. But someone hit on the idea of trading town lots in return for road work and in a few months the road was built.

The most celebrated event in Austin's early history occurred on this road. Reuel Gridley, one of the town's handful of Democrats, made a bet on the spring elections in 1864 with local Republicans. The loser agreed to carry a sack of flour up the road from the old camp into town. Taking his loss good naturedly, Gridley finished the haul and proposed the sack be auctioned off with the proceeds going to a hospital fund for war relief. That was so much fun that the high bidder turned the sack in so that it could be auctioned off again. By the end of the day, $10,000 had been raised. That gave Gridley an idea, and for the next few months he toured the mining camps of Nevada and California, auctioning off his flour sack again and again and raising money for the Union. Gridley's store still stands at the eastern end of town.

The miners at Austin also agreed to import several of the camels that were turned loose by the military in Arizona after a failed experiment in exotic desert transport (see U.S. 95 for a more detailed description of that episode.) For years afterwards, the beasts were a familiar sight here toting quartz for nearby mills.

Another curious sight is Stokes Castle, built in 1879 by a pair of brothers from Philadelphia who had invested heavily in the area's silver mines. A square, three-story granite tower built on the hilltop just west of town, the castle once contained living quarters but has been abandoned for decades. It is visible for miles.

Austin was the childhood home of Emma Wixom, who entertained the miners by singing at community functions. She went on to become one of the great coloratura sopranos of the European opera. At a time when most serious singers felt they had to adopt

European-sounding names to gain legitimacy, she decided to emphasize her American roots and changed hers to Emma Nevada. Her return to Austin in 1885 was a civic celebration, but it was one of the last the town saw. The mines had already started to decline and the biggest employer shut down two years later.

Austin today is one of the most authentically preserved mining towns in the West, a glimpse of the way Nevada used to be. The town pays tribute to the large number of Irish miners who came here with an annual St. Patrick's Day celebration and in mid-June old Reuel Gridley is saluted again with an old time fiddler's contest. Its courthouse is the oldest in the state as is its weekly paper, the *Reese River Reveille*.

And drop in at the Oldest Bar in Nevada. If you're lucky, someone may wander in from the hills and show you some Lander County turqoise, best in the world.

* * *

The road crosses New Pass through the Desatoya Mountains and enters Churchill County. We parallel the route of the Pony Express here and some of the best preserved stations of that legendary mail service are nearby. This run, from St. Joseph, Missouri to Sacramento, California was in operation for less than 19 months. It ended when the first transcontinental telegraph opened on October 22, 1861, sending messages almost instantaneously across country that it had taken the Express riders ten and a half days to cover. But while the Pony Express existed it had halved the previous mail delivery time and the image of the young, solitary riders racing across the plains and deserts of the West permanently captured the American imagination. The stations at Cold Springs and Sand Mountain, both just a short walk off the highway, give a sense of what a trip through this wilderness was like when a traveler's life depended on a fast horse. Sand Mountain is named for a

nearby dune, built of material piled up against a ridge by the western winds. It is known for moaning in a low tone when the breeze
stirs the granular pellets.

Continuing west, the highway crosses Eight Mile Flat, part of
the bed of ancient Lake Lahontan, which once covered all of western Nevada. Salt wells were once mined here, but transportation
costs made the project uncompetitive with other sources.
Unfortunately for its sponsors, a $175,000 processing plant was
built before that determination was made.

Another set of Indian petroglyphs are visible just beyond the
western end of the flat, at Grimes Point. Tours of the archeological
excavations in adjacent Hidden Cave are given on alternate weekends.

Fallon is a product of the first federal reclamation project,
Newlands, on the Truckee-Carson river system. The site was a
ranch owned by Mike Fallon when the project was approved in
1902 under the recently passed Reclamation Act. By the time the
first phase of the irrigation program was completed in 1908, it was
the county seat and a prosperous planned community. Hearts o'
Gold cantaloupe are the best known local crop and a festival held
each Labor Day weekend serves them up in rich, juicy portions.
The Churchill County Museum contains exhibits on the nearby
Pony Express stations, the building of the transcontinentnal telegraph through this area, and the Newlands project.

The highway divides just west of Fallon, with 50A jogging to the
north. We'll stay with Highway 50. At this point once stood the
community of Leeteville, which was also known as Ragtown. This
is where wagon trains began lightening their loads for the final
push across the Sierras. Now that the mountains were in sight, the
reality of the difficulties ahead of them hit home to the pioneers
and observers said the ground here was littered with discarded
belongings. Everything but the essentials of life was discarded. As
the wagon trains gathered here, the crossroads became a trade cen-

ter. Now traffic heading up on 50A will join Interstate 80 in a few miles to cross the mountains with hardly a tug on the steering wheel.

Lahontan Dam, the key element in the Newlands project, and its 16-mile-long reservoir, which is also named for the prehistoric lake that covered this area, are just west of town along the highway.

Dayton grew up around the quartz mill that processed the ore from the Comstock Lode. A few miles beyond is the turnoff to Virginia City, the fabled mining town that the silver from the Comstock Lode created. That's outside our scope, however, and we'll just proceed straight ahead to Nevada's capital, **Carson City**.

Once the smallest state capital in the country, it has grown all the way up to 12th smallest. Maybe that doesn't quite make it a metropolis but it does reflect what has happened in Nevada in the last few decades. Still, a sense of openness remains in this town on the eastern slope of the Sierra. Its rivers and trees were a welcome sight to the desert-weary pioneers, but not many of them lingered when the California gold fields were so close. A group of miners did backtrack into the area in 1851. Unsuccessful in California, they thought they might have better luck here. When one of them shot an eagle while building a cabin, the place, which was a stop on the Overland Stage route, became known as Eagle Station. Later, during a period of land speculation, it was decided to dignify it a bit by renaming it in honor of the frontier scout, Kit Carson. The speculation was fired by anticipation of this area separating from Utah. Until 1861, what is now Nevada was all part of the Utah Territory. But four years previously, Brigham Young had called Mormon settlers across the west back to Salt Lake City to help defend the settlement against an expected federal assault. That left a governing vacuum here and in 1859 settlers started organizing a new territory, a move that was welcomed in Washington when the Comstock Lode came in. The Carson City promoters argued that the old capital, Genoa, was too remote, whereas their town sat astride the stage and Pony Express routes. They carried the day and the new territorial legislature quickly voted to move here, abandoning Genoa to its fate (See U.S. 395).

The silver-domed State Capitol, completed in 1871, was a great advance from the first legislative sessions here, which were held in a hotel ballroom with a curtain hung down the middle to make it bicameral. The big money that came down from the nearby Comstock made this the home of the most wide open politics in the country, featuring characters that could have stepped right out of a Mark Twain novel. The handsome sandstone structure is still in use, surrounded by a park in the heart of the city. Historical displays about the building and some of its former denizens are located in the old Senate chamber. Four blocks north, in what used to be the U.S. Mint, is the Nevada State Museum. The machinery that stamped out silver and gold coins here from 1866 to 1893 is still in place. There are also large exhibits on a ghost town, an underground mine, and an Indian village. Also in the Capitol area is the Warren Engine Company Fire Museum, displaying antique fire-fighting equipment in a stone firehouse built in 1863. The handpumper that was imported from California as the state's first piece of fire apparatus is restored and exhibited.

The highway runs south along Carson Street and in a few miles reaches the State Railroad Museum. The core of the exhibits here are authentic engines and cars from the Virginia and Truckee Railroad, which brought ore down from the Comstock Lode. Two of the engines still operate and rides on the vintage equipment are given on weekends.

Highway 50 bends sharply west to begin its approach to the Sierra foothills. At Spooner Summit, you get the first glimpse of the sparkling blue waters of Lake Tahoe. This alpine jewel, framed by pines and mountains, was first seen by explorers when John C. Fremont was brought here by Indians in 1844. "A beautiful view of a mountain lake," he wrote in his journal, understating the matter nicely. Despite attempts to name it in honor of various politicians and explorers, the Washoe word for lake was applied to it in the first official mapping of the Pacific Coast in 1862 and it stuck. The lake is about 200 square miles in size and its average depth is 989 feet. It holds enough water to cover the entire state of California 14 inches deep, which is something to consider.

Tahoe was created by the same mountain-building process that uplifted the Sierras—a massive fault forming a trough between the main range and the Carson Mountains to the east. U.S. 50 traverses a rather small portion of its southeastern corner and you may be inclined to settle in here and make the circuit of the lake on state highways. That is understandable. On this road, however, you will pass several scenic overlooks, especially near the tunnel at Cave Rock, looking directly across to the California shore. Cruises along the southern end of the lake leave the dock at **Zephyr Cove** aboard the paddlewheeler M.D. Dixie and visit Emerald Bay, one of the most beautiful portions of the lake. The area around Stateline is a major casino and resort development and a side road here leads to Nevada Beach, for those willing to try the 68-degree summer water temperature.

There is also a state recreation area on the California side of the line, around the town of South Lake Tahoe. At one time, the lakeshore here was lined with wharves, serving the lumber camps clustered on the southern shore of the lake. The lumber was shipped across to Glenbrook, just north of where U.S. 50 reached the lake on the Nevada shore, then hauled off to the Comstock to line the mine shafts. The forests in this area were very nearly wiped out by this activity. Only the depletion of the Comstock enabled them to survive.

At this point, the road turns south, away from the lake. It runs through Tahoe Valley before starting its ascent to Echo Summit, at 7,382 feet, where it enters Eldorado National Forest. This was the main supply road for the Nevada mines from San Francisco and

Sacramento and six-mule team wagons paid a toll of $36 to make the run. It was also the first overland mail route to the gold camps from the east. The highway follows the South Fork of the American River through the mountains, passing through towns that grew up around former toll stations. One area is still known as Toll House Flat. Watch also for the waterfall at the edge of the Desolation Canyon Wilderness Area.

Just west of Pacific House, a politically charged stagecoach robbery took place in 1864. Three Confederate sympathizers made off with a gold shipment, probably the westernmost raid conducted in the Civil War. But two were captured within a day and the third made the mistake of killing a pursuing lawman and upon his apprehension he was executed. The funds never reached the beleaguered armies of the South.

For the last 60 miles of its run to Sacramento, U.S. 50 becomes a freeway. We'll only stay with it for a few more miles, into **Placerville**. This was the commercial center of the Gold Rush country, the great jumping-off place for the mines from the Overland Trail. Within a year of the gold strike, it was the third largest city in California, trailing only San Francisco and Sacramento. Fortunes were made here. Mark Hopkins started accumulating the capital that would build railroads by running a grocery store. Philip Armour owned the butcher shop. John Studebaker manufactured wheelbarrows. Back then it was called Hangtown, for the preferred method of dealing with lawbreakers. Placer, the name given to gold found in gravel, eventually became attached to this settlement. During Wagon Train Week, in mid-June, celebrations commemmorating Gold Rush days are held all along U.S. 50, back to the Nevada line, concluding with a parade through town. Placerville also operates a gold mine in Gold Bug Park, where you can see an exposed vein and an operating stamp mill. El Dorado County Historical Museum, at the fairgrounds, features exhibits on the Gold Rush era.

We have come to the end of U.S. 50, but as long as we're this close we'll take a brief drive north on California 49 to **Coloma**. This is where the rush began, where a man named John Marshall discovered flecks of gold in the river on January 24, 1848 near a sawmill on the land of Johannes Sutter. The find made California and destroyed Sutter. He was overrun by gold seekers who staked out claims on land that belonged to him, barred him from his own property, and when he sued for recovery, bought out judge and jury. Years later he was voted a $200 monthly stipend by the state legislature that was cut in half at the following session. Sutter died impoverished in 1885 while some of the greatest fortunes in America were made on his land. A monument marks the spot of Marshall's fateful find and a cabin that he occupied in later years is also part of the Gold Discovery State Historic Park. There is also a replica of Sutter's mill and a museum. Visitors can still flock to the banks of the South Fork of the American River to pan for a souvenir of their own and take away a piece of California's golden dream.

VISITING HOURS

NEVADA

Carson City: Nevada State Museum, (702) 687-4810. On U.S. 50, at N. Carson at Robinson Sts. Daily, 8:30–4:30, Admission.

Warren Engine Company Fire Museum, (702) 887-2200. In State Capitol area, at 111 N. Curry St. Daily, 10–5. Free.

State Railroad Museum, (702) 687-6953. South, on U.S. 50, at Fairview Dr. Wednesday–Sunday, 8:30–4:30. Admission. Weekend train rides, Memorial Day–Labor Day. Call for schedule.

Ely: White Pine Museum, (702) 289-4710. At 2000 Aultman St. Monday–Friday, 9–5, and weekends, 10–3. Free.

Fallon: Churchill County Museum, (702) 423-3677. At 1050 S. Main St. Monday–Saturday, 10–5 and Sunday, noon–5, June–September; closed Thursday at other times. Admission. Tours to Hidden Cave, east on U.S. 50, are given on the second and fourth Saturday of each month.

Zephyr Cove: Lake Tahoe Cruises, (702) 588-3508. Daily, mid-April–mid-October. Call for schedule and reservations.

CALIFORNIA

Coloma: Marshall Gold Discovery State Historic Park, (916) 622-3470. North of U.S. 50, on California 49. Museum open, daily, 10–5, Memorial Day–Labor Day; 11–4:30 at other times. Admission to park.

Placerville: El Dorado County Museum, (916) 621-5865. West, at the County Fairgrounds. Wednesday–Saturday, 10–4, and Sunday, 1–4, Memorial Day–Labor Day; closed Sunday, at other times. Donation.

U.S. ROUTE 54

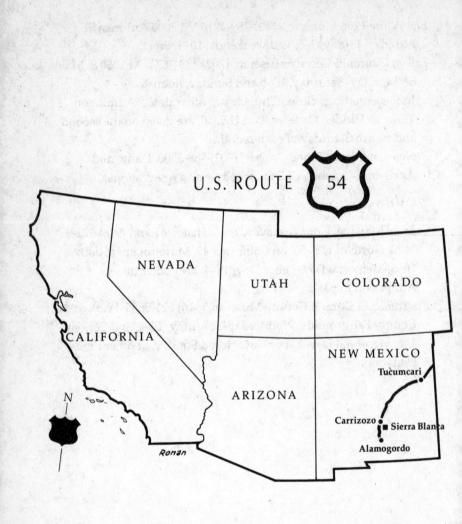

Rocket Country

U.S. 54

Nara Visa, N.M. to Orogrande, N.M.
344 miles

This is one of the country's great diagonals, heading on a steady southwestern course across the midlands to the Rockies, from the Mississippi River in western Illinois to El Paso, Texas. On the way, it parallels the Rock Island and Southern Pacific rail lines, and in Kansas it follows the military supply road of the Santa Fe Trail, linking the pioneer track with the old U.S. Army outpost at Fort Scott.

Its route through New Mexico maintains the same angle. The road crosses the endless horizons of the Staked Plains, then turns due south at the western edge of the White and Sacramento mountains. The stretch between Corona and **Alamogordo**, particularly, features spectacular mountain scenery on one side, and views of the Tularosa Basin, with its celebrated white sands, on the other.

MILEPOSTS

We start with a mistake. The crossroads of Nara Visa sounds unmistakably and descriptively Spanish. By all rights, it should mean something like "distant passage." Actually, the town gets its name from a nearby creek, which runs through land once owned by a man named Narvaez. Early Anglo settlers transformed this into something like "Norvis" but later arrivals, groping towards a spurious authenticity, pseudo-Hispanicized it to Nara Visa. The words mean nothing in Spanish.

Even the Spanish name for this entire region, *Llano Estacado*, is open to debate. It means The Staked Plains, but what this refers to no one is quite sure. The grasslands are the onetime hunting ground of the Comanche and cover about 60,000 square miles in New Mexico and Texas, with their western limits at the Pecos River. U.S. 54 slides into the picture at what is usually regarded as their northern boundary.

Some reference sources claim the name derives from yucca growths. Viewed from a distance by Spanish explorers, they had the appearance of stakes delineating the trackless plain. Anglo pioneers said that the routes to waterholes were staked out and that was the origin of the name. There are also Indian legends that tell of stakes driven into the ground to guide a Great Chief who would appear to lead the Comanches to victory.

The first town of any size is Logan, on the Canadian River. It was named for a captain of the Texas Rangers who filed a claim on the site. A dam forms Ute Lake just west of town and a 633-acre state park overlooks the rare splash of blue.

The Don Carlos Hills now come into view to the north, and occasional ravines and sandstone outcroppings break up the monotony of the grass sea.

Tucumcari grew up as a railroad junction town, where the Rock Island met the Southern Pacific. The mountain at its side, which rises to 4,957 feet above the Llano Estacado, was a landmark and a lookout for the Comanches and westward-trekking pioneers. In later years, it was a major stopping point along U.S. 66 (its route now usurped by Interstate 40) and its rhythmic name furnished the title for a popular song hit by Jimmie Rodgers in the late 1950s. The word is probably a variation of a Comanche phrase for "a place to lie in wait," referring to the strategic advantages of the adjacent mountain. The town dates back to 1901 when the Rock

Island Line arrived. A small museum, just south of the central crossroads, recounts its past.

The road links up with I-40 for the next 54 miles along the western extremity of the Staked Plains. About 12 miles out of town, bluffs rise on the southern side of the road. Through the early 1870s, Comanches raided the ranches of this area and then sold the stolen cattle to bands of Mexican or renegade Anglos. They became known as the Comancheros. These bluffs were one of their hideouts and a place at which the rustled goods were exchanged.

The hostility of the tribe towards the early Spanish settlers acted as a barrier to any move further north. At the same time, however, they ensured that French trappers working the Colorado mountains would not venture any further south. By 1875, the last Comanche bands were removed to Oklahoma reservations.

Near Cuervo, (the Spanish word for "crow") there is a view of the Pecos Valley, as the highway descends to the riverside settlement of Santa Rosa. Corazon Hill is visible to the north, where it rises to 6,270 feet.

The highway turns sharply south here, leaving the Interstate, and cuts across the vast sheep ranches of Guadalupe County. Some of this land carries titles that can be traced back more than 300 years. The original settlers were soldiers who first saw the country while serving with the Coronado expedition of 1540.

Vaughn is another old railroad town, where the Southern Pacific meets the Santa Fe. No fewer than three old roads converge on this little settlement of 800 people, as rail lines and onetime cattle trails turned this, for a brief time, into one of the territory's transportation centers. The cluster of shade trees in the town recalls that era, when it was referred to as "the oasis."

The road continues to ascend through the high plains with the Gallinas Mountains rising to an 8,615-foot crest on the west. The village of Corona, Spanish for "crown," marks what the early settlers regarded as the division point between plain and mountain country. The mesa to the north is known as Gallo, which means rooster, and the Gallinas Range is Spanish for chickens.

Speaking of fowl play, one of the legendary copper mines atop Gallo Mesa was called the Millionaire. Its owner was one of the great con men, a breed that proliferated amid the western mines. His surveys indicated that while the walls contained rich copper deposits, he already had hit bedrock at a depth of only 150 feet. So each year he sold the rights to the mine to a new pigeon, with the proviso that if 50 feet weren't drilled within a year, title would revert back to him. Of course, the new owners always failed and the grifter was able to repeat the process the next year.

The road now runs along the eastern edge of Cibola National Forest, through a narrow valley walled in by the Jicarilla Mountains on the east. Where the valley widens is the town of **Ancho**, which means "broad." In this almost deserted mining town, just off the highway, the former rail depot has been converted into a museum of local artifacts, called My House of Old Things.

The mines of the Jicarilla reached their peak in the 1880s when gold was discovered. The Old Abe Mine was kept in production for 80 years and more than $3 million was extracted from the strike. But the man who found it received just nine dollars for his pains. John Wilson was a fugitive from Texas, on the run across this part of the country to hide out with two friends. He climbed Baxter Mountain to get a better view of possible getaway routes and as he sat down to rest, he idly chipped away at the rock with his pick. He found gold. His friends were overjoyed to hear it, but Wilson knew the strike was worthless to him. If he dallied, he'd be back in the lockup. So his buddies sent him on his way with nine silver dollars and a new gun, and became wealthy men.

The settlement that grew up around the strike, **White Oaks**, is now one of the area's preeminent ghost towns. It reached a peak population of 2,000 by 1900 and some of New Mexico's most powerful figures, including its first statehood governor, W.C. McDonald, were residents. The schoolhouse, built in 1894, is open for tours.

Three miles south of the turnoff to White Oaks is another of the linguistic mishaps with which New Mexico is speckled. Carrizo is the name for a sort of reed grass that grows abundantly in the area. One early settler was so impressed by its plenitude that he decided to add an extra syllable for emphasis and called the new town Carrizozo. The peak of the same name, a 9,650-foot landmark, stands sentinel on the east.

The town sits at the northern edge of the Tularosa Basin, a broad valley shielded by towering mountains from extremes of climate. The moderate temperatures are now turning it into a retirement area, but in the 1940s many of the same attributes that make it so attractive to retirees today provided a setting for another sort of activity. Just beyond Carrizozo, you'll see the bulk of Oscura Peak on the western horizon. On its far side is the Trinity Site, where in July, 1945 the first atomic bomb was succesfully tested. We'll hear more about that in a few more miles.

There is a historic marker and little else remaining at the crossroads of Three Rivers. Some of the state's best-known cattle ranches were situated around this rail-loading point. Susan Barber, the Cattle Queen of New Mexico, took over her husband's holdings as a widow in the 1890s and ran them for the next 20 years. She eventually sold out to Albert Fall, who consolidated many of the ranches in the area to become the biggest landowner in the state. Fall met his downfall, however, as Secretary of the Interior in the scandal-ridden administration of President Warren G. Harding. He went to prison in 1929 for his part in the Teapot Dome oil lease hanky-panky.

Three Rivers is at the base of Sierra Blanca, the highest peak in this part of the state at 12,003 feet. It is snowcapped for most of the year and, viewed in the early morning, with the first light glimmering on its summit and on the white sands to the west, makes an unforgettable sight. Five miles east on the road to the mountain is the Three Rivers Petroglyph Site. Watch for the sign on the left;

it is small and easily missed. A short walking trail leads from the parking lot and ascends a small hill, with rock steps built into the incline. Climb to where the path divides. A loop trail leads to most of the pictures; faces, fanciful animals, and geometric designs on the black rocks. The meaning of the figures is not clearly understood, but it is felt that the location held some religious significance for the Mogollon Culture people who occupied this site from about 900 to 1400. The last of these pictures was made more than a century before the landing of Columbus.

The name, Tularosa is a combination of two Spanish words, meaning "reeds" and "roses." The settlers from flooded-out Rio Grande communities to the west found both growing here when they arrived in 1860. They also found Apaches and the site was quickly abandoned. But two years later they returned to stay and the town still celebrates a Rose Festival each May, as well as a fiesta for its patron saint at the Church of St. Francis de Paula. The Mexican influence is also strong at Christmas when the center of town is lit with *illuminaria*.

Just to the south is La Luz, first settled in 1705 and the oldest village in the valley. It is now an arts center, with shops specializing in weavings, pottery, and jewelry. Cottonwoods line the highway as we approach the outskirts of Alamogordo, named for the large size of these native trees.

FOCUS

When Robert Goddard was politely advised by the civil authorities to get out of Massachusetts and take his rockets with him, the scientist had the entire country from which to choose a new site for his experiments. He picked New Mexico, about 100 miles east of Alamogordo.

The preponderance of clear days, a necessity for tracking the results of his pioneering tests in rocketry, and its isolation from great population centers made the area a perfect choice.

Goddard arrived in 1930, and while his work attracted little attention at the time, it was the first step in America's space program.

Fifteen years later, the same sort of calculations figured in the selection of the area by the U.S. government for its own stepped-up program of rocketry research. In the closing days of World War II, the team of German scientists who had devised the V-2 rockets surrendered as a group to American forces. In a secret operation called "Paper Clip" they were transported to the New Mexico desert to continue their work.

The area had worked out well for the military in the development of the atomic bomb. Los Alamos was one of the primary research centers for the project and, as mentioned above, the area northwest of Alamogordo was chosen for the bomb's first successful test in 1945. (How odd that the two New Mexico cities associated with the development of nuclear weapons, while located hundreds of miles apart, carried the same Spanish name for cottonwood, the tree that marked the presence of water in the arid West and was a symbol of life.)

The White Sands Missile Range was established in the Tularosa Basin later that year, with Werner Von Braun placed in charge of the project. Along with the clear skies and isolation that had attracted Goddard, this area also contained an Air Force installation, a vast flat firing area, and adjacent mountains to hold observation points. While the research facilities were transferred to Huntsville, Alabama in a few years, the missile range is still an active part of the country's space and military program. It is also used as an alternative landing site for the Challenger shuttle and is officially designated as a Space Harbor.

On this range, the testing of rockets that first carried Americans into manned Earth orbit and, eventually, to the moon, was carried out. From the panicked response to the Soviet launch of Sputnik in 1957 to the triumphant landing of the first men on the moon 12 years later, Alamogordo was the proving grounds for the latest advances in rocketry.

Appropriately, the city's Space Center has become one of the country's foremost museums of the rocket age. Housed in a cube-like structure on a rise that overlooks both the city and the missile range, the Space Center is a combination of historical exhibits, hands-on displays of space technology, a planetarium, a Hall of Fame, a wide-screen movie theater, and an outdoor collection of actual spacecraft and launchers.

The museum traces the history of rocket research from the efforts of the ancient Chinese to Goddard to the Challenger and beyond. Visitors ascend to the top of the building and then make their way down along a winding ramp.

The turnoff to the Space Center, White Sands Boulevard, is clearly marked to the east on U.S. 54, White Sands Boulevard. Even if you miss the sign you can hardly fail to notice the white rocket that sits in front of it, outlined against the dark mass of Alamo Peak.

* * *

Almost opposite the turnoff to the Space Center is Alameda Park, a pleasant green space that contains a small zoo almost as old as the city. The town grew up in 1898 at the base of the Sacramento Mountains as a water supply point for the railroad serving the lumber camps in the heights. The zoo was intended by the rail line as a diversion for weary travelers who had just made the sooty cross-mountain trip. While the train stopped here to take on water, passengers were free to stroll through the animal exhibits. The zoo now has expanded to seven acres and houses more than 300 different kinds of mammals and birds.

South of the city, a side road leads east to Oliver Lee State Park. At the mouth of Dog Canyon, the park memorializes one of the area's early ranchers and is intended to preserve a piece of frontier history. Lee and Frenchy Rochas homesteaded here in the 1880s, in an area avoided by earlier settlers who had feared it as an Apache stronghold. The outlines of the Rochas ranch are visible and the Lee home can be toured. There is also a visitor's center that explains the natural and historical significance of the canyon. The town of Valmont that once stood on U.S. 54 to supply the Lee ranch and other small farmers in the vicinity disappeared after the Dust Bowl years of the 1930s forced most of them off the land.

The road now enters a long, arid stretch for its final run to the Texas border. Orogrande was the site of a gold strike in 1905 and turquoise mines in the area were once owned by Tiffany's of New York. Hardly any trace of the mining camp and its two smelters remain.

U.S. 54 passes the boundary into Fort Bliss, the military reservation that sprawls across the state line, and runs across the base all the way to the end of the road in El Paso.

VISITING HOURS

NEW MEXICO

Alamogordo: Space Center, (505) 437-2840. East of U.S. 54 at northern outskirts of town. Daily, 9–6. Admission.

Alameda Park Zoo, (505) 437-8430. North of downtown, on U.S. 54. Daily, 9–5. Admission.

Oliver Lee State Park, (505) 437-8284. South of city on U.S. 54, then east on Dog Canyon Road. Daily, 9–4. Admission.

Ancho: My House of Old Things, No phone. East of U.S. 54, on New Mexico 462. Daily, 9–5, May–mid-October. Admission.

Tucumcari: Historical Museum, (505) 461-4201. At 416 S. Adams St. Monday–Saturday, 9–6 and Sunday, 1–6, June–August; closed Monday, at other times. Admission.

White Oaks: (505) 648-2228. Call for information on schoolhouse tours.

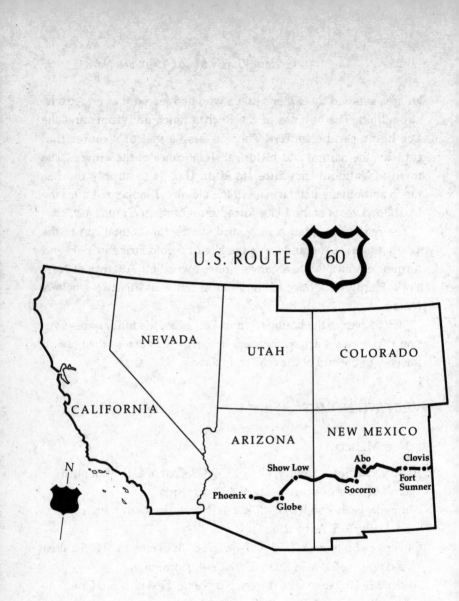

U.S. ROUTE 60

NEVADA

UTAH

COLORADO

CALIFORNIA

ARIZONA

NEW MEXICO

Abo

Clovis

Show Low

Socorro

Fort
Sumner

Phoenix

Globe

N

Missings and Copper

◊

U.S. 60

Texico, N.M. to Tempe, Ariz.
630 miles

This is another of the former transcontinental roads that will never
see the Pacific again. U.S. 60, in its prime, crossed the upper south
and linked the two coasts from Virginia Beach to Los Angeles.
Then, as with most of these routes, the Interstates took over in its
far western reaches and now the highway doesn't make it out of
Arizona.

Still, it gets further west than most and on its run through New
Mexico and Arizona it is blessedly free from freeway interference
for almost its entire length. In this journey from the high plains to
the low desert, the road runs through cow towns, ancient missions, memories of copper and gold booms and some remarkable
mountain and canyon scenery.

MILESTONES

Texico has nothing to do with the homophonic oil giant; getting its
name, instead, from its position on the state boundary. A railroad
town on the Pecos Valley line, it is a twin of the community on the
Texas side of the border, Farwell.

Railroad officials were very big into city-naming around these parts. The next city on the route was first named Riley's Switch when the Santa Fe came through in 1906. But this somehow didn't have the right ring to it when the road decided to move its shops and warehouses here. A more resonant name was called for. The daughter of a Santa Fe executive obliged with **Clovis**, the name of the king who founded the Frankish monarchy in 481 A.D. (although he is not believed to have ever visited New Mexico). One reference work credits Clovis's rise from tribal chieftain to king to "patience and murder." But he did convert to Christianity after attaining the throne.

Clovis is the trade center for a stock-raising area, with some of the largest feed lots and auction markets (sales every Wednesday) in the country. It is still a major division point on the Santa Fe, as well as a market area for surrounding beet and alfalfa farms. Music fans will fondly recall that rockabilly star Buddy Holly recorded many of his early hits in the Norman Petty Studios here, as did Buddy Knox. The studios are still active and the city hosts a Music Festival each summer. Hillcrest Park, on East 10th Street, contains sunken gardens, a zoo, and a homesteader museum with antique farm equipment and a sodhouse.

You pass another of Clovis's big employers on the road west, as Cannon Air Force Base sprawls to the south of the highway. U.S. 60 then parallels the Santa Fe tracks into Melrose, the place from which the line's yards were moved to Clovis. It is now a crossroads in the middle of extensive ranch and dry-land farming operations. An old spring just south of town, Canada de Tule, is the seat of Hart Youth Ranch, a working cattle operation for homeless boys.

Alamosa Creek runs alongside the road east of Taiban. It was just south of this area, at Stinking Springs, that Billy the Kid was captured by Sheriff Pat Garrett and his posse in December 1880. After holding out for two days in a sheepherder's hut with three companions, he surrendered and was taken off to stand trial for murder. But the denouement of the Billy the Kid saga lies a few miles ahead, at **Fort Sumner**.

Billy escaped from the Lincoln County jail in April 1881 (see U.S. 380) and made his way back here to hide out in the home of his friend, Peter Maxwell, on the grounds of the old fort.

The Maxwell family was the biggest landowner in this part of the Territory. Young Peter's father, Lucien Maxwell, had purchased the property from the federal government to house his ranch hands and used the former officer's quarters for his own residence. The fort had been built during the Civil War on the site of a Comanche campground and former trading post and named for the commander of the military district, General E.V. Sumner.

Its original purpose had been to watch over the Navajo, who had been forcibly transported from their ancestral lands hundreds of miles to the west. Federal authorities in New Mexico, faced with a Confederate invasion from Texas in 1862, were uneasy about having hostile tribes operating on their northwestern flank. In a brutal campaign directed by Kit Carson, the Navajo were burned out, starved, and rounded up to be marched to their new homes near Fort Sumner. But the relocation didn't take. Preyed upon by Kiowa and Comanche raiders, unable to adjust to the new climate and land, the Navajo went on the equivalent of a strike. They refused to plant crops in the spring of 1868. With the possibility of massive starvation ahead, federal authorities relented and permitted the Navajo to return to their former homes. That ended the need for a fort and the place was sold at auction to Maxwell.

The quarters were remodeled into a 20-room mansion from which Maxwell supervised his two million acres of holdings. After Lucien's death in 1875, his son Peter took over the property and wound up on the same side of the range wars as Billy the Kid. Garrett, knowing of their friendship, tracked Billy here and waited in ambush in Maxwell's bedroom. When the Kid entered the darkened room with his gun drawn and asked "Who is it?" Garrett responded with two fatal shots.

The property passed out of Maxwell's hands and, eventually, the mansion was torn down for lumber during the depression of the 1890s. A museum now marks the site of the post, just east of the town of Fort Sumner. Nearby is the gravesite of the famous outlaw. Another collection of memorabilia is housed in the town's Billy the Kid Museum on East Sumner Avenue.

The road crosses the Pecos and continues into sheep raising country, with the first range of the Rockies visible ahead. It passes the old cattle trail and rail junction of Vaughn and the "live oaks" that gave Encino it's name, with the Santa Fe tracks a constant companion. The summit of Pedernal Peak, at 7,576 feet, rises to the north.

The area west of Willard once boasted the world's greatest concentration of pinto bean fields. But drought in the 1950s forced most of the farmers out of the Estancia Valley and the area is now given over to ranching. At Mountainair, the road has climbed to 6,500 feet with the Manzano Mountains stretching off to the north. In this onetime bean-processing center, dominated by the ornate facade of the Shaffer Hotel, are the offices of Cibola National Forest and **Salinas National Monument**.

FOCUS

In the third decade of the 17th century, when English-speaking settlers still clung precariously to a handful of communities on the Atlantic seaboard, Spanish explorers and priests had penetrated hundreds of miles into the southwestern interior to replicate the civilization of Europe in New Mexico's mountains.

The missionaries ventured up from the Rio Grande Valley, through the pass traversed by U.S. 60 to the west, and found a thriving Native American culture. The Salinas were situated along the trade routes of the New Mexico pueblos and were a bridge between the two major groups—the Mogollon and the Anasazi.

Anthropologists think the Salinas may have arrived in the area 7,000 years ago and as settlement developed they found a niche as middle men in the trade between the villages on the Rio Grande and the plains to the east.

When the Spanish arrived, the Salinas settlements were among the most populous in the area. As many as 10,000 people are believed to have lived in the valleys around Mountainair.

Three such settlements and their Spanish additions have been preserved and are grouped under the designation of Salinas National Monument. Gran Quivira is twenty-five miles south of Mountainair on New Mexico 55, while Quarai is about eight miles north on the same road. Directly on our route, about seven miles west, is Abo, and that's the unit of the park on which we will concentrate.

A side road leads from U.S. 60 to the north and twists across an arroyo. Then, rising like a red stone vision from the western landscape, is the ruined mission church of Abo, San Gregorio. If you have seen the ruins of abbey churches in parts of northern England, this sight might summon up a memory. The first Americans who came upon it, during a survey party in 1853, were thunderstruck. They recognized it as a church, but had no idea of its age or who had built it. "The tall ruins standing there in solitude had an aspect of sadness and gloom," wrote the expedition leader, Major J.H. Carleton. "The cold wind...appeared to roar and howl through the roofless pile like an angry demon."

The ruins and 40-foot-high walls belong to the second church built on this site. The first was completed in 1627 under the supervision of Fr. Francisco Fonte. It became the center of missionary activity for the region and within 15 years had outgrown its facilities. So Fr. Fonte's successor, Fr. Francisco Acevedo, set about enlarging it in the style of contemporary European churches. An accomplished architect, Fr. Acevedo used exterior buttresses to support the higher walls and roof and added a graceful bell tower. Sunshine poured into the interior through clerestory windows raised eight feet above the top of the nave. Adjoining the church itself, an entire mission community arose, with dining and sleeping facilities for the Franciscans and Indians visiting the church.

Behind the church was the pueblo itself, parts of which date back to about 1150. Nothing remains but mounds, many of them unexcavated.

The Salinas culture could not survive its collision with Spain. The first explorers came to the area looking for the seven cities of gold. They never found them, but there were other riches to exploit, including the salt deposits for which this area was named, *Salinas* in Spanish. Civil authorities imposed confiscatory taxes on the pueblos and while the missions tried to alleviate the harshness of the system they were powerless to stop it. Worst of all, as far as the Salinas people were concerned, the Spanish forced them to assist in slave-raiding expeditions against the Apache. That won them the lasting hostility of that tribe, which began raiding the Salinas pueblos in retaliation. When drought and epidemics caused by a lack of immunity to European diseases also swept the area in the 1670s, the Salinas could not withstand the blows. They abandoned their pueblos and after just 50 years of activity, San Gregorio of Abo found itself deserted and all but forgotten for almost two centuries. The Salinas themselves drifted to the south and were absorbed by tribes in the El Paso area, losing their identity as a distinct people.

Stop at the Visitor's Center in Mountainair for an overview of the national monument and a short film on the history of these pueblos. There is also a smaller center at Abo, at which you can pick up a brochure to guide you through the ruins of the church and pueblo.

It is a haunting sight, these towering sandstone walls surrounded by emptiness, one that enables you to feel the weight of years in this place and the astonishing degree to which the culture of a land thousands of miles away once penetrated it.

* * *

The road goes on through Abo Pass and opens on a spectacular view of the Rio Grande Valley. Straight ahead is the 9,176-foot-high bulk of Ladron Peak The name means "robber" in Spanish; the peak was known as a gathering spot for Apache and Navajo rustlers during colonial times.

At Bernardo, the road joins the route of the Camino Real, which has been taken over by Interstate 25. There is a State Waterfowl Area along the river here, at which many migratory birds can be observed, and a few miles south is the Sevillita National Wildlife Refuge. The Interstate bypasses several villages that trace their origins back to Piro Indian pueblos that were here when the Camino Real was opened up in 1598. La Joya, the most northern of them, was an important stopping point on that road.

The Camino Real began in Chihuahua, connecting with other highways that led to Mexico City. It had been blazed as early as 1581, but not until Juan de Onate and 130 men-at-arms with their families came north along the road to settle the new colony did it attain its status as a main thoroughfare of the Spanish Empire. Incidentally, the butte near the town of San Acacia, a landmark on the old trail, is also the point at which the principal meridian for the New Mexico topographic survey was placed in 1855.

When the Onate party reached the site of **Socorro** they found a large, friendly Piro settlement. The pueblo supplied the famished travelers with corn, and two priests were left behind to establish a mission. Thirty years later, as a tribute to this first encounter, the place was given its present name, which means "assistance."

Socorro became a mission center at about the same time that Abo did to the northeast, and it declined for many of the same reasons. Unlike Abo, the Spanish did manage to protect the Piro from Apache raiders. But in 1680, the northern pueblos rose in revolt and drove the Spanish out of the colony. The Piro had remained loyal to the Spanish, however, and, fearing reprisals, they abandoned the settlement and retreated south to El Paso. The deserted mission was sacked and not for 137 years did colonists return to rebuild Socorro.

Then 21 families received land grants from the Spanish crown and established a farming community here. The place prospered and spurted in growth during the Civil War as a supply base for Union troops at Fort Craig, which was located just to the south. Two years after the war's end, silver was found in the nearby hills and Socorro's serenity was shattered. By 1880, it had become the biggest town in the territory, and one of the wildest. Forty-four saloons lined the main street, a thoroughfare jammed with teamsters hauling supplies to the mining towns. When the price of silver collapsed in the 1890s, so did Socorro. It is now a trade center and college town of about 7,600 people.

The New Mexico School of Mines (now New Mexico Tech) was established here in 1889, at about the same time that the legendary lawman, Elfego Baca, was taming the town. The two are linked today in a rather unusual way—on the links. The golf course at Tech, regarded as the most challenging in this part of the state, is the site of the Conrad Hilton Open, which is named for a native of nearby San Antonio, (see U.S. 380) each June. A featured event of the tournament is the Elfego Baca Shoot, in which competitors try to get down from "M" Mountain to the second hole of the course. Par is 50. A more scholarly attraction on campus is the Mineral Museum, housed in the school's Workman Center. It contains an exceptionally varied collection of minerals as well as fossils from around the state and information on rockhounding in the area.

The main attraction in the town is the San Miguel Mission, built on the site of the original church of the Onate expedition. The south wall dates from 1598 and is among the oldest church structures on the continent. Most of the church was built during the resettlement in 1821, but it contains many artifacts of the earlier missions. San Miguel is located a few blocks north of the Plaza, which is lined with late 19th-century structures, including many associated with the Baca and Hilton families.

The road leaves Socorro and begins its ascent to Cibola National Forest, dominated by South Baldy, a 10,783-foot-high peak. **Magdalena** is an old cattle town, once the end of the line for rail traffic to the west. Sheep and cattle ranchers between this point and the Arizona line had to drive their stock here on the trail across the San Agustin Plains, now crossed by U.S. 60. The plains today are the site of a stranger adventure. About 20 miles west of Magdalena is the turnoff to the Very Large Array radio astronomy observatory. Here 27 dish-shaped antennas, each of them 82 feet in diameter, collect radio waves from the skies and compose a picture of their source. The antennas can be moved by rail into different receiving positions to vary the patterns of the transmissions they are picking up. A visitor's center explains all this and also directs you on a walking tour around the installation, which opened in 1981.

Datil was a major stopping point on the cattle trail to Magdalena. The well here was an important source of water along the route, but is now a campground in the Cibola National Forest. The town was named for a cactus plant that produces date-like fruit found growing in the area.

Now the highway enters the Datil Mountains on its way to the Continental Divide, which it crosses at 7,796 feet, just east of Pie Town. This highway stop was named, logically enough, for a filling station at which travelers could buy freshly baked pies. Omega's derivation is less clear. Towns named for the last letter of the Greek alphabet are usually the last stop on a given route, but we still have 40 more miles and two more settlements to go before we leave New Mexico. The town was originally known as Sweatzerville, though, and it may be that later residents just liked the sound of Omega better.

Quemado was named for an Apache chief who burned his hand in a campfire, the word being Spanish for "burn." Then it's through Red Hill and into Arizona.

The White Mountains rise to the south while a high plateau stretches away to the northern horizon. At the edge of the mountains is the Valle Rodondo, "Round Valley," and the resort town of Springerville, which is the administrative center of the surrounding Apache-Sitgreaves National Forest. The place grew up around a trading post run by Henry Springer on the Little Colorado River and its elevation of almost 7,000 feet makes it a top summer resort for overheated Arizonians. There is a Madonna of the Trails monument in the middle of town, one of a dozen placed in communities on the main pioneer roads west.

West of here is cattle country, with the 8,000-foot high summits of Cerra Quemado (named for the scalded chief we encountered back in New Mexico) and Cerro Montosa. The road then cuts into the national forest and the community of Show Low, which bears its name as the result of a game of cards. The two ranchers who settled the area in the 1870s, C. E. Cooley and Marion Clark, decided to split up, and since they didn't think the area could support two operations they agreed to play cards to decide who would go and who would stay. With Cooley nearing victory, Clark decided on an all-or-nothing proposal. He told Cooley that if he could show the low card in the hands they were holding, he'd accept defeat. Cooley tossed down the deuce of clubs, and Clark, true to his word, moved out. The main street in Show Low is still called Deuce of Clubs.

The highway turns south and crosses the Mogollon Rim, the

1,000-foot deep gash that divides the Colorado Plateau from the southern deserts. At the far side is the Fort Apache Reservation. The name has an almost mythic quality. It has entered the language as symbolizing the epitome of danger. More than a century later, American soldiers refer to hostile territory as "Indian country." Fort Apache was also the name of a book and movie about a police precinct in the highest crime area of the Bronx in New York City. The Apaches, unlike many other tribes, actually received prime rangeland for their Arizona reservations and have also converted much of their holdings into resort developments. The actual fort lies 23 miles east of this highway from Carrizo, a bit beyond the bounds of this book. One of the most bitter battles in the fort's history, however, raged right across this area.

A detail from the fort, established in 1870, was sent to arrest a medicine man who was stirring up the settlement of Cibecue, to the west of here, late in the summer of 1881. This was not a good idea. Even the Apache scouts turned against the detachment and seven men, including the officer in charge, were killed at the site. The surviving 78 cavalrymen were forced to retreat 40 miles to the fort, right through Carrizo, fending off Apache attacks every mile of the way. Two days later, the assembled Indians attacked the fort itself. With the garrison cut off from relief, Will C. Barnes, a scout, was able to slip away and by muffling his horse's hooves in blankets managed to skirt the Apache outriders and bring reinforcements from Fort Thomas. It sounds like it came right out of a John Ford movie...and maybe it did. The facts themselves make a great Western.

From here the road drops down to the Salt River Canyon and one of the great scenic drives in the state. The road dips 2,000 feet in about five miles through deeply colored sheer rock walls that have been carved into fantastic shapes. Only in a state that also contained the Grand Canyon could such a natural wonder be almost unknown.

The nearly deserted village of Seneca was once the center of asbestos mining operations in the nearby canyons. The material was carried out by 100-burro trains to the railroad at **Globe** over the trail that became U.S. 60. The town was once the headquarters of the Cross S Ranch, which dominated the cattle industry in this part of Arizona.

The ghost town of McMillenville, just to the west of the road, was the site of an 1874 silver strike and the town was named after a miner who was sleeping off a drunk. The actual find was made by Charles McMillen's partner, who didn't recognize the metal in the rock he had chipped from a nearby ledge. When McMillen awoke from his nap and saw what his partner was holding he sobered up in a hurry and filed the claim on the Stonewall Jackson Mine, which eventually produced more than $2 million.

During the ensuing excitement, a globe-shaped boulder was found on the San Carlos Apache Reservation. It turned out to be almost solid silver and a 12-mile strip was quickly carved out of the Indian lands with mineral rights taken away from the tribe. It was a clear case of theft, but there was money to be made.

The town of Globe grew up as a supply center for the mines. This was one of the most remote locations in the country. The closest railhead was in Silver City, New Mexico and goods had to be brought in overland, along the route now followed by U.S. 70 to the east. The camps were further isolated in 1881 when the Apache, disgusted by the repeated broken promises of the territorial government, rose up under Geronimo and started attacking everything that moved on the road to Globe.

By this time, however, it was discovered that silver was only a sideshow. The big news in Globe was copper and when word of the Old Dominion mine got out it took more than Geronimo to stanch the flow of eager prospectors into the area. By 1886, Globe bullion was being used to mint most U.S. copper coins. Nine years later, the Lewisohn family of New York bought the Old Dominion and upgraded it, bringing in a railroad and building a new smelter. For the next 25 years it would be one of the richest copper mines in the world and Globe took to calling itself the "Capital of the County with the Copper Bottom." But in 1909 an unexpected rival appeared when the Inspiration Mine opened in the neighboring town of Miami. That touched off a bitter rivalry between the two cities, the richest in the state for many years. Globe declined further after a rancorous strike at the mine during World War I was broken by federal troops. The San Carlos reservation closed its range to grazing by cattle owned by outsiders, decimating the cattle business. Finally, the Old Dominion shut down in 1931.

The town is trying to restore its atmospheric downtown area, laid out along Broad Street. The thoroughfare follows the course of Pinal Creek, where miner's shacks once were slapped up back to back. The county jail, St. John's Episcopal Church, and Pioneer Hotel have all been restored and the Gila County Historical Museum has exhibits on the colorful past of the area.

Also on display at the museum are artifacts from the ancient Salado Indian village located south of town. Inhabited from about 1225 to 1400, the town was known as Besh-ba-Gowah, or Metal Camp, indicating that the copper deposits were known 650 years before Europeans found them. More than 200 rooms have been excavated in the pueblo, which may be reached from Broad Street by way of Ice House Canyon Road.

The site of the Old Dominion is just to the north of the road as it leaves Globe.

Miami had an even more rapid rise and precipitous decline than its rival. While Globe grew rich, Miami remained a small settlement along Bloody Tanks Wash, a stream named for a massacre of Apaches in 1864 by territorial militia. The town had been named by pioneers from Miami, Ohio. Having given it a name, they then gave it up as a bad bargain. But in 1907, advances in technology made reduction of low grade ores feasible and the Inspiration Mine was opened. Globe newspaper publisher Cleve Van Dyke promoted the building of a new town on the site, a move bitterly opposed by businessmen in the older city as well as the mine operators who wanted their workers living in a company town. Undeterred, Van Dyke moved his presses to Miami and by the start of World War I, the upstart had passed Globe in population. The highway was extended from Phoenix in 1922 (over the same route west we are about to follow) giving Miami an additional advantage over its more eastern rival.

Van Dyke and his newspaper were enthusiastic supporters of George W.P. Hunt, the first Arizona governor after statehood and the winner of six more terms after that. Although Hunt came from Globe, it was the support of the Miami claque that held the balance of power for him. The bitter rivalry between the two neighboring towns divided the entire state politically, and eventually, Hunt was toppled when his old hometown turned against him as a way to get back at its hated competitor.

But the Depression saw the Inspiration shut down, and Miami never regained its onetime prosperity. In recent years, the community has been the biggest loser in this high growth state. Its current population of 2,500 is only about one-third of Globe's. Just west of town and north of the highway, however, the Pinto Valley Mine remains in operation, the third largest open pit mine in the world.

Two miles west of Miami is the site of Bloody Tanks, in which 19 Apaches were killed when a peace parley turned unfriendly. Some historians insist, however, that this encounter actually took place at another location and the killing here was accomplished by leaving corn meal laced with strychnine where the Indians would find it. Both sides agree that Colonel King S. Woolsey was in charge of the campaign and that he was a man who believed in killing Apaches by any means at hand.

In a few more miles, after the road twists its way past the narrow defile of Devil's Canyon and through the 1,217-foot-long Queen Creek Tunnel, we come to another spot of unhappy memory to the Apaches. Just west of the tunnel, to the north of the highway, is Apache Leap. Cavalrymen from nearby Camp Pinal cornered a party of about 75 Indians on these cliffs. The campaign against the Apaches had turned into a bitter war of extermination in the 1870s, with stories of atrocities committed widely repeated on both sides. Rather than allow themselves to be captured, the Apaches jumped to their deaths from these rocks.

Superior is another of the old mining towns in this district, and like Globe, its cycle went through silver and then to even greater riches in copper. The Magma Mine opened beneath the played-out diggings of the Silver Queen in 1910. The place is best known today, though, for the Boyce Thompson Southwestern Arboretum, a desert biology station operated by the University of Arizona since 1927. Plants from semi-arid regions around the world have been brought here and may be seen on the two miles of hiking trails that lead across the site.

Seven miles past the arboretum is another reminder of the sufferings of the defeated Indians in this area. A digging area off the road allows rock hounds to look for the rounded pieces of obsidian that are known locally as Apache Tears (also the name of an adjacent cave).

But the Apache had a final, mysterious triumph. If you have been observing the horizon, as far back as Devil's Canyon, you will have noticed a towering, thumb-like rock formation rising to the northwest. This is Weaver's Needle, named for pioneer scout Pauline Weaver. It marks the start of the Superstition Mountains and one of the great, enduring legends of the Southwest: The Lost Dutchman. The location of this fabulous mine, supposedly, is hidden somewhere near the Needle, but the only ones who knew for sure were killed by the Apaches long ago.

Even the name of the mountain range carries an aura of legend. Indian tales described this area as the site of a prehistoric flood. Many people were given refuge in the hills by the gods on the condition that they make no sound. But they broke their promise as the waters receded, and were turned to stone, their human forms still visible on the mountain's rocky slopes. This equivalent of the Genesis stories of Noah and Lot's wife is the source of the name, Superstition.

According to the tales, the gold mine was first found when the land belonged to Mexico. An entire community traveled here to enrich itself, but on the way home they were ambushed by the Indians and killed to the last man, except for two little boys. The boys kept the mine's secret and returned as adults, around 1870. But while two men went into the mountains, only Jacob Wolz, a white-bearded prospector known as The Dutchman, came out alive. The Mexicans were never seen again. Until his death in 1891, Wolz claimed ownership of the mine and also said that he'd killed eight men who had tried to follow him into the mountains to find it. He gave directions on his deathbed to a friend, but they could not be deciphered and no one has been able to find the mine since.

Oh, they certainly try. Every February the nearby town of Apache Junction holds Lost Dutchman Days and the state has even designated part of the Superstition Range as Lost Dutchman State Park. Both amateur and professional expeditions set off annually to locate the mine. But a century after Wolz's death, the Dutchman's golden secret remains unsolved.

Apache Junction is also the starting point for the famous Apache Trail, Arizona 88—a scenic drive that leads to Roosevelt Dam. The road was built in 1905 to carry supplies up to the dam construction site. This irrigation and power project on the Salt River, completed six years later, made possible the vast urban concomitation of metropolitan Phoenix. Many oldtime Arizonians feel that is a mixed blessing, at best. Also on the route are the cliff dwellings in

Tonto National Monument. (This Spanish word, by the way, which was given to the Lone Ranger's faithful Indian companion, literally means "fool." Given that information, one can only wonder what "Kimosabe" means.)

Now we enter the Valley of the Sun and greater Phoenix. The suburb of **Mesa** started out as a cotton-raising town settled by Mormons in 1878. Now the third largest city in Arizona, it has retained a strong Mormon identity. The temple, built in 1927, is surrounded by striking gardens and while it is not open to the public, a visitor's center explains its historic setting. The temple is located just off Main St., U.S. 60 in Mesa.

The Mesa Southwest Museum, just north of the highway at MacDonald Street, has fine collections of Indian and pioneer history and displays about the myth and reality of the Lost Dutchman and other famous mines.

As it passes into **Tempe**, the road changes its name to Apache Boulevard. The settlers of Tempe, the location of Arizona State University, obviously had some academic training themselves. They named it for a site in classical literature, the Vale of Tempe, which lay between Mt. Olympus, home of the ancient Greek gods, and Mt. Ossa. Since their desert outpost bore no other resemblance to that mythical place of plenty, the settlers can also be described as a fairly optimistic bunch. But sometimes optimism is justified. The pioneer trading post was owned by Charles T. Hayden, whose son, Carl, went on to serve in Congress and the U.S. Senate for more than half a century.

The highway curves around the edge of the university campus and at its southwestern corner passes the Grady Gammage Center for the Performing Arts. This structure, named for a longtime president of the university, was the last major design of Frank Lloyd Wright. It opened in 1964. If you park the car to have a closer look, you might as well take a walk around the rest of the campus with its covering of towering royal palm trees. Look for the Matthews

Center (maps of the 649-acre main campus are posted near its entrances) which houses the school's art collection, noted for its Latin American section.

Just across the Salt River, the highway enters Phoenix and begins a slow crossing of this sprawling urban center. But we'll end our trip at this corner of the university campus.

VISITING HOURS

NEW MEXICO

Clovis: Hillcrest Park Museum, No phone. East of downtown on 10th St. Saturday, 10–4, April–September. Free.

Fort Sumner: State Historic Monument, (505) 355-2573. East of town, on U.S. 60. Thursday–Monday, 9–6. Admission.

Billy the Kid Museum, No phone. Near old fort cemetery. Daily, 9–5. Admission.

Magdalena: Very Large Array Telescopes, (505) 835-7000. On U.S. 60. Daily, 8:30–dusk. Free.

Salinas National Monument: Abo Ruin, No phone. North of U.S. 60, west of Mountainair. Daily, 9–5. Free.

Visitor Center, (505) 847-2585. On U.S. 60, in Mountainair. Daily, 8–5. Free.

Socorro: New Mexico Mines Mineral Museum, (505) 835-5420. On campus, in Workman Center. Monday–Friday, 8–5. Free.

San Miguel Mission, (505) 835-1620. Two blocks north of Plaza, at 403 El Camino Real. Daily, 6–6. Free.

ARIZONA

Globe: Gila County Historical Museum, (602) 425-7385. On U.S. 60, north of downtown. Monday–Saturday, 9–5. Free.

Mesa: Mormon Temple Visitor Center, (602) 964-7164. At 525 E. Main St. Daily, 9–9. Free.

Southwest Museum, (602) 644-2230. North off U.S. 60, at 53 N. MacDonald. Tuesday–Saturday, 10–5 and Sunday, 1–5. Admission.

Superior: Thompson Arboretum, (602) 689-2811. West on U.S. 60. Daily, 8–5. Admission.

Tempe: Arizona State University Art Collection, (602) 965-2787. In Matthews Center. Monday–Friday, 8:30–4:30; Saturday, 10–4; Sunday, 1–5. Free.

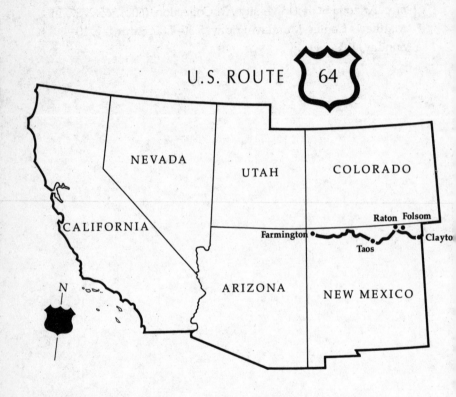

U.S. ROUTE 64

The Trail to Taos

U.S. 64

Clayton, N.M. to Farmington, N.M.
380 miles

By the time it reaches our turf, U.S. 64 has wandered from the Outer Banks of North Carolina on a jagged journey through the Middle South. It has cut through the Great Smokies and the Ozarks and meandered through the river valleys of the Arkansas and Cimarron.

Its run through New Mexico may be the best part of all. The highway enters the state in the Kiowa National Grasslands and follows a determinedly western course across a series of mountain ranges along the state's northern tier. It visits some of New Mexico's most historic settlements, and one place that predates history. Although this is a tremendously scenic route, portions of it between **Taos** and **Chama** are not advised for travel during the winter months.

MILEPOSTS

One of Clayton's early residents was a chap named Black Jack Ketchum, who, on the occasion of his being hanged, on April 26,

1901, instructed his executioner: "Hurry it up; I'm due in Hell for dinner." He also asked to be buried face down; the faster to get at his meal, possibly. This was a spirited community in its younger days. It began in 1888 as a camp for cattle drovers on the Denver and Fort Worth Railroad and it still wears the look of a cattle town. Some of the country's biggest feedlots are just to the north and the Clayton Livestock Research Center is part of the Kiowa National Grasslands to the east. This facility conducts research on bovine management and health. Look in at the Eklund Hotel, a two-story rock structure built in 1892. The original bar is still in place and there are many antiques in the building. It has no overnight accommodations, but its restaurant has been restored and serves meals.

Rabbit Ear Mountain, at 6,062 feet, is just northwest of town. Usually places with this designation are named for a distinctive rock outcropping, but this Rabbit Ear was a Cheyenne chief who had his ears frozen. The mountain was also the site of a battle between the victorious Spanish and the Comanche in 1717.

The road passes through a succession of small railroad towns. Des Moines was named after the Iowa capital and originated as a station at the base of 8,720-foot-high Sierra Grande. The town wasn't built until 1907.

Now we'll take a circle trip on New Mexico 325, which heads north to **Folsom**. This little cattle town burst into the headlines in the 1920s, when a cowboy found some old bones and everything anthropologists thought they knew about dating the human arrival in North America was tossed out the window. George McJunkin was trying to track some lost cows in an arroyo west of town when he saw the bones in the dry stream bed. He dismounted and knew immediately that what he had found was part of an animal bigger than any cow. Moreover, he also saw several flints that were different from any arrow heads he was familiar with.

McJunkin reported the find and within a year an expedition from the Colorado Museum of Natural History was excavating the site. It was determined that the bones belonged to a bison that had been extinct for 10,000 years. When one of the flints was found embedded between two animal ribs, it provided a direct link that placed human hunters at the site at the same time. All the animal skeletons lacked tails, indicating that they had been skinned, and that clinched the case. Until that time, the best estimate of human activities on the continent went back no more than 2,000 years. Carbon dating of these artifacts pushed that estimate back to 14,000 years. The Folsom Museum on Main Street has exhibits of material found at the site. The location itself is seven miles west, on New Mexico 72, and is identified by a historic marker.

Now swing back south on Highway 325, past **Capulin Volcano National Monument**. This is an exercise in symmetry, a perfectly shaped cone rising 1,000 feet from the surrounding plain. Lava escaped from fissures in the volcano's side instead of blasting through the mountain top to form this cone. This all happened about 4,000 years after the Folsom Man was hunting his bison a few miles to the north. The cone is about one mile in circumference and 415 feet deep. A loop road encircles the summit, while a foot trail descends into the crater itself. The name Capulin is Spanish for choke-cherry and refers to the growths found in the area by early explorers.

U.S. 64 continues west into gradually rising country and hits Interstate 25 just south of **Raton**. The town grew up at the foot of Raton Pass, the toughest segment of the old Santa Fe Trail. This famous pioneer route opened in 1822, when Mexico won its independence from Spain and encouraged commerce with the United States, not realizing that the contact would whet American appetites for these rich Southwestern lands and bring on war. The route over Raton Pass was the earliest and most arduous of the trail's variations, but it was also the safest. In later years, the Cimarron Cutoff, which roughly paralleled the current route of U.S. 64, would be favored. The great cattle trails running from west Texas to Denver also passed through Raton. Realizing the difficulties presented by the original trail, local entrepreneur Dick Wootton blasted a new, better-graded route through the mountains in 1866 and then got rich on the tolls he charged. When the Santa Fe Railroad came through 13 years later, they bought Wootton's trail for their right of way.

There is still a wealth of 19th-century buildings along First Street, including the Palace Restaurant in a hotel dating from 1896. Nearby is the Raton Museum, housed in the former Coors Brewery, which contains historical displays on the town and Santa Fe Trail. You can see the original trail by following Moulton Avenue north from town. The ruts made by wagons braking as they came down the mountain are still visible.

The road runs south with the Interstate for a few miles, then turns west for **Cimarron,** one of the most colorful old towns in the Southwest. It was a favorite of Kit Carson and Buffalo Bill, who both savored this area on the edge of the Sangre de Cristo range of the Rockies. Carson intended to retire on land that is now the Philmont Ranch, south of town. Cody organized his Wild West shows at the historic St. James Hotel, which is still standing, and usually returned each Christmas to spend his holiday. Cimarron was built by yet another of the Southwest's fabulous characters, Lucien Maxwell. A scout with John C. Fremont's expeditions through the area, Maxwell later married into the Beaubien family, which was engaged in a legal dispute over the title to one of the largest Mexican land grants in the Southwest. It dragged on for 41 years but at its settlement, Maxwell was left with 1.7 million acres throughout northeastern New Mexico, making him the richest man in the territory. His home in Fort Sumner was a showplace and later the scene of Billy the Kid's demise (See U.S. 60).

Maxwell eventually made a succession of bad investments in gold, banking, and railroads and lost most of his holdings before his death in 1875. A gristmill he built in Cimarron in 1864, now called the Old Mill, is a historical museum of the town and of Maxwell's career.

Philmont Ranch is now the national camping center of the Boy Scouts of America. A replica of the house Carson built there in 1849 is now a museum of the famous scout. Also on the property is the Ernest T. Seton Library and Museum. It preserves the artwork and artifacts collected by the naturalist and author who founded a woodcraft organization that later merged with the Scouts.

The road runs through Cimarron Canyon, a scenic passage through a narrow gorge bounded by 400-foot-high granite cliffs. There is a state park with fishing and picnic facilities on the way, just east of Ute Park. Eagle Nest Lake is at its western end. Formed by a dam built in 1912, the lake is famous for its trout fishing and mountain location.

The road turns sharply south here and begins its ascent to **Angel Fire**, a ski resort that has developed into a four-season recreational area. Just where U.S. 64 turns west from the road to the resort is the Vietnam Veterans National Memorial. Not as well known as the memorial in Washington, D.C., this striking hilltop chapel, with its soaring curvilinear construction and views into the Sangre de Cristo, is a deeply moving and dramatic place. It is maintained by the Disabled Veterans of America. The chapel is always open.

The highway crosses 9,101-foot-high Palo Flechado Pass, named for a Taos Indian custom of shooting arrows into a tree after a hunt, and enters Kit Carson National Forest. In a few miles we'll be in sight of the home of the forest's namesake.

FOCUS

There is magic here. You can feel it. Nowhere else in the Southwest do its three cultures—Hispanic, Indian, and Anglo—meet in such a mystical setting. Artists come to **Taos** and never leave, enchanted by the clear light and the mountains and the sense of timelessness that clings to its old stones. The Spanish town was built five years before the Pilgrims landed at Plymouth, Massachusetts. The Indian pueblo which drew the Spanish to the area was already old then, and has remained virtually unchanged since 1540, when European explorers first saw it. The Anglo artists, who began arriving in the 1880s, have become a fixed presence and a vivid part of the historical tapestry.

Taos has survived three revolts, fire, and the hippie invasion of the 1960s. While it may seem to contain more art galleries than homes, it still retains the ambience of a small town in the West, which is its greatest appeal. Of course, not many small towns have boasted D. H. Lawrence, Georgia O'Keeffe, and Willa Cather as residents.

Not to mention Kit Carson. The frontiersman built a home in Taos in the 1840s and lived here for the last 25 years of his life. Carson was the first American to visit parts of the West in the earliest days of exploration, but this is where he chose to make his home. That's a fair testimonial.

As with so many other places in American history, the settlement of Taos began with soldiers. Veterans of the Spanish military expeditions to the area returned as civilians, remembering the well-watered fields and sunny skies they had seen on their campaigns. The first town was adjacent to the pueblo, but after a few years the Indians complained that the Spanish were ruining the neighborhood and asked them to move. They felt the traditional way of life was being threatened by the proximity of Europeans. This strong sense of independence remains a defining characteristic of the pueblo and is probably why it has gone 450 years without a change.

The Spanish obligingly moved the town to its present location in 1615, but tensions continued to develop between the two peoples. In 1650, a revolt, planned at Taos pueblo, swept across the area. It was repeated 30 years later by a more widespread uprising that drove the Spanish completely out of the New Mexico colony. But by 1692 the military had reconquered the area and the settlers moved in for a 150-year stay. It was still Mexican territory when Carson moved here in 1843, but the growing traffic on the Santa Fe Trail was bringing in an irresistible Anglo presence. Within three years, at the close of the Mexican War, Taos was ceded to the United States. But in 1847, the Taos Indians rose up, just as they had against the Spanish hundreds of years before, and killed the American governor, Charles Bent, in his home. They moved on to threaten Santa Fe itself before the army dispersed them.

Carson made sure that there would be no further upheavals during the Civil War. At the outbreak of hostilities, he marched to the plaza and raised the American flag. Then he stood guard through the following night to make sure Secessionist sympathizers understood that Taos was one place in New Mexico that would remain with the Union. The plaza still shows the flag 24 hours a day to commemmorate that event.

Carson died in 1868, three years after the war's end. Within another generation, Taos had been transformed from frontier town to art colony. Joseph Henry Sharp was the first landscape artist to visit and his reports of the area encouraged two of his Eastern friends to investigate it themselves. Ernest Blumenschein and Bert Phillips intended to make a camping tour of New Mexico in 1898 but some of that Taos magic intervened. A wheel came off their wagon here and while they were waiting to have it repaired they fell under the spell. They decided it wasn't necessary to go any further and settled in to stay. The two of them and Sharp were the shaping forces of the colony and formed the Taos Society of Artists in 1912. Their activities attracted Mabel Dodge Luhan, a wealthy mystic who sought to fuse artistic expression with the Pueblo Indian religion. She publicized Taos in the 1920s and brought D. H. Lawrence here from England to write about the area and ponder its religious implications in three short books. Psychiatrist Carl Jung also visited during this time and engaged in a discourse with an Indian religious leader who told him that white men were mad because they thought with their heads and not their hearts. This, somehow, seemed to clarify many things for Jung.

Since then the art colony has thrived and expanded until it now forms the core of the community. Galleries line the historic plaza, the center of the old town, and its adjoining side streets. A fire destroyed several original structures on the plaza in 1932 and the sidewalk arcades were added in the reconstruction, but some of the walls date from at least one century earlier.

The Blumenschein Home, two blocks from the plaza, was purchased by the artist in 1919 and is now a showcase for the works of the early Taos painters. Nearby, also on Ledoux Street, is the Harwood Museum, with more of the early Taos landscapes and a greater sampling of contemporary artists.

As you enter Taos on U.S. 64, you'll pass the Kit Carson Home. It contains many of the frontiersman's belongings and other displays of the era of exploration he represents. Carson is buried just to the north of the plaza in a memorial state park named for him, which is also the resting place of Mabel Dodge Luhan. The home of Governor Bent, one block away, is now a museum of history and Western art, recapitulating the early years of American rule and the governor's untimely demise.

U.S. 64 becomes the town's main street, Pueblo Road, and it passes two more of Taos' artistic landmarks. Stables Art Center mounts changing exhibitions of the work of contemporary local artists. The Fechin Institute was the home of Russian sculptor Nicolai Fechin from 1927 to 1933 and is filled with his elaborately carved wood creations.

This is also the highway to Taos Pueblo. This remarkable community, with the tallest apartment-style pueblos in the Southwest, is dedicated to the preservation of traditional ways. Visitors must pay a fee to enter and another to take photographs. There is no electricity permitted, nor running water. During certain ceremonies the area is closed altogether to outsiders. The earth tones of the pueblos, the creek that bubbles through the middle of the settlement, the stunning mountain backdrop, all combine to make this one of the most unforgettable settings on the continent. If you can't feel the magic here, you never will.

* * *

As the highway leaves the Taos area, there is one final stop to make. The Millicent Rogers Museum concentrates more on the Native American and Hispanic artistic legacy than the other Taos institutions. In the 1940s, Rogers was among the first collectors to recognize the importance of the work being done in the Rio Grande pueblos. The museum's holdings in this field, especially the pottery of Maria Martinez and her family from San Ildefonso, are the most highly regarded in the country.

The road continues west and crosses the Rio Grande in spectacular fashion, 650 feet above the rushing stream. This is the second highest bridge in the country and the view is stunning.

Tres Piedras means "three stones" in Spanish and the town is named for the sandstone formations around it. West of here the road embarks on the most mountainous portion of the trip, a spectacular crossing of the San Juan Mountains through Kit Carson

National Forest. Hopewell Lake Recreation Area is a choice stop for a picnic or to stretch your legs and view some mountain scenery and wildlife.

In the valley just north of Tierra Amarilla, watch for the settlement of Los Ojos. Churro sheep are raised here and the villagers hand-dye and weave their wool using traditional patterns.

Chama is an old railroad town that grew up during a silver boom in the 1880s. Its antique rail equipment is now used for one of the west's great excursions, the Cumbres and Toltec Scenic Railroad. The route crosses Cumbres Pass into Colorado and winds up in Ossier, a town inaccessible by car. At that point, it connects with another scenic line, the Colorado Limited (see U.S. 285). Passengers have the option of transferring to that train, which runs to Antonito, and then making the return trip by van, or turning around on the same train. Either way the run takes in some spectacular scenery in a means of travel that quite literally transports you to the previous century.

The road winds through rugged country to Dulce, largest town in the Jicarilla Apache Reservation. The tribal name means "little baskets;" the tribe itself is known for its skill in this type of handicraft. Dulce is also the site of the Little Beaver Roundup, a combination rodeo and Indian festival held in mid-July. (Fred Harman, the cartoonist who drew Little Beaver in the Red Ryder comic strip, lived just north of here, near Pagosa Springs, Colorado. See U.S. 160).

After cutting through another band of the Carson National Forest, the road runs a few miles south of Navajo Lake. Formed by a dam on the San Juan River, it is the largest body of water in this part of the state. A short jog north on New Mexico 539 will take you to a scenic overlook and also gives access to the lake's recreational facilities.

The dam's primary purpose was irrigation, which makes nearby **Bloomfield** an aptly named town. It is a trading center for an extensive farming district, but its chief attraction is named for a Salmon. Ruins of an Indian people known as the Chaco Culture are found throughout this portion of New Mexico. The largest concentration is about 60 miles south of here at Chaco Culture National Historical Park, but on the ranch of George Salmon a 250-room structure constructed by the same people was found. Built in the late 11th century, the C-shaped building covered about two acres. It was abandoned in the 12th century and then taken over by an offshoot of the Mesa Verde Culture, who occupied it for another 100 years. Many of the ruins in this area were irreparably damaged by souvenir hunters, but Salmon zealously guarded this find and was rewarded by having his name attached to it. There is a museum on the site, which is two miles west of town, on the highway.

U.S. 64 is four lanes wide as it rides into **Farmington**, the biggest town in this corner of New Mexico. An agricultural community, the place grew up at the confluence of three rivers—the San Juan, Las Animas and La Plata—on the site of ancient Indian settlements. It boomed in the 1950s with the exploitation of nearby gas, oil, and, especially, coal reserves. Two massive developments, the Four Corners Power Project, one of the Southwest's greatest energy sources; and the Navajo Indian Irrigation Project, which supplies water to adjacent Indian lands, are transforming this area economically. But it still takes time out to celebrate an apple blossom festival every April in honor of the area's staple crop, and to remember its origins with an Anasazi Pageant, recalling Indian legends and rites, which runs through the summer. The Farmington Museum shows off both its archeological past and geological present with several hands-on displays, many of them geared towards children.

The road pushes on into the Navajo Reservation and ends, 53 miles ahead, just across the Arizona state line, in the community of Teec Nos Pos. If you want to continue on U.S. 666, the road combines with that highway at the next major town, Shiprock. But if

you've decided that Farmington is far enough, this is as good a
place as any to end the drive.

VISITING HOURS

New Mexico

Angel Fire: Vietnam Veterans National Memorial, no phone. On
U.S. 64. Daily, 6:30–5:30. Free

Bloomfield: Salmon Ruins Museum, (505) 632-2013. West on U.S. 64.
Daily, 9–5. Admission.

Capulin Volcano National Monument: (505) 278-2201. North of U.S.
64, on New Mexico 325. Daily, 8–5:30, summer; close at 4:30,
other times. Admission.

Chama: Cumbres and Toltec Scenic Railroad, (505) 756-2151. Depot
is off U.S. 64, on New Mexico 17. Call for reservations. Trains
leave at 10:30, Memorial Day–mid October. Fare.

Cimarron: Old Mill Museum, (505) 376-2466. South of U.S. 64, on
New Mexico 21. Friday–Wednesday, 10–4, May–September.
Admission.

Philmont Ranch, (505) 376–2281. South on New Mexico 21.
Monday–Saturday, 8–noon and 1–5, April–October. Free.

Farmington: Museum, (505) 327-7701.

Folsom: Museum, (505) 278-2155. North of U.S. 64, on New Mexico
72.

Raton: Museum, (505) 445–8300. At 148 S. 1st St., in former Coors
Building. Tuesday–Saturday, 9–4, June–September;
Friday–Sunday, 2–5, at other times. Free.

Taos: Blumenschein Home, (505) 758-0330. East of Plaza, at 13
Ledoux St. Daily, 9–5. Admission.

Harwood Foundation, (505) 758-3063. At 25 Ledoux St.
Monday–Friday, 10– and Saturday until 4. Free.

Kit Carson House, (505) 758-4741. East of Plaza, on Kit Carson Rd.
Daily, 8–6, June–October; 9–5, at other times. Admission.

Governor Bent House, (505) 758-2376. North of Plaza, on Bent St.
Daily, 9–5 and Sunday 10–4, March–December. Admission.

Stables Art Center, (505) 758-2036. On U.S. 64, N. Pueblo Rd.
Monday–Saturday, 10–5 and Sunday, noon–5. Free.

Fechin Institute, (505) 758-1710. At 227 N. Pueblo Rd. Late
May–early October. Call for times.

Taos Pueblo, (505) 758-4604. North on U.S. 64. Daily, 8–6 summer;
9–4:30, at other times. Admission and photography fee.

Millicent Rogers Museum, (505)758-2462. North on New Mexico
522. Daily 9–5. Admission.

U.S. ROUTE 66

NEVADA

UTAH

COLORADO

CALIFORNIA

N

Seligman
Oatman • Kingman

NEW MEXICO

ARIZONA

Shadow of a Legend

◯

U.S. 66

Seligman, Ariz. to Oatman, Ariz.
119 miles

That's all there is. Just 119 miles remain of what was once ranked among the most famous highways in the world. Route 66; celebrated in literature, in song and television. John Steinbeck's "Mother Road" and the bearer of the dreams of generations of California-bound travelers.

It wound from Chicago to Los Angeles. But now its entire route has been replaced by the Interstate system. There is no more U.S. 66, except for this little segment designated Arizona 66, which is the last remaining continuous portion of the old road. If you go looking diligently, you will find chunks of Route 66 in other areas. Illinois, Oklahoma and New Mexico all try to direct travelers to "Historic Route 66." But these are just snippets, running for a few miles before the Interstate swallows them up again. This Arizona route is the real thing, the way U.S. 66 was in the heyday of the old roads.

MILEPOSTS

The town of Seligman is quite conscious of the distinction it carries. It now bills itself as the "Birthplace of Historic Route 66." Interstate 40 dips to the south here over a route built by highway engineers, but Highway 66 sticks to the route pioneered by Lt. Edward F. Beale in 1857, when he was charged with laying out a wagon road from Santa Fe to Los Angeles and came marching through with a pack of camels carrying his supplies. This was also the route followed by the Santa Fe Railroad when it arrived here in 1883. Seligman grew up at the junction of the main line with the spur that ran south to Prescott, the old territorial capital. The railroad later established repair yards here and the roundhouse erected in 1897 has been preserved.

The road heads west through the Aubrey Valley to **Grand Canyon Caverns**. Here is a nice old-timey sort of roadside attraction, the kind that once proliferated all along Route 66. As soon as you see the dinosaur statue at the entrance, you know that this is tourist hoke the way it used to be. The caverns are 210 feet underground and make an interesting stop, with colorful formations and the vast Chapel of Ages. But it's the style that is important here.

The road now crosses the southernmost portion of the Hualapai Reservation. This is the home of the people who, along with the Havasupai and Yavapai, controlled the lands along the South Rim of the Grand Canyon. The name means "People of the Tall Pines" and before the arrival of Europeans they were nomadic, hunters who lived in dome-shaped huts covered with thatch. However, in its wisdom, the federal government decided to transport them to the searing desert heat near La Paz, far to the southwest, after they were subdued in 1874. The Hualapai could not adapt to the drastic change in environment and died by the dozens. This reservation was established for them in 1883. The administrative center of the one-million acre reservation is Peach Springs. Look for shops selling baskets and dolls, the tribe's most highly developed crafts.

Peach Springs is also the place where early travelers took off for a look at the Grand Canyon. Before the rail spur north from Williams to the present site of Grand Canyon Village was built in 1907, Peach Springs was the closest point the Santa Fe Line came to the Canyon. Travelers would disembark and board stage-coaches for a ten-hour haul to the Canyon floor. It was a far less impressive view than the one we're familiar with today. The Canyon is only about half as deep at this point, but the road did go right down to the level of the Colorado. The Diamond Creek Hotel there was the first of the Canyon's famed hostelries. No trace of it remains, but you can still make the trip. It's a 21-mile haul along the dirt road of Diamond Creek Wash and it is strongly suggested that you don't attempt it in rainy weather.

Valentine became a sub-agency of the Hualapai Reservation in 1900 when a boarding school for Indian children opened here. Some of the old buildings have been preserved.

The road jogs around the Peacock Mountains for its straight run into **Kingman**. Another of the railroad towns that sprung up along the Santa Fe, Kingman was named after the line's head surveyor. Conoisseurs of highway lore will also note that it is the only town on this route mentioned in the lyric of the song "Route 66," by Bobby Troup, which celebrated the wonders of this road.

Kingman was a celebrated stopping place on Route 66, where drivers could rest up before setting off across the Mohave at night in the days before cars were air conditioned. It was also where Clark Gable and Carole Lombard eloped in 1939, too trendy to take the more obvious Nevada nuptials. Andy Devine, the tubby, good-natured sidekick to dozens of cowboy heroes in movies and TV, was a local boy. The main road into town is named for him and there is a display of his memorabilia in the Mohave Museum of History and Art. This facility also contains exhibits of the turquoise mined in the vicinity, some of the most highly prized in the world. The town of Chloride, 20 miles north, still has some small operations going (See U.S. 93).

Kingman has also preserved one of its earliest residences, the Bonelli House, as a museum of domestic life on the frontier. The Bonellis were Swiss-born Mormons who arrived in the Kingman area in 1894. Many pieces in the home are original family possessions, including the wall clock that was the only timepiece in Kingman when the Bonellis arrived. But, then, they *were* Swiss.

Kingman is the end of the route that is still marked Highway 66. You can take a worthwhile extension to the ghost town of Oatman, over the route actually followed by old U.S. 66. One of the most atmospheric old mining towns in the state, Oatman has been painstakingly preserved to look as ramshackle as possible. The ruins are real enough; they're just lovingly maintained as authentic ruins. In the first decade of this century, Oatman's population reached 10,000, and $3 million in gold was taken from the surrounding hills. Now artists live in many of the old miners' shacks. The place has been used frequently as a movie set, including several sequences of *How the West Was Won*. Wild burros still roam the streets and are a prominent feature of the annual Gold Camp Days celebration on Labor Day weekend.

VISITING HOURS

ARIZONA

Grand Canyon Caverns: (602) 422-3223. On Highway 66. Daily, 8–6, mid-June–Labor Day. 10–5 at other times. Admission.

Kingman: Mohave Museum, (602) 753-3195. Off Beale St. exit of Interstate 40, at 400 W. Beale. Monday–Friday, 10–5 and weekends, 1–5. Admission.

Bonelli House, (602) 753-3195. At 310 N. 4th St. Thursday–Monday, 1–5. Free.

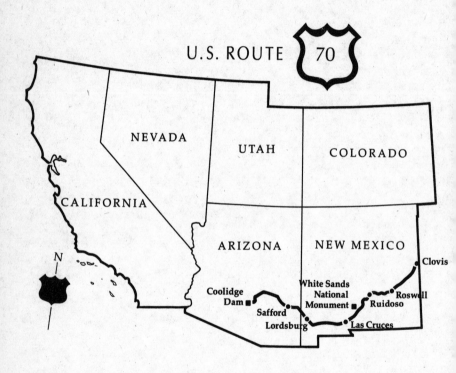

U.S. ROUTE 70

NEVADA

UTAH

COLORADO

CALIFORNIA

ARIZONA

NEW MEXICO

Clovis

Coolidge
Dam

White Sands
National
Monument

Roswell

Ruidoso

Safford

Lordsburg

Las Cruces

N

Gadsden's Corner

$\bigcirc$

U.S. 70

Clovis, N.M. to Coolidge Dam, Ariz.
561 miles

This is another of the attenuated bicoastal highways. Starting on
the Atlantic shore, in the Outer Banks of North Carolina, U.S. 70
remains a major route across the Middle South, bobbing in and out
of shadowing Interstate highways most of the way. But while it
once reached the Pacific at Los Angeles, U.S. 70 now goes no further west than the old copper town of Globe, Arizona.

It does make a scenic and inviting scoop-shaped run through
this area, even with 20 percent of it shared by an Interstate. You'll
cross the Rockies near the resort of **Ruidoso**, dip down to historic
Las Cruces, then angle northwest through the Gila Valley of
Arizona, following one of the most dangerous routes on the frontier. After all, it was along this road that the *Stagecoach* of the classic Western movie made its perilous run and turned John Wayne
into a star.

MILEPOSTS

The trip starts where the road branches away from U.S. 60 in
Clovis; the highway ends where it rejoins U.S. 60 in Globe. In

between, U.S. 70 has a nice chunk of territory to itself. It's a territory that has seen some spectacular geological change. A prehistoric river once ran through this part of New Mexico until an upheaval drained it into the course now followed by the Pecos, several miles to the west. This area was left dry, but portions of the abandoned bed can still be seen. One of these is Blackwater Draw, in which a wealth of fossils and 12,000-year-old human artifacts have been recovered. A museum at the site along the highway, operated by Eastern New Mexico University, explains what happened here and displays what was found in the ancient riverbed.

The main campus of the school is just down the road in **Portales**. This entire area was developed fairly recently. The town grew up when underground wells were discovered in 1890, enabling an irrigation system to be built. The area now produces a variety of crops, the mightiest of which is the peanut. Portales, in giddy moments, refers to itself as "The Peanut Basin of the Nation" and in late October dedicates a festival to the goober. The college was founded here in 1934 and, as indicated by the museum at Blackwater Draw, has a fine school of Paleo-Indian studies. The Miles Museum in Roosevelt Hall contains more displays of the ancient Indian cultures of the area.

The road now runs along a spur of the Santa Fe line, through the great cattle ranches of Roosevelt and Chaves counties. The towns are barely crossroads, with a few hundred in population. It's a typical pattern on the Staked Plains, the Llano Estacado, whose endless flat expanse makes up the landscape here.

Elida was probably named for the daughters, Ella and Ida, of an early settler. West of Elkins, the rounded form of Haystack Mountain, with an elevation of 4,188 feet, breaks the monotony of the view to the north. The turnoff to Bitter Lake National Wildlife Refuge leads to a 24,000-acre sanctuary for wintering waterfowl, sandhill cranes, and about 300 other varieties of birds. Between

October and February this wetland area, lying between the plains and the desert, is a bird watcher's delight. Loop trails lead to prime observation areas and picnic shelters overlook the water, too.

Roswell, now the fourth largest city in the state, started off as a trading post along the old cattle trails to Texas. The post was run by a gambler, Van C. Smith, although why a man whose livelihood depended on some semblance of community would choose to live off in the middle of nowhere is not quite clear. Smith sold his holdings to cattle-baron Joseph Lea in 1877, but he stayed long enough to name the settlement after his father, Roswell.

While neighboring Lincoln County erupted in a bloody range war, the Leas managed to keep peace on their lands. When artesian wells were discovered in 1891, the town prospered as a farm center. It also was chosen as the site for the New Mexico Military Institute, a Roswell landmark since 1898. The campus on the northern edge of town has an enrollment of 900 young men, who receive high school and junior college training here. The Alumni Memorial Chapel is near the entrance and nearby is the General Douglas L. McBride Military Museum, with displays on the contributions of graduates to national history and memorabilia of the Bataan Death March.

It wasn't military matters that drew Robert C. Goddard to Roswell in 1930. Its clear climate and lightly populated surroundings happened to be ideal for the experiments he was conducting in rocketry. However, his pioneering work in the field helped establish New Mexico as a center for such research (see U.S. 54.) and enhanced the military presence in the state enormously. Goddard's workshop and many of his instruments are preserved at the Roswell Museum and Art Center, which also shows off its collection of paintings by Georgia O'Keeffe and Peter Hurd, who we'll meet again a bit further along this road. It is one of the most wide-ranging small museums in the Southwest.

The road joins U.S. 380 as it approaches the eastern slope of the Rockies, through the fruit-growing Hondo Valley. There are great views over this terrain as the road begins to ascend near the town of Sunset. Hondo is Spanish for "deep" and the valley is named for the river which runs alongside the road. It branches off at the town of Hondo and we swing to the south, along the Ruidoso ("noisy") River.

Near **San Patricio** is Sentinel Ranch, former home of Peter Hurd, whose paintings of the New Mexico landscape filled a wing of the museum back in Roswell. Hurd became nationally famous in 1967, when President Lyndon B. Johnson referred to Hurd's portrait of him as "the ugliest thing I ever saw" and suggested that Hurd study the work of Norman Rockwell if he wanted to learn how to be an artist. The portrait now hangs in the Smithsonian's National Gallery in Washington, D.C.

Hurd's studies of light and shadow in the isolated reaches of the southwestern deserts established him as a leading force in American art. He dropped out of West Point after two years to study with Andrew Wyeth, married that artist's daughter, Henriette, and came back to this ranch to spend the rest of his life. He hung a sign on his studio door that read: "If it is the Second Coming, call me. Otherwise, let me alone." He was rarely disturbed. "A painting should be a prolonged and haunting echo of human existence," he wrote. "I would like future viewers to say of my work, 'Here is what the southwest looked like in the 20th century.'" At the time of his death in 1983, Hurd occupied a position at the pinnacle of American art, despite the presidential demurral.

The area around **Ruidoso** has grown into one of the most popular resorts in the state, with excellent golf three seasons of the year and skiing on the slopes of snow-crowned Sierra Blanca. But the core of its development is a shrine to the quarter horse, Ruidoso Downs.

This is the favored breed of the west, the paradigm of the ranching cowpony. Its name actually originated in Virginia, where quarter-mile tracks were carved for it in the colonial forests. Shorter and more heavily muscled than the thoroughbred, the quarter horse can get off to a quicker start, turn more adeptly and develop more speed on a short course. But it also tires more easily over a longer distance, and as tastes in racing changed the thoroughbred, which was developed for sustained speed, supplanted the quarter horse. But not in New Mexico. Quarter horse racing here began as competitions between ranches, then expanded at Ruidoso into the three richest events in the sport. The four-month season culminates in the All-American Futurity on Labor Day with a $2.5 million purse.

In the track's Turf Club is the Hubbard Museum, an outstanding collection of western art, with several paintings by Charles Russell and Frederic Remington. There are also many art galleries in the center of town, which is built along the Ruidoso River. Look for the century-old waterwheel of the Dowlin Mill nearby.

The highway crosses into the **Mescalero** Apache Reservation, some of the best-developed Indian land in the country. Grazing and logging bring in revenue to the tribe, but the big moneymaker is tourism. The resort on the reservation, Inn of the Mountain Gods, has the top-rated golf course in the state and the tribe runs several ski areas in the vicinity. There is a museum of tribal history and culture at the Community Center in the town of Mescalero. The Maidens' Ceremonial and The All-Indian Rodeo, held on the Fourth of July weekend, top the annual calendar of events.

The Mescalero broke out of their former reservation lands near Fort Sumner in 1866 and for the next 16 years were the most feared raiders on the New Mexico and Texas frontier. Their ability to vanish into Mexico, then suddenly recross the border miles away from the original point of departure, enhanced their reputation for speed and deception. Finally overcome by force of numbers and the U.S. Cavalry's strategy of staking out water holes to trap them, the Mescalero were restricted to these lands in 1883. It turned out to be a better deal than most tribes received.

You can make out the distinctive shape of Round Mountain on the north as you pass through Bent. The mountain was the site of a fierce battle between cavalry and Apaches that ended in a standoff but thwarted a planned raid on the town of Tularosa in 1868.

At Tularosa, the highway combines with U.S. 54. The 13-mile segment between here and Alamogordo is described in that chapter.

The road swings west as a four-lane, high-speed thoroughfare, past Holloman Air Force Base and down to the Tularosa Basin. This area has become famous as the testing ground for the country's missile program, and the road is occasionally closed for brief periods when firing is scheduled across the range. (See U.S. 54 for a more detailed decsription of this area's link to rocketry.)

Long before that, however, the basin was a landmark because of its white sands. This sea of gleaming gypsum, stacked by the wind into dunes 60 feet high, is one of the southwest's signature sights. This is the material from which plaster of paris is made; it has a coarser texture than the sand you'd find at the beach. It was carried here from surrounding mountains by rainwater runoff and deposited into the bed of ancient Lake Lucero. When the lake evaporated, the gypsum crystals were broken down and carried to this valley by the wind.

This is no wasteland, though. In some places, plants have extended their roots down 400 feet or more to survive amid the sands. Animals also adapted and many species have become as white as the surrounding sands to escape predators. Just a few miles north, at Valley of Fires State Park, on U.S. 380, the animals have become coal black to blend in with the lava flow. A Visitors' Center at **White Sands National Monument**, north of the highway, explains both the geological and natural history of this unique area.

From White Sands, the road speeds across the basin, gradually climbing toward San Agustin Pass, the gateway to the Rio Grande Valley. This was the road that linked the old territorial capital of La Mesilla to the ranching settlements in Lincoln County. Somewhere along this stretch of road is where one of New Mexico's great unsolved mysteries occurred. In 1896 Colonel A. J. Fountain, one of the territory's most prominent citizens, was on his way home to La Mesilla after prosecuting several rustlers in Lincoln, when he was ambushed. His wrecked wagon and some of his papers and belongings were found east of the pass, but the colonel and his 12-year-old son were never seen again and their attackers never discovered. We'll meet the Fountains once more, however, a few miles ahead in La Mesilla.

Now, on the western horizon, is the outline of the Organ Mountains, named for their pipe-like peaks shaped by wind erosion. Just east of San Agustin Pass is a turnoff south to Aguirre Spring, a recreation area with hiking trails and close-up views of those towering organ pipes.

From the 5,719-foot-high pass, U.S. 70 descends into the outskirts of Las Cruces. This fast-growing city, a retirement center and seat of New Mexico State University, is now the third-biggest community in the state. Surrounded by rich farmland, it is best known for its chili production. Each October, it observes the Whole Enchilada Festival, topped off by the annual concoction of the world's largest specimen of that Mexican treat.

The town's origin is a far darker story. It was named for a massacre. Spanish for "the crosses," it refers to the graves of a party of Mexican pioneers, traveling north along El Camino Real, who were killed by Indians here in 1830. The site became a somber landmark on the road and the settlement that grew up nearby was named for it.

This is also the route of the Butterfield Stage, the line between Texas and California. It ran north from El Paso along El Camino Real and turned west here. Las Cruces grew up in earnest, though, when it became a terminal for the Southern Pacific Railroad in 1881. Before that, it was merely a small settlement outside the region's most important town, La Mesilla, which is where we are headed.

The easiest route is to leave U.S. 70 on southbound Interstate 25. Take it to westbound University Avenue, which runs past the New Mexico State campus. If you want to take a look at the campus, park near Solano Drive and walk around, stopping off at Kent Hall to see the University Museum. It has changing exhibits of local historical interest. Continue on University to New Mexico 28 and turn right to La Mesilla.

FOCUS

Throughout the ominous 1850s, as the country plummeted towards war, everything in America was viewed through a regional prism. Even while serving the federal government, men searched for some advantage for their part of the country. So when Jefferson Davis of Mississippi was named Secretary of War in the Pierce Administration, the events that would redraw the international boundary in America's most remote southwestern frontier were put into motion.

The Mexican War of the previous decade had placed more than half of Mexico's former land area under American control. But it wasn't quite enough. One of Davis's most critical policy tasks was to choose a route for a proposed transcontinental railroad. Early reports favored a northern route—but railroads meant power. Davis was not about to permit such an enormous economic and political weapon to fall into the hands of the north. So in 1853 Davis looked over the possibilities and decided that the route running through southern New Mexico was clearly the best. There was just one problem: the land west of the Rio Grande still belonged to Mexico.

The United States had expressed no interest in this barren territory south of the Gila River when the Mexican War ended. Now it
had become essential. Fortunately for Davis's designs, the minister
to Mexico, James Gadsden, was an old railroad man from South
Carolina who understood the situation perfectly. Mexico's former
dictator, Antonio Lopez de Santa Anna, had just returned to
power and he was strapped for cash with which to buy the loyalty
of his leading military officers. He was more than happy to dis-
pose of another slice of his country for the $10 million offered by
Gadsden. Purchase was approved on December 30, 1853, and the
United States had acquired the last piece of property in its continental holdings. The railroad, however, was built along the northern route after all. It would be decades before the Southern Pacific
came through along the route Davis had chosen.

On July 4, 1854, the American flag was raised over the plaza of
La Mesilla to officially mark the passing of this territory to U.S.
control. The action was not universally popular. Most residents of
the town had moved here from other parts of New Mexico after
the war because they preferred to remain under Mexican rule.
Now America had swallowed them anyhow. Accepting the
inevitable, they remained to build. With a population of 3,000, La
Mesilla was already the largest settlement in the area, and when
the Butterfield Stage came through in 1858 it was a thriving community that boasted the only hotel between San Antonio and Los
Angeles.

In three more years, however, another flag would be raised on
the plaza. Confederate troops from Texas seized La Mesilla and
made it the capital of the newly proclaimed Arizona Territory.
Within a year, however, this force would be shattered at the Battle
of Glorieta and decimated in its long retreat across the desert. A
Union detachment from the west, the California Column, reached
La Mesilla in the summer of 1862 and secured it for federal control.

Late in 1880, Billy the Kid was brought here for trial. It was felt, quite reasonably, that a fair hearing would be impossible in Lincoln County, where the killings of the long range war had stirred hatreds that could not be confined within a court of law. So he was brought to the opposite end of the territory and tried in the courthouse on La Mesilla plaza. After his conviction, Billy was returned to Lincoln. He escaped and was subsequently shot by Sheriff Pat Garrett. Garrett later returned to this part of the territory as a lawman and was himself shot dead in Las Cruces.

A few months after this excitement, the railroad arrived in Las Cruces. La Mesilla, content in its prosperity on the stage line, could not see that its removal from the rails meant its eclipse. Maybe that was for the good. It has changed very little over the last 100 years. The plaza over which the Stars and Stripes were raised to salute the Gadsden Purchase on that long ago Independence Day looks much the same. The courthouse in which Billy the Kid was tried still stands as a store on the southeastern corner of the plaza. The adobe church of San Albino was replaced by a more substantial brick structure in 1906, but it remains at the head of the plaza and the original bells are still rung. The La Posta restaurant occupies the old Butterfield station, one block to the east, and many other historic buildings have been converted to dining places and art galleries.

A walk around this historic place—its plaza and adjacent side streets—is about as close as you can come to recapturing the texture of the late-19th-century Southwest.

Be sure and look in on the Gadsden Museum, too, on the far side of Highway 28. It displays many items relating to the town's past and its range of cultures. Included is the original painting of the Gadsden flag-raising by Albert J. Fountain Jr., father of the man who would mysteriously vanish near San Agustin Pass 42 years later. The museum was established in 1931 by members of the Fountain family.

* * *

Follow highways 28 and 292 north to westbound Interstate 10 and in a few miles you'll be reunited with U.S. 70. Some reunion. For the next 109 miles, unfortunately, Interstate and old road are one. They run parallel to the Southern Pacific tracks that would so gladden Jeff Davis's heart. This was also the Butterfield Stage route. But that road and the U.S. 70 that was built in its tracks are gone. So we'll grit our teeth and forge ahead on the Interstate.

Deming is a good stop if you're a rockhound. There is, in fact, a state park named for you just southeast of town, and within Rock Hound State Park you may find opal, jasper, agate, and many unpronounceable minerals of assorted hues. You reach it from southbound New Mexico 11 and a paved park road. To the south looms Florida Peak (given the Spanish pronunciation of Flor-eeda in this part of the country) at 7,295 feet.

If you continued south on Highway 11 for another half-hour, you'd come to Columbus, the border town raided by Mexican bandit Pancho Villa in 1916. Deming was the command center for the military action following the raid and the punitive expedition sent into Mexico after him. Troops were bivouacked in the National Guard Armory, which was then just nearing completion. The old armory is now the Luna Mimbres Museum, named for the county and the river valley in which Deming is located. It contains exhibits on local history, including the Villa expedition and artifacts of the Mimbres Indians who once inhabited the region. The Mimbres River, incidentally, disappears into the earth just south of here and doesn't re-emerge until it reaches Chihuahua, deep into Mexico, much like Villa's raiders.

Deming still observes Butterfield Trail Days each July in memory of the stage line. It was the stretch of trail between here and **Lordsburg** that was traveled by the fictional *Stagecoach* of movie fame. A tastier tribute is the Klobase Festival in October, during which the area's Czech settlers serve up the sausages which give the celebration its name.

We finally part company with the Interstate at Lordsburg, after gliding effortlessly across the Continental Divide at the Grant County line. The place was first named Lordsborough, after a construction engineer with the railroad, but the spelling was sensibly shortened. It's situated in the midst of a vast ranching area, and mines are also worked in the nearby Pyramid Mountains. One of these old mining camps, Shakespeare, is maintained as a private ghost town. An entrance fee is charged and events are staged there throughout the year. But the degree of authenticity is kept high and commercial hoke reduced to a minimum. The place was first named Ralston City in 1870, but nine years later some literary mine promoters changed it to honor the Bard; in the hope, no doubt, that when their claims were assessed, measure for measure, the result would be as you like it.

The last mine closed in 1935 and three years later the place was purchased by a local family and seven historically significant structures preserved. These include the Butterfield station and the Stratford Hotel, where Billy the Kid once worked as a dishwasher. If you like your ghost towns in the rough, this may not be for you. But for those who don't mind tame ghosts, it does present a good idea of what an old mining town looked like when everything was still standing.

The road veers off to the northwest and in 26 miles crosses the Arizona line, into the Gila Valley. Duncan is an old railhead for surrounding cattle ranches, and the landscape is dominated by the 10,717-foot mass of Mt. Graham on the west. Mormon settlers came into this area in the late 19th century, but until the road reaches the river, at Solomon, the area is still lightly populated, open land, with yucca and cholla plants along the roadside making the dominant visual statements.

It was along this passage that General Stephen Kearney headed west with his army in the first year of the Mexican War. Kearney had easily taken Santa Fe for the United States in 1846. Named

General of the West, he was ordered to go ahead and take California, too. But scout Kit Carson met him near here and told him that the northern part of the territory was already in American hands. Carson then turned back and led the army towards the Los Angeles settlement, to complete the California conquest.

This was all Mexican territory then, but it was controlled by the Apaches and almost unpopulated. Solomon wasn't even settled until 1873. It was named for a pioneer merchant, Isador E. Solomon; who, surprisingly, found himself a gentile when the place became a predominantly Mormon community after 1879.

Safford is the biggest town in the area, with a population of 7,000. It is also the oldest, settled as a farming town in 1872 and named for the territorial governor, A.P.K. Safford. Cotton and alfalfa production remain the economic mainstays, as well as fruit and vegetable farms watered by the Gila. (For a further description of this area at the base of Mt. Graham, see U.S. 666.)

The highway continues angling northwest, past a succession of riverside farm towns. Central is named for the irrigation canal on which its prosperity is based. Fort Thomas is on the site of an army post situated here during the campaigns against the Apaches in the 1870s. The next town on the route is named for the adversary of that era, Geronimo.

Now U.S. 70 enters the second Apache reservation along its route, the San Carlos. Like the Mescalero in New Mexico this is good grazing land and the tribal cattle operation is the biggest of its kind in the country. The road passes the Indian settlement of Bylas, named for a chief, then leaves the river to angle towards the village of Peridot, named for a green stone found in the area.

From here, a 13-mile trip on reservation road 3 takes you to the place to which this trip through the Gila Valley has been leading. The growth of Arizona is the triumph of engineering over nature. The dams that were the decisive elements in this story are all named after U.S. Presidents: Hoover on the Colorado River,

Roosevelt on the Salt, and Coolidge on the Gila. By the time Coolidge Dam was completed, in 1930, Calvin Coolidge had already been out of office for a year, but he stopped by to dedicate it anyway. It immediately sextupled the cultivated acreage in the Gila valley, primarily in the area through which we have just driven.

The 259-foot-high dam sits just inside the San Carlos land and it was the Apaches who opposed it most adamantly. The reservoir it formed, 23-mile-long San Carlos Lake, inundated Apache lands, including tribal burial grounds. They viewed its construction as a violation of tribal treaty rights. The government finally agreed to place a concrete cap on the cemetery so that the dead would not be disturbed and the project was allowed to go forward.

U.S. 70 runs another 19 miles from Peridot to the copper town of Globe. But Coolidge Dam is as good a place as any to end this ride: atop its crest, in an Arizona canyon, looking at the splash of deep blue that brings life to the land.

VISITING HOURS

NEW MEXICO

Deming: Rock Hound State Park, (505) 546-1212. South on New Mexico 11. Daily, 7:30–dusk. Admission.

Luna Mimbres Museum, (505) 546-2382. At 301 S. Silver St. Monday–Saturday, 9–4 and Sunday, 1:30–4. Donation.

Las Cruces: University Museum, (505) 646-3739. On New Mexico State campus, in Kent Hall, University Ave., west of Interstate 25. Tuesday–Saturday, 10–4 and Sunday, 1–4. Free.

Gadsden Museum, (505) 526-6293. In Mesilla, see text for directions. Daily, 9–11 and 1–5. Admission.

Lordsburg: Shakespeare Ghost Town, (505) 542-9034. South of town. Call for hours.

Mescalero: Tribal Museum, (505) 671-4494. In town center. Call for hours.

Portales: Blackwater Draw Museum, (505) 562-2254. North on U.S. 70. Tuesday–Sunday, 9–4. Donation.

Miles Museum, (505) 562-2651. On Eastern New Mexico University campus, Roosevelt Hall. Monday–Friday, 9–4. Free.

Roswell: McBride Museum, (505) 622-6250. On campus of New Mexico Military Institute, at College and N. Main Sts. Tuesday–Friday, 9–3. Free.

Roswell Museum, (505) 624-6744. At 11th and Main Sts. Monday–Saturday, 9–5 and Sunday, 1–5. Free.

Ruidoso: Hubbard Museum, (505) 378-4431. In Clubhouse of Ruidoso Downs. Daily, early May–Labor Day. Admission.

San Patricio: Sentinel Ranch, (505) 653-4331. On U.S. 70. Monday–Friday, 9–4, and Saturday, 10–4. Free.

White Sands National Monument: (505) 479-6124. North of U.S. 70. Daily, 8–7, Memorial Day–Labor Day; 8–4:30, at other times. Admission.

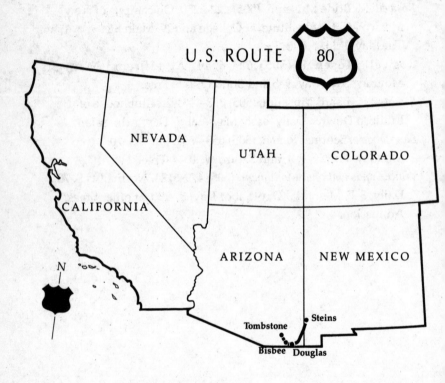

U.S. ROUTE 80

NEVADA

UTAH

COLORADO

CALIFORNIA

ARIZONA

NEW MEXICO

Tombstone

Steins

Bisbee

Douglas

N

Tombstone Territory

$$\bigcirc$$

U.S. 80

Steins, N.M. to Benson, Ariz.
153 miles

Once it was the road across the baseboard. Running from the beaches of Savannah, Georgia to the beaches of San Diego, California, U.S. 80 was the southernmost transcontinental highway. But in the Southwest, the Interstates have gobbled up its former route and pushed it into a corner of Arizona.

Of course, it isn't a bad corner to be in. It runs through the old haunts of Geronimo, then enters some of the most colorful mining towns in the world: Douglas, **Bisbee**, and **Tombstone**, the Town Too Tough to Die.

MILESTONES

The ghost town of **Steins** actually is two miles west of the point where U.S. 80 dips south to slip away from Interstate 10. But it's worth the short jog west. While most ghost towns in this area were once mining camps, Steins is a railroad wraith, a specter of the Southern Pacific. It first was a station on the Butterfield Stage route, named for a major in the U.S. Cavalry who was a member of an early exploring party. The major's name was also given to a nearby peak and the pass leading to Arizona.

While the railroad maintained a depot and water stop here,

Steins thrived. But in 1945 both were closed and the town shut down, too. Still standing along its main street are portions of the hotel, several stores, a saloon, and a house of illicit assignations. For those of a more serious bent, houses belonging to the railroad section crews have been restored and furnished in late 19th-century style, as a domestic museum of Mexican–American life.

Now backtrack to U.S. 80 and head south. Four miles beyond the intersection with New Mexico 9, a paved road leads west across the Arizona line to the town of Portal. The place got its name because it sits at the entrance to Cave Creek Canyon, on the edge of Coronado National Forest. Towering rocks of red rhyolite rise from the canyon floor and are reflected in the creek. It is a beauty spot well worth the short detour. Portal itself, surrounded by mountains, is a striking place, removed from Arizona's heaviest tourist traffic.

Retrace your route to U.S. 80, which crosses back into Arizona after a few miles. Near the town of Apache, the road reaches a memorial to the last of that tribe's great chiefs, Geronimo. It was near this spot, in Skeleton Canyon, that he surrendered to federal troops in September 1886, ending the final military campaign against the Apaches. So vivid were its memories, however, that 50 years later, when the memorial was dedicated, many pioneer families were incensed and urged the state to reconsider.

Historians have described Geronimo as a clever politician and a ruthless leader. The less sympathetic compare his personality and skills to that of a contemporary mob boss. Nonetheless, they enabled him to gain the leadership of the Chiricahua band by 1881. He was then a man in his early 50s and too restless, too much a leader, to be satisfied with reservation life. Repeatedly over the next five years he led members of his band on brief raids; slipping across the Mexican border to obtain cattle and coming back to the American side for ammunition. The last break started in May 1885 and was occasioned by new federal regulations prohibiting home-brewed beer and wife-beating. Geronimo regarded this as unwarranted interference with tribal folkways. His top assistant, Nana, told cavalry Lieutenant Britton Davis that "you can't advise me how to treat my women. You are only a boy. I killed men before you were born."

With that chilling pronouncement, the Chiricahua were off once more. Davis, who later wrote a history of the campaign, described it this way: "Thirty-five men and eight half-grown boys, encumbered with the care and sustenance of 101 women and children, with no base of supplies and no means of waging war or obtaining food or transportation other than what they could take from their enemies, maintained themselves for 18 months against 5,000 troops, 500 Indian auxiliaries and an unknown number of civilians."

Although the death toll of military and settlers reached close to 100, there were never any doubts about how this campaign would end. The days when the Apache were a serious threat to the Arizona frontier were well in the past. There was too much of an American presence in the state by this time. But a recognition grew that this was to be the last of the Indian campaigns in the West. Urban Americans shuddered in civilized safety and enjoyed the final chapter for all it was worth. The large Eastern newspapers sent correspondents to cover this "Apache War," and their lurid accounts of Geronimo's activities turned him into a legendary name in American history.

Finally, exhausted and surrounded, Geronimo surrendered and was shipped off to captivity in Florida with what was left of his band. He found himself a national celebrity, posing for photographs in towns around the country as he toured with Wild West shows. For the last 23 years of his life he served as a benign symbol of a fierce and vanished past.

Incidentally, you can blame a western movie for the traditional paratrooper cry of "Geronimo!" According to historians of the 101st Airborne Division, paratroopers training at Ft. Benning, Georgia during the early days of World War II started the custom.

A private bet his buddies that he would be so calm on his first jump that he could yell anything they chose when he leaped from the plane. The unit had just seen a movie about Geronimo, so they told him to yell that. He did, and a tradition was born, although in the interests of accuracy it should be pointed out that the proper pronunciation is *Hee-ronimo*, since it is derived from the Spanish.

Skeleton Canyon was not named because of anything to do with the Apache campaigns. Instead, it commemorates the ambush of a group of Mexican smugglers by American outlaws in 1882. The bodies were left to turn to bone.

The road crosses the eastern edge of verdant Sulphur Spring Valley, with its fruit and vegetable farms and pecan groves. The Pedregosa Mountains rise to the northwest and the Sierra de San Bernardo are visible across the Mexican border.

Douglas perches right on that border, across from the Sonora community of Agua Prieta. Even more important to its history is that Douglas sits at the foot of the Mule Mountains. When the copper smelter at Bisbee, 23 miles further and 1,400 feet higher up U.S. 80, reached capacity in 1900, the Phelps Dodge Co. selected this site to build new ones. Transporting the ore here was easy enough, since it was downhill all the way.

Within four years, the smelters were in operation. The place now named for the Phelps Dodge president had become a boomtown and residents figured it was time to build a grand hotel. Western copper towns loved building grand hotels. They meant permanence in a business that was transitory almost by definition. The one in Douglas was called the Gadsden, named for the railroad man who had arranged the land deal by which this slice of Arizona came to be American territory. The hotel opened in 1906 and is still a Douglas ornament today, with its wealth of stained glass, its skylight, and richly adorned lobby. From its roof, spectators watched Pancho Villa lay siege to Agua Prieta in 1915. The fabled bandit leader retreated and later claimed that he had been fired on by American artillery. As an act of revenge, he carried out

his raid on the border town of Columbus, New Mexico the following year.

The copper industry is part of the past. Douglas has built up a
diversified economic base and is an active trading partner with
Mexican businesses. The two border cities hold several joint celebrations throughout the year, but the biggest local attraction is
September's College Rodeo, with star performers drawn from the
unique rodeo school of Cochise College. The highway runs past
the modern campus west of town as it climbs towards Bisbee.

The contemporary brochures are fond of noting Bisbee's "Old
World Charm" but it's hard to figure out to what in the world
they're referring. The place certainly couldn't be found anywhere
else but the American Southwest. In its setting, clinging to the
walls of a series of steep ravine; and in its purpose, the mining of
copper, it is intrinsically a part of Old Arizona. What makes it
unique is the number of historic structures that have been preserved and the sense of appreciation and reverence with which
they are treated today. The old mining camp has transformed itself
into a bed-and-breakfast, antique-filled center of charm, in which
the past can be recaptured on every corner.

The first strike was made here in 1877 and within three years
Phelps Dodge had arrived to consolidate various holdings and
form the Copper Queen Mining Co. For the next 40 years, the town
steadily expanded to become a city of 20,000 (almost three times its
present size), adding the amenities that one would expect in the
communities of the east. One service that never was established,
though, was home mail delivery. The steep slopes on which Bisbee
is built made that impractical and the place remains the largest
town in America where you still have to walk to the post office to
pick up your mail. In the peak years you could take a streetcar, an
amenity that no longer exists. A disastrous fire in 1908 wiped out
the business district, so older shanties were cleared out and the
buildings in the center of town have a unified appearance since
they all date from the reconstruction. The removal of the smelter to

Douglas helped improved the quality of life as well.

Bisbee reached its peak production years during World War I, but when the price of copper began falling afterwards it went into a steady decline. The Lavender Pit, which adjoins the Copper Queen, was developed after World War II in an effort to exploit the ore more economically. Almost one mile wide and 950 feet deep, the pit produced more than $41 million. But in 1975, after $2 billion had been taken from the ground here over 98 years, all large-scale mining stopped and the town concentrated on exploiting its past instead.

The old Phelps Dodge offices in the center of town are now the Bisbee Mining and Historical Museum, a good place to start for an orientation. The museum sits at the entrance to Brewery Gulch, once the home address of more than 40 saloons, which now are art galleries and antique shops. The Muheim Brewery, which gave the thoroughfare its distinct air, is gone, but the museum has restored the Muheim House, built in 1914 by its proprietor on a nearby hill.

Another place to seek out the story of Bisbee's past is the Restoration and Historical Society Museum, on Main Street, which is also liberally laced with crafts shops and galleries. The Copper Queen Hotel, dating from 1902, with the names of Teddy Roosevelt and General John Pershing in its register, still receives overnight guests in its 43 rooms. Many great homes have also been converted into smaller inns.

U.S. 80 runs along the edge of the Lavender Pit and a viewpoint overlooks the massive hole. Tours of both the pit and the Copper Queen Mine leave from the mine offices in the middle of town. The pit tour takes 75 minutes by bus and the mine tour, which descends into the Copper Queen by mine car, lasts about the same amount of time. The underground temperature is only in the high 40s, though, so take a warm garment with you.

The road heads west through Mule Pass Tunnel, the longest in the state at 1,400 feet. The Mule Mountains were named for their two most prominent peaks, which resemble a mule's ears.

Now U.S. 80 drops steadily into the desert, with the snow-capped Huachuca Mountains in the distance to the west.

FOCUS

Shots were fired and three men died. In the movies, right prevailed. But history has fewer certainties than Hollywood. The epitaph on the grave marker in Boothill reads: "Murdered on the streets of Tombstone."

Exactly what happened on the afternoon of October 26, 1881, in the street outside the O.K. Corral, is as much the province of legend as any event in the history of the West. Wyatt Earp, his brothers, Morgan and Virgil, and their shady associate, Doc Holliday, challenged the McLaury brothers, Frank and Tom, and the Clantons, Billy and Ike, sons of the largest rancher in the area. The gunfight was the culmination of a feud between the two factions. But while the Earps wore badges, there are many historians who still wonder which side of the law they really were on, and the gunfight at the O.K. Corral remains as controversial as it is celebrated.

Three years before the fight the corral, the street, the whole town of Tombstone didn't even exist. Then prospector Ed Schieffelin struck gold here in 1877, having ignored warnings that all he would find in these hills deep in Apache country would be his tombstone. When he hit the Lucky Cuss strike, he touched off the wildest decade any town ever knew.

Within three years, 14,000 people had crowded into the area. Many of them were not the type to be welcomed by the chamber of commerce. Some came after tapping out in the dwindling goldfields of California and Australia; some had been invited to leave by older towns that had attained minimal levels of respectability. They came to strike it rich or to get the money of those who had already done so by any means possible. The saloons and dance halls and bordellos that sprang up here were as wild and lusty as any in Western fiction. The law was a convenience, to be observed or ignored as the occasion dictated. This year's town marshal could be holding up the stage next year. Deputies could drop their badges and become part of a lynch mob. Lawmen could double as private gunfighters for hire. That was the normal course of events in Tombstone in the 1880s.

The Earps and Holliday were part of this migration, coming down from the Kansas cattle towns where all four had worked on both sides of the law. Television shows and movies have taught us to view Wyatt Earp, especially, as an heroic figure, a town-tamer, "brave, courageous, and bold," in the words of the theme song. Actually, Earp was dismissed from the Wichita police force for taking part in a street brawl and withholding money he had collected in fines. After he paid up he was thrown out of town for vagrancy. He served parts of three terms as marshal of Dodge City, interrupting his service to visit Deadwood as a gunman. He arrived in Tombstone in 1879 as a stagecoach messenger, became a deputy sheriff, then quit to become a private guard for a gambling house. His brother, Virgil, was appointed marshal by a vigilance committee and followed up by pistol-whipping troublesome cowboys from the Clanton ranch with his brothers. Threats were made, and the Earps called on Holliday, a dentist turned gambler and gunman, to assist them. When they confronted the cowboys as they were picking up their horses at the corral, the gunfight followed. A court hearing cleared the Earps but public opinion turned against them. Morgan was shot to death while playing billiards, Virgil was wounded in an ambush, and Wyatt left for healthier surroundings and ultimate glory.

That was the bloodiest day in Tombstone's history. By 1887 underground water was seeping into the mines and the cost of pumping it out made them unprofitable. Tombstone could never find the answer to this engineering problem and the 1890 census saw only 1,875 hardy souls remaining, about the same population it has today.

Small-scale mines and individual claims continued to be worked, though, and unlike played-out mining towns in less amiable climates, Tombstone remained a community. It held on to the county government until 1931, possibly because other communities were too scared to try and take it away. Its storied past attracted those who were fascinated by western lore and many of them settled in to make the town their avocation. They researched and restored what was left. Tombstone became, in its own proud boast, The Town Too Tough to Die. Now it is the perfect epiphany of respectability, a National Historic Site.

Much of the local preservation was the achievement of Harold O. Love, an attorney from Grosse Pointe, Michigan. He drove through town in 1963, stopped at the Crystal Palace Saloon, found it was for sale and bought it. Then he started to restore it to its former splendor. "We tried to locate the original," he said, "only to find that it was like the artist who had painted 2,500 pictures—5,000 of which were still in existence. So we reconstructed it from old pictures in the newspaper, the *Epitaph*." Over the next 20 years, he invested several million dollars into returning the luster to others of Tombstone's famous and notorious monuments—the O.K. Corral, Schiefelin Hall, the *Epitaph*—in what became a true labor of Love.

Most of these places are located along Allen Street, between 3rd and 5th, one block south of U.S. 80. The Crystal Palace and its even naughtier neighbor, the Bird Cage Theatre, present entertainment once more. The O.K. Corral recreates its gunfight at 2 p.m. each Sunday. The offices of the *Epitaph*, now published as a monthly journal of Western history, display antique printing equipment.

At 3rd and Toughnut, one block beyond Allen, is the Tombstone Courthouse, containing the best historical exhibits of the town. There are the original courtrooms from frontier days and mementoes of John Slaughter, the less-celebrated rancher and lawman who tamed the town in incorruptible style after the Earps departed. A gallows, which actually saw effective use, is also on the property. And, of course, there is Boothil.

No visit to Tombstone should end without a visit to this cemetery, meticulously restored from the tangle of weeds it had become. Here lie the gunmen, the miners, the ordinary citizens who had a part in one of the country's most colorful communities. Here are the Clantons and the McLaurys, buried near John Hicks who was shot in a saloon brawl, and Joseph Wetsell, stoned to death by Apaches who didn't want to alert his friends by using guns. Here lie two unnamed cowboys, hanged; Margarita, stabbed by another dance hall girl; and poor old Lester Moore "Four slugs from a .44, No Les, no more." A pamphlet on sale at the Boothill entrance provides a complete rundown on the graveyard lineup. It is well worth the price, for the insights it provides on those who met their end in the town too tough to die.

∗ ∗ ∗

The highway runs along the San Pedro River as it nears the old Mormon settlement of St. David, an area that opened up to agriculture when an earthquake revealed artesian wells in 1887. The Coronado Party followed the San Pedro north through here in 1540 (see U.S. 666) on the quest for the Seven Cities of Gold. This was also the route in 1846 of the Mormon Battalion, recruited to fight in the Mexican War and open a wagon road from Santa Fe to San Diego. On the way, it also captured Tucson. The battalion saw no combat, but as the troopers crossed the San Pedro near this point they were attacked by a herd of wild bulls and suffered one dozen injuries in the engagement.

Benson's site on the San Pedro was occupied by Indian villages since the 17th century. It was at the ford of the Butterfield Stage Road and also became a railhead for the Southern Pacific, the access point to the mining camps which we just passed through. The main line still runs through the middle of town, with the business district lying across the highway. With the growth of Interstate 10, Benson has developed a tourist industry to serve travelers on that road. This old road stops here, though, the rest of its route to San Diego part of the Interstate.

VISITING HOURS

NEW MEXICO

Steins: Ghost Town and Museum, (505) 542-9791. West of U.S. 80, off Interstate 10. Call for hours. Donation.

ARIZONA

Bisbee: Mining and Historical Museum, (602) 432-7071. Copper Queen Plaza, downtown. Daily, 10–4. Admission.

Muheim House, same phone as museum. At 207 Youngblood Hill. Friday–Monday, noon–4.

Lavender Pit, (602) 432-2071. On U.S. 80. Tour daily, at noon. Admission.

Copper Queen Mine, same phone as above. On U.S. 80. Tours daily at 10:30, noon, 2 and 3:30. Admission.

Tombstone: O.K. Corral, (602) 457-3456. Allen St., between 3rd and 4th. Daily, 8:30–5. Admission.

Bird Cage Theatre, (602) 457-3421. Allen and 6th Sts. Daily, 8–6. Admission.

Courthouse Museum, (602) 457-3311. At 219 E. Toughnut St. Daily, 8–5. Admission.

Boothill Cemetery, (602) 457-3348. North of city, on U.S. 80. Daily, 7:30–6. Donation.

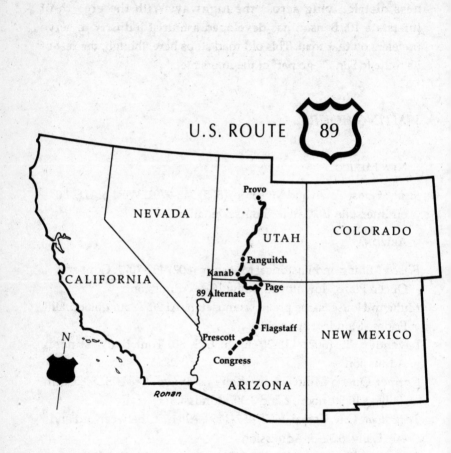

U.S. ROUTE 89

Southwestern Wonderland

⬡

U.S. 89

Provo, Utah to Congress, Ariz.
497 miles by way of Jacob Lake, 499 miles by way of Page

Visitors to the West know U.S. 89 as the National Park Highway. In its journey from the Montana border of Canada to the vicinity of the Mexican border of Arizona, the route links a succession of scenic wonderlands. It leads to Glacier, Yellowstone, and Grand Teton in the Northern Rockies, and in the area covered by this book, it is the way to Bryce, Zion, and Grand Canyon.

We'll pick it up at the end of its less appealing, Interstate-crowded run through the Utah Valley, where most of that state's population and commerce is jammed. **Provo** is the gateway to the comparatively untouched desert and canyon country of south-western Utah. The road then skirts the eastern edge of the Grand Canyon before wending past the unforgettable scenic and historic glories of northern Arizona.

MILEPOSTS

Provo is the second largest city in Utah, tucked neatly into the space between the Wasatch Mountains and Utah Lake. It is a college town, with one of the country's largest church-supported schools, Brigham Young University, as a major presence. It is also something of a resort, with lake beaches on its western doorstep

* 163 *

and ski resorts and mountain scenery to the east (see U.S. 40). It is part of the state's industrial heartland, as well, with steel and iron production in the area. It even became an entertainment center, briefly, when the singing Osmond Family taped their weekly television show from studios here in the 1970s.

The area was visited by the Spanish priests, Escalante and Dominguez, who skittered about central Utah in search of a California passage in 1776. Half a century later, French–Canadian trapper Etienne Provost made his way here from the summer rendezvous at Ogden. His exploring efforts were memorialized in the town's name after a Mormon colonization party planted a settlement here in 1849. Nine years later, Provo became, temporarily, the largest city in Utah, when the more northern settlements were abandoned under threat of federal invasion.

It had become politically expeditious to ease growing public concern over the slavery issue by ringing the alarm over the practice of polygamy. President Buchanan declared the Mormons to be in rebellion against the United States and dispatched a force to Utah under the command of General Albert Sidney Johnston, who would later be killed at Shiloh fighting on the Confederate side. Brigham Young determined to resist the invasion and ordered a withdrawal of settlers to the Provo area to make a stand. But before any harm was done, the expedition, highly ridiculed in the Eastern press, was called off and a truce agreed upon. The episode did end the isolation of the Mormon colony from the rest of the country and led the way to the eventual statehood of Utah.

The university was established in 1875 as an academy for teachers. It did not become a full-fledged college until 1903. The beautiful 634-acre campus, in the eastern part of town, is a fine place for a stroll. Just look for the Centennial Carillon Tower, rising 112 feet, bells ringing away several times daily, to get your bearings. The Harris Fine Arts Center has two galleries, one concentrating on 19th-century Utah and American art, the other on rare musical instruments. The Monte L. Bean Life Sciences Museum has an outstanding collection of dinosaur bones in a state famous for them. The Museum of Peoples and Cultures specializes in the art of Southwestern Native Peoples.

There is a state park and beach in the western part of the city, on the shore of Utah Lake. At 140 square miles, it is one of the largest lakes in the mountain states.

The town of **Springville**, just to the south, is one of the state's leading cultural centers. A first-rate collection of Utah painters and sculptors, going back to 1862, is housed in Springville's Museum of Art, developed as a program of the Works Progress Administration during the Depression. Its Spring Salon, held each April, is a first-rate national competition, and in August the town hosts the World Folkfest, a celebration of folk dancing.

The highway turns east to run with U.S. 6 for a few miles before dipping south once more at Thistle, named for the burrs found here by construction gangs when the railroads came through. The road enters the Sanpete Valley, snuggled between the Mt. Nebo Range to the west and Manti-Lasal National Forest to the east. This is a rich agricultural area, among the leading producers in the nation of turkeys, sheep, and alfalfa. The area was originally referred to as "Little Denmark" because so many of its settlers came from that country. While the scenery is far more mountainous than the European country, its neat farms and fields live up to the nickname.

Wild hay meadows attracted settlers to **Fairview**, named for its overlook onto the valley. The Museum of History and Art here is a pleasant repository of pioneer farm memorabilia. There are also a good number of vintage commercial structures in its business district.

Mt. Pleasant, a center of Danish settlement, has been a sheep-raising town since the introduction in the early 1900s of the highly productive Rambouillet breed. Wasatch Academy, opened here in 1875, is the oldest secondary school in the state.

In Spring City, every building in town is listed on the National Historic Register. The town was founded by James Allred, the personal bodyguard of the founder of the Latter Day Saints, Joseph Smith. The spring that gave the place its name is still gushing in the town center.

The wild birds that once flocked here gave Pigeon Hollow its name. (By the way, is there any other place in the West in which all the communities bear names as nice as the ones we've been passing through? Fairview; Mt. Pleasant; Pigeon Hollow. Sanpete Valley residents must be happy folks.) Ephraim is another pleasant farming town with a vintage business district and lots of turkeys in its environs. Its old department store, the Ephraim Mercantile Cooperative, was restored in the 1980s and each Memorial Day the place celebrates a Scandinavian festival.

You have been able to see the Mormon temple, sitting high on the hillside above Manti, back up the valley for miles. It has been one of the landmarks of Utah since its opening in 1888. The state's largest historical-religious observance, the Miracle Pageant, is held on its grounds each July, retelling the story of the Mormons. Manti itself is named for a city mentioned in the Book of Mormon, and is one of the oldest settlements in this part of the state, dating back to 1849. Palisade State Park, just south of town, offers a swimming beach in scenic surroundings.

Captain John W. Gunnison was a topographic engineer who was the first to survey much of southern Colorado and Utah. A city and river are named for him in Colorado but he also left a good impression in Utah. Gunnison was favorably disposed towards the Mormons and his reports to the government reflected that. After he was killed by a band of Pahvants, in 1853, the settlers of this town renamed the place for him. Gunnison was also the site of a short-lived agricultural experiment by Jewish emigrants from Eastern Europe. They settled here in 1911 and helped organize the Utah Poultry Co-operative Association, which standardized egg sizes.

Many of the socialist ideals that later were practiced by Israel's kibbutz movement were tried out here, but the place folded in 1920.

At Salina, named for its rock salt mines, the valley narrows perceptibly between the Pahvant and Fishlake Ranges. From here on it is called the Sevier Valley, named for the river running through it.

Richfield is the valley's commercial center, in the midst of a beef-raising area. It was also the center of the state's most severe Indian war, the Black Hawk engagement of 1865-1868. Raids forced the abandonment of several settlements in southern Utah after infuriated Utes blamed white settlers for a smallpox outbreak that began in Manti. The treaty ending the war was signed here under a cedar in front of the Mormon Tabernacle.

Elsinore, as those of you who remember Hamlet's castle may have guessed, is another of the Danish settlements in this area, dating from 1874.

Just past **Sevier**, at the junction with Interstate 70, Fremont Indian State Park displays artifacts of an Anasazi Indian culture uncovered at nearby Five Fingers Hill. The Fremont People lived here for about a millenium before leaving for unknown reasons in 1300. Trails lead to examples of rock art and an interpetive center explains what little is known about these people and their way of life.

There is, indeed, a Big Rock Candy Mountain, and if it is not quite the toothsome treat Burl Ives sang about, the formation does look very much like chunks of rainbow-hued hard candy. The prevailing flavor, judging from the color, would be lemon.

Marysvale was named by Spanish priests and has profited from the potash deposits in the surrounding hills. The landscape gets considerably more rugged beyond here, as U.S. 89 descends to the desert country and the spectacular scenery of Utah's extreme south.

The road passes Piute Reservoir, known for its duck hunting and rock hounding. At Junction, where the Sevier River's two branches meet, watch for the old Piute County Courthouse, built of adobe in 1903.

Circleville was the boyhood home of the highwayman, Butch Cassidy, who was not nearly as gentlemanly as Paul Newman made him out to be on film. During the peak of Cassidy's career, in the 1890s, he favored banks in the eastern part of the state (see U.S. 191). His real name, incidentally, was George L. Parker.

Panguitch is known for its large number of red-brick pioneer houses on its shady residential streets, many of them put up in the 1870s. This was another of the Danish towns, its first settlers being led by Jens Nielsen. It may have been their Viking blood that kept them alive through their first winter when they had to survive on frosted wheat and beef fat. The town prospers now as a cattle ranching center and a tourist stop on the way to nearby Bryce Canyon and Zion National Parks. This was also the jumping-off point for Mormon settlers who ventured east to colonize the San Juan area (see U.S. 163) through terrain so forbidding that there is still no road that makes the trip.

The highway continues along the Sevier through the village of Hatch, named for a pioneer family. It then cuts across a corner of Dixie National Forest, through Long Valley Junction, before descending into high-desert sagebrush country.

Glendale was renamed from its original Berryville because pioneer settler James Leithead wanted to be reminded of his home in Scotland, which it does not resemble in the least.

Orderville was named for another experimental community, much like the agricultural cooperative back in Gunnison. This one, however, was organized by the United Order, a Mormon offshoot that believed in strict communal living and abolition of private property. It survived for 11 years after its founding in 1875, not a bad track record for communities such as these. But high pay in the nearby mines drew younger men from the settlement, and when they returned and those who had stayed behind saw how well they were living, it was curtains for the Order. A small museum, run by the Daughters of Utah Pioneers, contains exhibits on the colony.

Mt. Carmel Junction is the eastern entrance to Zion, but our road bends to the southeast, through Three Lakes Canyon and into **Kanab**. Just outside of that town, named for a Paiute word for *willows*, you'll pass a small memorial to Jacob Hamblin. He was the leading Mormon missionary to the Indians of southern Utah and the man most responsible for encouraging that back-breaking trek from Panguitch across the state. And they still built a monument to him. Remarkable!

Kanab is movieland, one of several spots in the Southwest preferred by makers of Western films since the age of the silents. (See Monument Valley on U.S. 163, Moab, Utah on U.S. 191 and Lone Pine, Cal. on U.S. 395.) The Kanab Movie Ranch is visible east of the highway, north of town. In Kanab itself is a false-front street used frequently as a set, called Lopeman's Frontier Movie Town. Look for it just west of Main Street, downtown.

The town is extremely photogenic, with the towering Vermilion Cliffs, which rise at the end of its streets, forming the backdrop. Zane Grey lived here for a time in 1912 and drew inspiration for several of his novels from the surroundings. This was another of the southern Utah communities founded by missionaries inspired by Hamblin. They arrived in 1870 and built the place on top of a fort that had been abandoned because of Ute raids.

There are several homes dating from the 1880s and 1890s. The Henry Bowman house, with its foundation built of rocks from the nearby red cliffs, was built in 1894 and is now the town historical museum, Heritage House. You can pick up a map there for a short walking tour to other old homes in Kanab. Maybe the most intriguing is the Swapp House on First Street West, which was built in 1912 out of a kit ordered from the Sears Roebuck catalog. It was shipped here and assembled for a cost of $664.

Until the late 1950s, the highway simply continued south from this point to Fredonia, Arizona (see below for U.S. 89A). But with the construction of Glen Canyon Dam, U.S. 89 was extended east across the Paria Canyon wilderness area to the dam site. It is now the major access route from the west to Lake Powell and its National Recreation Area. This is a fast, scenic drive past towering, eerily contorted rock formations and mesas, with Paria Canyon just to the south. There is a ranger on duty at the turnoff to the trailhead if you feel the need to take a hike through that remote area.

At Big Water, on **Wahweap** Creek, you get your first glimpse of the startling splash of deep blue in the barren desert. Lake Powell began to fill in 1963 and now covers 161,390 acres, the second largest manmade lake on the continent. It is named for John Wesley Powell, leader of the expeditions that explored the Colorado River and who, in turn, named Glen Canyon on his voyage of 1869. Powell was struck by the diversity of landscape features he saw in the area "...carved walls, royal arches, glens, alcove gulches, mounds and monuments. From which of these features shall we select a name? We decide to call it Glen Canyon." Just like that. It must be fun to be an explorer and get to name things because you feel like it.

Just across the Arizona state line is Wahweap Marina. You can rent a boat here or take a variety of cruises through the National Recreation Area. Many of its attractions, including Rainbow Bridge National Monument, are only accessible by boat and the scenery is dazzling. If you only take one cruise in the parched Southwest, this should be the one.

A few miles beyond is the dam itself. Planned for this site as early as the 1920s, it is part of the Colorado River Storage Project, a federal program that combines irrigation, hydroelectric power, and recreational uses for all the Southwestern states. Power generated by this dam, in fact, is sent to small communities as far away as Wyoming and Nebraska. This 710-foot high structure took nine years to complete, being formally dedicated in 1966, and it truly transformed this area of northern Arizona and southern Utah. Until the late 1950s, this was one of the most isolated corners in the

United States. Now more than one million people a year come into the Recreation Area. You can get the best view of the dam from the Carl Hayden Visitor Center, named for the U.S. Senator from Arizona who was its most ardent backer. There is a self-guided tour of the powerplant and movies show highlights of the arduous construction.

On the far side of the dam is **Page**, the town built by the U.S. government to house construction workers, and named for a former Commissioner of Reclamation. Built in 1957, it was turned over as an incorporated Arizona community in 1975. Unlike many such towns that withered away when the construction was done, Page continues to grow as a retirement and resort center, and now has a population of more than 7,500. A very orderly sort of place, it has the look of a planned community. As you drive in from the main access road, for example, you'll notice its 12 churches lined up all in a row. But it's a pleasant place for all that. It is an outfitting center for Lake Powell trips. Cruises and air tours to any place on the lake can be arranged.

There is a museum dedicated to Powell here, with a replica of the boat on which he made his voyage of discovery. The Powell Museum also presents a useful overview of the entire Colorado River Basin, its topography and its peoples.

From here, the road curves back southwest, across Echo Cliffs, and rejoins U.S. 89A near the Navajo Reservation outpost of Bitter Springs.

If you elect to take the alternate route (while there really is little to choose scenically between them, I lean towards regular Highway 89), U.S. 89A heads due south from Kanab towards Fredonia. The name is a tipoff about this community just across the Arizona border. Connoisseurs of the Marx Brothers will remember Fredonia as the name of the mythical duchy in their classic comedy, *Duck Soup*. Long before that, however, it was coined as ersatz Latin to represent the ideals of freedom. Early in the 19th century, Fredonia was even suggested as the official name for the United States, but found few takers. The reform-minded settlers of western New York did give the name to one of their towns. So did the Mormons who came here from across the line from Utah seeking pasture land. The northernmost slice of Arizona was known as the Mormon Strip because of the influence of these early settlers, and the name of the town is an indication of their hopes for religious tolerance.

There are great views back into Utah as the road swings east to Kaibab National Forest. The word *Kaibab* is Paiute for "on the mountain"and this high plateau is very much like a mountain lying on its side. We climb 4,400 feet in the 30 miles between Fredonia and Jacob Lake, to one of Arizona's most atypical corners. The climate and forms of plant and animal life on the Kaibab Plateau more closely resemble areas hundreds of miles to the north than any place in Arizona. Some species here differ widely from those found just over on the South Rim of the Grand Canyon. It is 10 miles across from rim to rim, but the North Rim on the Kaibab Plateau is more than 1,400 feet higher. The North Rim is open only from May to October because of the harsher weather conditions. Arizona 67 runs to the North Rim from Jacob Lake, but Highway 89A continues east, slowly descending towards its crossing of the Colorado at Navajo Bridge.

The Vermilion Cliffs rise as a sheer, 1,000-foot high red wall for about 20 miles along the road, a dazzling background to the Houserock Valley.

Marble Canyon is the easternmost extremity of Grand Canyon National Park, and the last crossing of the Colorado until Hoover Dam, hundreds of miles to the west. Before the Navajo Bridge was built here in 1929 there was no crossing going upstream, either, until Moab, Utah. Marble Canyon had been a traditional Colorado ferry point since 1872 when John D. Lee established a service a few miles upstream, at the mouth of the Paria River. John Wesley Powell gave

Marble Canyon its name when he passed through the steep, smooth-walled gorge on his exploring expedition of 1869. Powell had to abandon one of his craft here and three years later Lee salvaged it for use as his first ferry. This was an important crossing point for Mormon settlers heading into Arizona and a wagon road ran south from the far side of Lee's Ferry. Unfortunately, Lee's past eventually caught up with him and he was executed in 1877 for his role in a wagon train-massacre 20 years before. The Mormon Church took over operation of the ferry and ran it for several years, but 616-foot long Navajo Bridge, suspended spectacularly above the river at the height of a 40-story building, ended the perilous crossings by ferry. For those with acrophobia, however, braving the river rapids may be preferable to the view from the bridge.

The highway enters the western edge of the vast Navajo reservation on the far side of the bridge and turns sharply south. A few scattered trading posts are all that break the emptiness of this richly colored landscape, sealed off by the towering Echo Cliffs to the east. The two Highway 89s then rejoin at Bitter Springs.

The reunited road passes through The Gap (named for a natural opening in the surrounding mesas) and reaches the trading post at **Cameron**. Founded in 1890, this is one of the oldest posts still operating in the Southwest, and carries an extensive collection of craft items that have been exchanged for groceries and staples. (See U.S. 191 for a discussion of Hubbell Trading Post National Monument.)

Immediately south of Cameron is the turnoff to the South Rim of the Grand Canyon, on Arizona 64. U.S. 89 continues south, however, and passes out of the reservation, to the entrance to **Wuptaki National Monument**. Wuptaki means "tall house" and the three-story structure that contains more than 100 rooms is the most impressive of the ruins at this place. It was inhabited by farming people during the 12th century, who left about 800 red sandstone structures when they departed around 1225 A.D.. One of the most unusual of the structures is a ball court, but archeologists have not come up with any statistics or explanations for the games played there. Several such courts have been found in Mexico, but this one is the furthest north that has been located. A self-guiding trail leads to the most important sites and there is also a visitor's center.

Wupatki was settled because of what happened a few miles further along this road. At about the same time that William of Normandy was making plans to conquer England, in the summer of 1065, an extremely violent volcanic eruption blew the top right off a mountain here in Wupatki. The deposit of ash that filtered down to nearby fields enriched the soil to such an extent that farms were then able to support large communities, such as Wupatki. Only a 1,000-foot-high stump remains of the volcano, with mineral stains around the top, giving it a glow that resembles a desert sunset. As a result, it became known as **Sunset Crater**, a name credited to Powell during a later voyage through this country. It is now a National Monument, with a foot trail around the lava flows at its base and a vistor's center.

The San Francisco Mountains are immediately to the west here, with the snow-capped summit of Humphreys Peak, the highest point in Arizona, in plain sight.

The first settlers arrived in this area in 1876 and on the Fourth of July in that centennial year, F.F. McMillan stripped a pine of its branches and ran up the flag to great cheers and enthusiasm. But when no minerals worth mining were found in the area, the enthusiasm waned and the early arrivals left for more promising diggings. The flagpole remained, however, and became a landmark along the Beale Wagon Road from Santa Fe to California. And when the Santa Fe Railroad arrived in 1882 to give the town a second life, **Flagstaff** seemed the natural choice for a name. There were lots more pines where the original staff came from and the basis of its economy was lumbering. It also became the center of a sheep-raising area.

Arriving in Flagstaff, along with the lumberjacks and shepherds, was a Boston brahmin whose gaze was directed much higher than the pines. Astronomer Percival Lowell showed up in 1894, drawn by Flagstaff's 7,000-foot elevation and its clear weather. Many other observatories would also locate in the Southwest because of its clean, cloudless skies. But Lowell's privately endowed institution, placed atop Mars Hill on the western edge of town, was the first.

Lowell's area of specialization was Mars and he advanced scientific knowledge of that planet enormously. He received more publicity for his speculations, however, which could run a bit on the eccentric side. Lowell was an advocate of the theory that striations on the planet's surface were canals made by intelligent beings. His writings on the topic fostered the branch of science fiction which focused on Mars as a source of inter-planetary aggression and a threat to Earth. But Lowell had more useful theories, too. In 1914, two years before his death, he postulated the existence of an unknown planet because of computations he had made on irregularities in the orbit of Neptune. These irregularities could only be explained by the gravitational pull of a yet unseen body beyond Neptune. The Lowell Observatory dedicated itself to verifying his prediction, and in 1930 its efforts were rewarded with the discovery of Pluto by Dr. Clyde W. Tombaugh. The furthest-flung planet in the solar system turned up exactly where Lowell said it would.

The observatory itself is still a working scientific installation. It can be reached off Santa Fe Avenue, just west of the point at which Highway 89 swings away from that main thoroughfare and turns south.

The road then runs along the western edge of Northern Arizona University, established here in 1893 as a boy's home. When there weren't enough wayward youths to populate the place, it was turned into a mental hospital. But that didn't work, either, and finally, almost as an act of desperation by local officials who feared the loss of legislative funding, it became a teachers' college in 1899. Now it has an enrollment of 13,000. Just off the campus is Riordan State Park, preserving the connected mansions of one of Flagstaff's leading pioneer families. Built in 1904, the homes were occupied by the families of Timothy and Michael Riordan, brothers who had their hands in cattle, banking, and various other enterprises. This is apparent from the lavish fixtures and furniture in the interiors. (For more on the Flagstaff area, see U.S. 180.)

Highway 89 runs west with Interstate 40, but we'll go with 89A, which is by far the more interesting route. It goes through Oak Creek Canyon, built as the first direct route between Flagstaff and Prescott in the 1920s. The highway drops 4,500 feet through the canyon, and is one of the great scenic drives in the West. Descending amid sheer red rock walls, with thick stands of trees filling the space between, and the rushing creek far below, it is a trip of incredible beauty. You can understand why even back in the 1920s, when environmental damage from highways was still slight and little understood, opposition to this road was strong among those who feared it would diminish the canyon. You'll have to make up your own mind on that, but these miles in Oak Creek Canyon are among the best of any on the old roads. Slide Rock, containing a natural sandstone water slide and restored pioneer homestead, is a state park within the canyon. Other areas are also being developed under state controls.

At the southern end of the canyon is **Sedona**, an old Mormon ranching town that has grown up as an art colony and resort since the 1960s. One of the most delightful places in the Southwest, Sedona's streets are filled with galleries, crafts shops, and romantic restaurants, all set against the backdrop of Oak Creek Canyon's soaring walls. This is not a drive-through. Just park the car and walk—you'll find delight in any direction. Notice especially the architecture of the homes here, designed to incorporate the natural setting with the life within. The Sedona Arts Center, just north of the town center, has ongoing exhibits by local artists. You'll also want to stroll through Tlaquepaque (which is fun to say once one of the locals teaches you the hang of it), a Mexican-style complex with shops grouped around fountains, shaded walkways, and patios.

Just south of Sedona, on Arizona 179, is Chapel of the Holy Cross, a striking contemporary shrine perched between two red monoliths.

Once you can bring yourself to get on the road again (and you lose no points for wanting to settle in here for a while) you'll drop into the Verde Valley, with Mingus Mountain imposing its 7,743-foot bulk on the southern horizon. Cottonwood is a pleasant ranching town, named for the growth of trees that pioneers found on the site along the Verde River. Just north of town is Dead Horse Ranch State Park, a lovely spot along the Verde with hiking trails and fishing.

A bit beyond the park is the turnoff to **Tuzigoot National Monument**. Here are the excavated ruins of a pueblo once occupied by a branch of the Sinagua people, who also built Wupatki. But this place was inhabited far longer. Archeologists put its occupancy at between 1000 A.D. and 1450 A.D. and artifacts found here indicate that in its last years it had developed trade with communities as far away as California.

The signature of Clarkdale is the smokestack on the old copper smelter, one of the tallest unsupported masonry structures in the world. Clarkdale was a planned town built by United Verde Copper to process the ore taken from the mines in Jerome, 3,000 feet up the side of Mingus Mountain. Named for one of the company's owners, U.S. Senator William A. Clark, of Montana, the town was built around the huge smelter, completed in 1915. It shut down 35 years later, functioned as a cement plant for a while, and is now simply an astounding sight.

Now we start the ascent to **Jerome**. Its copper deposits were worked by the Indians for hundreds of years and were known to the first settlers of the Verde Valley. But not until 1882, when the

Santa Fe Railroad reached Ash Fork, to the north, did it become economically feasible to develop them. The aforementioned Senator Clark was one of the major developers, as was New York financier Eugene Jerome, a cousin of the famous beauty who was Winston Churchill's mother. The town was named for their family. When further exploration brought in the Little Daisy Mine in 1900, Jerome embarked on its most prosperous era. Among those employed here at the time was Pancho Villa, who contracted to supply the place with burro-trains of water before embarking on a career as a revolutionary.

With demand for copper peaking during World War I, Jerome grew to a city of 15,000. But then the slow decline began and when the mines finally closed in 1953, there were fewer than 500 residents left. By the end of the following decade, the place had been discovered by artists, attracted by its splendid hilltop location and its atmospheric old streets. Much like Sedona, it has become a place for galleries and historic restorations. Jerome literally has to be propped up, with many of the buildings dug into the hillside on stilts and braces. After a mine explosion in the 1920s, several structures slowly shifted as many as 225 feet from their original locations. Much of the town is now a State Historical Park. A museum in the restored home of Rawhide Jimmy Douglas, one of the leading citizens in the boom days and a developer of the Little Daisy, relates the history of this colorful copper town. Several of Jerome's historic homes are open on the third weekend in May during the *Paseo de Casas*.

From Jerome, the road drops again through grazing land into the broad Chino Valley. Just before it rejoins Highway 89, you can see a two-mile long band of rock formations known as the Granite Dells, which is a public park. To get a closer view, turn north at the junction on U.S. 89, which passes right through their midst. Then turn around and head back into the old territorial capital of **Prescott**.

FOCUS

When Sharlot Hall came to the Arizona Territory as a child of 12, Prescott was still the capital. Gunmen walked the streets of Tombstone and Holbrook, and Geronimo was a name that struck very real terror into the hearts of its settlers. Sharlot's birthplace in Kansas was tame by comparison, although it hadn't been many years since Kansas had been a frontier. But in 1882 Arizona still was the real West and Hall never forgot it.

Almost half a century later, she came to Prescott. A writer and historian, she saw the Arizona she had known as a child in danger of being obliterated and forgotten. Sharlot set out to rescue it, here in its former capital city. She built a cabin on the grounds of the Old Governor's Mansion and opened a museum to show off the collection of frontier artifacts she had spent a lifetime assembling. The Sharlot Hall Museum today is an evocation of Prescott's past, as well as a tribute to a remarkable woman.

It is reasonable to suppose that this city would have become a repository of the past since it is named for an historian. The New Englanders who settled the place were enthusiastic readers of William H. Prescott's histories of the Spanish conquests of Mexico and Peru. Moving into an area that had actually been part of Mexico less than 20 years before fired their imaginations. They even named the streets after the historical figures in Prescott's books: Montezuma and Cortez.

When gold was discovered in the vicinity in 1863, the first settlement grew up. But as the Civil War started to rage, the federal government grew alarmed at the number of Confederate sympathizers in Tucson. Having already survived a Southern invasion of New Mexico by way of Texas, Congress decided to separate Arizona and form a new territory to secure it for the Union. Accordingly, a party of hand-picked Union loyalists was appointed to the governing posts, sent out to the new territory, and told to establish a capital away from Tucson's hotbed of sedition. They arrived in 1864 after a three-month journey and set up shop at Fort Whipple, a newly established Army post near the present town of Chino Valley, about 20 miles north of Prescott. After a few months, both post and town moved to the banks of Granite Creek. By September, the loyalists had built a two-room log cabin courthouse, called Fort Misery, and a more substantial structure to house the legislature and serve as Governor John Goodwin's official residence. This is the core of the Sharlot Hall Museum.

The Governor's Mansion gives you some idea of what life on this remote frontier was like. Its crude furnishings reflect its appearance during the first winter of occupancy. Historical displays humanize its first occupants, capturing the grief of the first governor at the death of his wife in this place so far from home.

When the Civil War ended, there was no longer any compelling reason for the capital to remain here, so off it went to Tucson in 1867. But new gold strikes were made in this vicinity and efforts to recruit new settlers from the East were succesful. So in 1877, the capital returned to bustling Prescott and stayed for 12 years. This era is represented by the two other large homes on the museum grounds. The John C. Fremont House was occupied by the politician and explorer. As his public career was winding down, he served as Territorial Governor here from 1878 to 1881. The William Bashford House was the residence of a prosperous local citizen. Both indicate how far comforts had advanced in the decade since the Governor's Mansion was built.

Also on the grounds are other historically significant buildings and the original exhibit hall opened by Sharlot Hall in 1934. The complex is located a few blocks west of the courthouse square, at the center of Prescott.

In recent years, the city has grown as a retirement center and resort because of its mild climate in a mile-high setting. Its Frontier Days Rodeo, first held in 1888, is reputedly the oldest such event in the country. It takes place every Fourth of July weekend.

Take a walk around the Courthouse Square to get a feel for the old town. There is very little evidence of Spanish architecture here. The area looks more like New England than Arizona. Dominating the courthouse lawn is the heroic statue of Bucky O'Neill, the frontier lawman who organized the Arizona Rough Riders during the Spanish–American War and was killed in the charge up San Juan Hill in Cuba.

There are two other first-rate museums in Prescott. The Smoki Museum, built in the shape of a pueblo, contains an outstanding collection of Indian art and objects from several area archeological digs, including Tuzigoot. Just north of town, at the intersection of Highways 89 and 89A, is the Phippen Museum of Western Art, which exhibits contemporary work by both national and local artists. Named for a local resident who was the first president of the Cowboy Artists of America, the museum sponsors an outdoor show on Courthouse Square each Memorial Day weekend.

* * *

The road leaves town through Prescott National Forest, winding in well-graded curves through the hills above the city and into Peeples Valley. The crossroads of Kirkland Junction was named for the man who ran a stagecoach station here and, in 1860, was credited with being the first European settler to be married in Arizona. The same applies to Mrs. Kirkland, of course.

The highway climbs once more, an easy four-lane ascent into the Weaver Mountains past the town of Yarnell. The mountains are named for Pauline Weaver, a frontier scout and prospector whose grave is on the Sharlot Hall Museum grounds back in Prescott. Congress, at the base of the mountains is now a ghost town, named for a gold mine that once flourished in the nearby hills. The view from here widens to encompass an enormous range of desert, stretching out endlessly to the southwest. U.S. 89 heads in that direction, combining with U.S. 60 all the way to the far side of Phoenix. But we'll end our trip through the heart of Arizona here.

VISITING HOURS

UTAH

Fairview: Museum of History and Art, (801) 427-9216. At 85 N. 100 East. Monday–Saturday, 10–5, late March–late September. Donation.

Kanab: Heritage House, (801) 644-2542. At 100 S. Main St. Monday–Saturday, 9–5. Free.

Provo: Harris Fine Arts Center, (801) 378-7444. On Brigham Young University campus. Monday–Friday, 8–5. Free.

Monte L. Bean Life Sciences Museum, (801) 378-5051. On Brigham Young campus. Monday–Saturday, 10–5. Free.

Museum of Peoples and Cultures, (801) 378-6112. At 710 N. 100 East. Monday–Friday, 9–5. Free.

Sevier: Fremont Indian State Park, no phone. South, on U.S. 89 at Interstate 70. Daily, 9–6, May–October; 9–5 at other times. Admission.

Springville: Museum of Art, (801) 489-9434. At 126 E. 400 South St. Tuesday–Saturday, 10–5 and Sunday, 2–5. Free.

ARIZONA

Cameron: Trading Post, (602) 679-2231. On U.S. 89. Daily, 8–4:45. Free.

Flagstaff Lowell Observatory, (602) 774-2096. West of U.S. 89, by way of Santa Fe Ave. Monday–Saturday, 9:30–4 and Sunday, noon–4, June–August. Call for schedule at other times. Donation.

Riordan State Park, (602) 779-4395. South of city, off U.S. 89 on Milton Rd., at 1300 Riordan Ranch St. Daily, 9–11 and 2–4, mid-

May–mid-September; 1–4 at other times. Admission.

Jerome: State Historic Park, (602) 634-5381. Off U.S. 89A. Daily, 8–5. Admission.

Page: Glen Canyon Dam, (602) 645-2511. West, on U.S. 89. Daily, 7–7, June–August; 8–5 at other times. Free.

Powell Museum, (602) 645-9496. In town, on Lake Powell Dr. at Navajo Dr. Monday–Saturday, 8–6, and Sunday, 10–6, June–September; Monday–Friday, 9–5, March, April, November; Monday–Saturday, 8–6, May and October. Free.

Prescott: Sharlot Hall Museum, (602) 445-3122. West of courthouse square, at 415 W. Gurley St. Tuesday–Saturday, 10–5 and Sunday, 1–5, April–October. Closes at 4 at other times. Donation.

Smoki Museum, (602) 445-1230. East, at Gurley St. and Arizona Ave. Tuesday–Saturday, 10–4 and Sunday, 1–4, June–August. Free.

Phippen Museum of Western Art, (602) 778-1385. North of town, at 4701 U.S. 89. Monday, Wednesday–Saturday, 10–4 and Sunday, 1–4, mid-May–December. Wednesday–Monday, 1–4 at other times. Admission.

Sedona: Arts Center, (602) 282-3809. North, on U.S. 89A. Tuesday–Saturday, 10:30–4:30 and Sunday, 1:30–4:30. Free.

Chapel of the Holy Cross, (602) 282-4069. South, on Arizona 179. Daily, 8:30–6, April–October; 9–5 at other times. Free.

Sunset Crater National Monument: (602) 527-7042. East, off U.S. 89. Daily, 8–5. Admission.

Tuzigoot National Monument: (602) 634-5564. Off U.S. 89A, near Cottonwood. Daily, 8–7, Memorial Day–Labor Day; 8–5 at other times. Admission.

Wahweap: Lake Powell Cruises, from Marina, (602) 645-2433 for reservations. East of U.S. 89.

Wupatki National Monument: (602) 527-7040. East, off U.S. 89. Daily, 8–6. Admission.

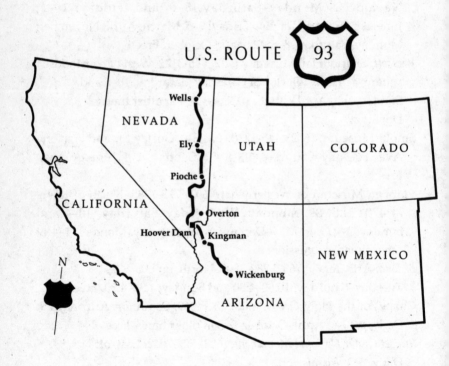

U.S. ROUTE 93

Wells

NEVADA

Ely

Pioche

UTAH

COLORADO

CALIFORNIA

Overton

Hoover Dam

Kingman

NEW MEXICO

N

Wickenburg

ARIZONA

Nevada Sampler

⬡

U.S. 93

Jackpot, Nev. to Wickenburg, Ariz.
742 miles

One of the great mountain roads of the West, U.S. 93 begins at the British Columbia border of Montana and makes its way south through stunning scenery on the Rockies' western slope. It becomes the Salmon River Route in Idaho and, for a time, joins the old Oregon Trail. At Twin Falls, it drops straight south to Nevada on the historic cutoff from the northern trail to California.

In this area, we'll track its run through the eastern corridor of Nevada, a land that is not nearly as empty as it seems. It couldn't be. We'll also turn off for a look at Lake Mead and then cross Hoover Dam, which has shaped the new West just as emphatically as the Oregon Trail shaped the old.

MILEPOSTS

The biggest promoter of this road was Johannes Sutter. Eventually, its success destroyed him. The Swiss-born Sutter owned vast land holdings east of Sacramento and was eager to build up an American presence in that part of California. He felt that such an emigration would offset the much larger Mexican population in the area. He hired agents to work the Oregon Trail and deflect pioneers south towards California instead. Caleb Greenwood was the most succesful of these. After 1843, he managed to build up a lively traffic from Fort Hall, Idaho, down this road to its link-up with the Humboldt Trail, one of the main routes to California. When gold was discovered on Sutter's land, the traffic became a torrent. They poured across in such numbers that Sutter, eventually, was driven right off his holdings.

U.S. 93 parallels that passage of the 49ers, which actually ran a bit to the east. The existing road follows the course of the Little Salmon River as it crosses the border at Jackpot. This is another of the border towns that dot Nevada's perimeter and bring the allure of liberal slot machines right up to the borders of its neighboring states. Jackpot grew up after 1959 to serve the urgent need of Idaho residents to be separated from their cash. It is now a lively casino and resort development on the eastern edge of the Jarbridge Wilderness Area, which is dominated by the 10,839-foot spike of the Matterhorn.

Miners gave Contact its name because it lay at the point where limestone deposits touched granite. The road runs south through a wide valley, with the Independence Mountains far to the west and the Toanas, nearly to the Utah border, on the east. Thousand Springs was a water stop for parties on the original Fort Hall cut-off.

Wells was the major stop on this route. This is where the cut-off turned west along the Humboldt Trail, now Interstate 80. Again, it was the water supply that gave the place its importance. Long before a town grew up the area was known as Humboldt Wells, the stopping point where emigrant trains gathered strength and supplies for the long trek west across the desert to the Sierras. You can still see the ruts made by thousands of wagons in the rock just outside of town. Wells didn't really start to grow until the Central Pacific arrived in 1869. Its downtown, laid out opposite the tracks, is regarded as one of the best preserved rail towns in the state. The place celebrates its frontier heritage with chariot races every Sunday from January to March and a Pony Express relay race in May. A beautiful 11-mile side trip from Wells, which can be taken only in the summer, leads to Angel Lake in a mountain-rimmed valley, by way of Nevada 582.

The highway now runs along the eastern edge of the Humboldt Range, dominated by 11,276-foot-high Hole of the Mountains Peak. This is ranching country, with vast livestock operations spreading across the Clover Valley. It was also the site of a historic mistake. One California-bound party in 1846 was misled into thinking that this route was a short cut from the established Humboldt Trail. They were told that a mountain passage existed just to the south. Instead, the Humboldts give way to the Ruby Mountains, one of the most rugged areas in Nevada. The traveling party lost precious weeks making their way south beyond the Rubys before they could start heading west again. That's one major reason the Donner Party began its crossing of the Sierras too late in the season, became trapped by autumn snows, and went through the horrors of death and cannibalism.

As the highway continues south, the peaks fall away to the west and the country becomes more arid. Currie developed as a shipping point for the surrounding sheep ranches on the Nevada Northern Railroad, which came up from the copper mines at Ely to connect with the Union Pacific main line. The highway parallels its route the rest of the way to Ely. It crosses the dry alkali bed of Goshute Lake, named for an Indian people whose reservation is just to the southeast, straddling the Utah border.

Ghost town alert number one: The mining camp of Cherry

Creek, which had a peak population of 6,000 around 1880 and was emptied out within a decade, is nine miles to the west on Nevada 489.

Mountain ranges define the horizon both east and west as the road descends the Steptoe Valley, through miles and miles of miles and miles. McGill was the smelting town for the copper mines of nearby Ely. Nevada Consolidated opened the plant here, then the largest in the state, in 1906. The last copper mine in the area closed in the 1970s.

East Ely was built as the rail connection for Ely. It was promoted as a residential suburb for company executives and technical workers. But older residents of Ely were so offended by the high-handedness of this plan that they set out to block water access for the new community. This was accomplished by the simple expedient of posting guards with shotguns over the proposed route of the pipeline and running off the construction crew. The company soon abandoned its scheme. East Ely's rail heritage remains strong, though. The former depot has been converted into the Nevada Northern Railway Museum and on weekends the Ghost Train, made up of authentic cars once used on the railroad, takes a ninety-minute trip through Ely into the old mining areas.

For the next 26 miles, U.S. 93 runs along the route of U.S. 6, described in that chapter.

U.S. 93 cuts to the south at Majors Place, offering fine views of 13,061-foot Wheelers Peak—the centerpiece of Great Basin National Park—to the east. Between here and Alamo, a distance of 161 miles, the road has been designated a scenic highway by the state, and presents a brilliant succession of high desert panoramas, vividly colored rocks, and hazy mountain ridges. One range succeeds another as the highway continues south through Lake Valley.

Pioche was one of the roughest, most free-spending towns on the Nevada frontier. It claimed that 75 men were buried in its cemetery before the first interment from natural causes took place. Rival mining interests fought pitched battles in its streets, as hired gunfighters protected their claims. The first strike in the area was made in 1863, but development began in earnest around 1870 when French-born financier F.L.A. Pioche invested in the district. The place had a population of 6,000 by 1874. It was at about this time that its residents decided they required a court-house. It was budgeted at $30,000, but in a case of financial hanky-panky notorious even by Nevada's liberal standards, the final bill came in at a cool one million dollars. It shut down in 1933, and was finally paid off three years later. The restored Million Dollar Courthouse is now the leading sight of Pioche. There is also the Lincoln County Historical Museum, with arti-facts from the area's lively past.

The road passes through Cathedral Gorge, where soft clay has been shaped by erosion into intricate spiral patterns that resemble the spires of a medieval cathederal and other fantastic forms. There are picnic areas and scenic trails in this state park.

At its southern end is Panaca, an agricultural town settled by Mormons in 1864. The word is Paiute for a ledge of ore. The road runs along a raised embankment above Meadow Valley Wash. Echo Canyon Dam to the east controls the floodwaters that once swept through these washes each spring and predicated the eleva-tion of the highway.

Caliente is the biggest city in this corner of Nevada, although with a population of about 1,000 there is no danger of gridlock. It was built around natural springs, which gave the place its name, Spanish for "hot." Like so many other isolated communities along U.S. 93, Caliente grew up when the railroad came. In this case, it was the Union Pacific and the tracks bisect its main street. The Spanish-style depot, built in 1909, is still used by Amtrak. Its chief function now, though, is as city offices and a tourist attraction.

Murals inside depict many of the top attractions in the area, in case you've lost your road map.

At this point, the road turns sharply west to cross Oak Springs Summit at a 6,231-foot elevation. This is the start of the Delamar Valley and you can see the gradual growth of joshua trees, a desert bloom that becomes a symbol of this road in Arizona. This is a stretch of the route on which pioneers made another terrible mistake, thinking they could get to California this way faster and easier. The Manly Party came through here in 1849 and got itself into just as bad a spot as the Donner bunch did further north: Death Valley in midsummer. Even then it was best to stick to the main roads when going to California.

Ghost town alert number two: Where the road turns south again, head north instead on Nevada 318 and in five miles you'll come to Hiko. This was the mining boomtown that preceded Pioche in this area and was county seat for a few years before everybody decamped for the new diggings in 1871.

Ash Springs is another geothermal watering hole, named for the ash trees that cluster around it. This is the start of the Pahranagat Valley, a green oasis in the middle of the vast desert basin. It was used as an Indian campground for generations because of its springs. Cottonwoods and poplars dot the landscape here and migratory waterfowl pass overhead, heading for the two Pahranagat Lakes and Maynard Lake, just to the south. There is a rest stop near the water and in the spring and fall you can observe geese, ducks, blue cranes, and swans. This was cattle country in the 1870s and was notorious as a rangeland for rustlers from Utah and Arizona.

Across the Clark County line, the country turns rugged and more arid again with mesa land stretching off to the distance. The original route of U.S. 93 turned back to the east here, along what is now Nevada 168. If you're in a rush, you can follow the current road, which will soon hook up with Interstate 15 and come out on the other side of Las Vegas. But the side trip on the former route is more interesting.

We run alongside the Muddy River into the Moapa Valley; the reservation of the tribe that gave the place its name is just to the south at the town of Moapa. Mule teams once hauled gypsum from the mines here before the road was cut through. This valley also brought all kinds of confusion and grief to the Mormon settlers. They were under the impression that they had settled in Arizona and dutifully paid taxes to that territory. But a survey party in 1869 determined that this was actually Nevada soil, and the state immediately demanded back taxes. The argument that the money was already in Arizona's pockets made no impression, so Brigham Young simply ordered the settlers back home to Utah. The loss of income almost bankrupted the county. Eventually, many people returned to reclaim their farms.

Jog back north briefly on Interstate 15 and then get off at Nevada 169, heading towards **Overton**. This town became the center of the Mormon community when they returned to the valley in 1881. Long before that, however, this site on the Muddy River was the core of an Indian civilization that extended for 30 miles. The 2,000-year-old settlement, known as Pueblo Grande de Nevada, was believed to have been built by ancestors of the Hopi. Much of the area, which is called the Lost City, was inundated by Lake Mead when Hoover Dam was built. Rescued artifacts are displayed in the Lost City Museum and reconstructions of the ancient habitations are also exhibited.

Highway 169 hooks west to make a scenic run along the shoreline of Lake Mead. But we are getting ahead of ourselves here, because this whole area was created by the engineering marvel that is the fulcrum of the entire Southwest. That is where we are headed.

FOCUS

It is hard to imagine what the Southwest was like at the start of the 20th century. Los Angeles was the largest city in the entire region, with a bit more than 100,000 people. San Diego and Phoenix were little more than towns. Las Vegas didn't exist. The Southwest was still, by and large, an untamed land, and the most unpredictable element in it was the Colorado River.

Its water brought life to the arid soil. But in spring the river could suddenly turn killer, sending its water on a torrent of destruction across farms, towns, and rail lines. In 1905 it inundated much of southern California, forming the 500-square-mile Salton Sea and not returning to its course for 16 months. That disaster provided the impetus for the plans that would lead 30 years later to the construction of Hoover Dam.

This massive cork in the river was the largest concrete dam in the world when it was built and is still the highest in America. It provides power and irrigation and recreation and drink for the fastest-growing part of the United States. Indeed, you can argue that this growth is possible only because of the dam. It made the Southwest.

Planning didn't really get underway until 1922 when the Colorado River Compact, allotting shares of the water to the affected states, was approved. Arizona later challenged the formula, arguing that California had used its greater political clout to snare an inequitable share of the water. The argument was upheld by the U.S. Supreme Court after decades of wrangling.

Secretary of Commerce Herbert Hoover presided over these meetings and the construction of the dam took place all through his presidential administration. His successor, Franklin D. Roosevelt, dedicated the dam in 1935 and the generators were turned on the following year. By that time, however, Hoover was popularly blamed for causing the Depression so the name was changed back to its original title, Boulder Dam. But this, too, presented problems. The first plan did call for the dam to be built in Boulder Canyon, but later surveys indicated that Black Canyon would be the better site and that's where it stands. In an effort to duck a political stigma, the dam-namers simply perpetuated an error. But passions cooled and in 1947 the name was changed back to Hoover. Its reservoir, the largest in the hemisphere, was named for Elwood Mead, head of the Reclamation Service during the construction. There was never any controversy about that.

They like throwing numbers at you here. The dam is 726 feet high, and 1,244 feet wide at the crest. Lake Mead has an 822-mile shoreline and can store 35.2 billion cubic meters of water. There are 17 generators that can turn out 1.9 million kilowatts. It has also become the second biggest tourist attraction in Nevada after the Las Vegas Strip. More than 700,000 visitors a year ride the elevators down to its innards and take a short walking tour. It is so popular that a system of satellite parking lots had to be set up with shuttle buses bringing visitors to the dam itself.

It is an astonishing sight; that wall of concrete backed by waters that sparkle improbably blue with the stark desert cliff of Fortification Hill rising on the Arizona side. But you can also understand how 96 men died placing it here.

Coming from Overton, the route follows the Northshore Road. Side roads lead to recreational areas at Overton Beach, Echo Bay and Callville Bay. The last site was the location of a loading dock from which Mormon traders ran boats down the river to the Pacific.

Continue south along Lakeshore Road to Lake Mead Marina. You can board an excursion boat here for a 75-minute cruise along the lake to the base of the dam. There is swimming at adjacent Boulder Beach. The road then hooks up to connect with U.S. 93.

Turn left, to the north, for a few miles to enter **Boulder City**. This was the town put up by the federal government to house 4,000 workers and supervisors during construction of the dam. In its early years there was no private ownership of property; inhabitants leased from the government. The central residential area is a National Historic District, while the business section along Arizona Street has a strikingly contemporary look. As part of the agreement for its construction in 1932 gambling was not allowed here, and that restriction is still in force. So Boulder City has an ambience unlike most places in Nevada. A number of artists have located here, drawn by the picturesque surroundings, and their galleries are along Arizona Street. The Boulder City–Hoover Dam Museum in the center of town displays artifacts from the project and shows a film, using some original newsreel footage, on how it went up. There is also a display on the less glamorous part of the story, the Ragtown tent city in which many of the less fortunate workers were housed.

Now head south again on U.S. 93. There is a magnificent vista of Lake Mead as the road sweeps around the mountain side to start its descent to the dam. The first satellite parking lots are on the right in a few miles, but except on busy weekends you can get a lot closer than this. There is usually better parking in the lots on the Arizona side of the dam.

Tours leave every few minutes from ticket booths atop the dam. Also take in the Exhibit Building on the Nevada side, with its scale-model representation of the Colorado River Basin and the role Hoover Dam plays in the Southwest. But as we said before, it really plays no role in the Southwest. It *is* the Southwest.

∗ ∗ ∗

The road now angles directly southeast, through the Detrital Valley. There is a turnoff west to Willow Beach, another developed area of Lake Mead National Recreational Area. This one offers swimming on Lake Mohave, which is what the section below the dam is called. Dolan Springs, just off the road to the east, is a retirement community at the base of 6,900-foot Mt. Tipton. Some small-scale silver mining still goes on at Chloride, in the Cerbat Mountains, but the turquoise mine once owned by Tiffany's is only a memory. The road cuts around Kingman on the freeway, with a fine view of the high-desert city as it passes by. (For more information on Kingman, see the chapter on U.S. 66.)

The road runs east with Interstate 40 for 23 miles before breaking away to the south. For the final 102 miles of its life, it is called the Joshua Forest Parkway. Remarkable stands of this giant yucca, given its name by Mormon pioneers because its upstretched arms recalled the biblical description of Joshua leading the Israelites into battle, cover the hillsides and desert floor. Several turnoffs along the road lead to dramatic viewpoints of the trees. Other than that, however, the country is uninhabited for almost the entire route. Wickiup, named for an Indian brush house that was standing here when the first road came through in 1922, is the last settlement of any size until **Wickenburg**. It's a fast ride and the best thing to do is simply settle back and enjoy the joshua trees.

Just outside of Wickenburg, the comfortingly named Vulture Mountains rise to the southwest. They contained plenty of comfort for Henry Wickenburg. He discovered gold there in 1862 and the mine produced $20 million before it was played out, turning the town of Wickenburg into one of the largest in the territory. But Henry's luck ran out in his later years. A dam on the Hassayampa River gave way in 1890 and Wickenburg's land outside of town was buried in silt, making the holdings he had purchased with his gold almost worthless. Fifteen years later, he walked out of his house and shot himself. The town prospered as a travel center in the days before the Interstates, because three of the state's old roads, U.S. 60, 89, and 93, converge on it. But now that Interstates 10 and 17 carry most traffic a good distance away, Wickenburg has transformed itself into a resort, with many guest ranches in the area. It has also rediscovered its past. Frontier Street has been preserved as it appeared around 1900, with a restored rail depot, hotel, and several other commercial buildings. The Desert Caballeros Western Museum, at 20 North Frontier, contains exhibits on the town's history and displays by area artists. A local landmark nearby is the Jail Tree, at Center and Tegner. The mining activity went at such a furious pace here that no one wanted to take time out and build a jail. So they just chained prisoners to this tree until they were transported to the territorial prison at Yuma or released.

From here on Highway 93 becomes fettered as well, as a state road, so we'll wind up our trip here at the Jail Tree.

VISITING HOURS

NEVADA

Boulder City: Hoover Dam, (702) 293-8362. South on U.S. 93. Tours. Daily, 8–6:45, Memorial Day–Labor Day; 9–4:15 at other times. Admission.

Lake Mead Cruises, (702) 293-3484. From Lake Mead Marina, east of Boulder City, on Lakeshore Rd. Daily, 10:30, noon, 1:30 and 3. Fare.

Hoover Dam Museum, (702) 294-1988. Off U.S. 93, on Arizona St. Daily, 9–5. Admission.

East Ely: Nevada Northern Railway Museum, (702) 289-2085. At 11th St. E. and Ave. A. Wednesday–Sunday, 9–5, mid-May–September. Admission.

Overton: Lost City Museum, (702) 397-2193. East of U.S. 93, by way of Nevada 168 and 169. Daily, 8:30–4:30. Admission.

Pioche: Lincoln County Historical Museum, (702) 962-5207. Main St. Monday–Saturday, 9–12:30 and 1:30–5; Sunday opening at 10. Free.

ARIZONA

Wickenburg: Desert Cabelleros Museum, (602) 684-2272. At 20 N. Frontier St. Monday–Saturday, 10–4 and Sunday 1–4. Admission.

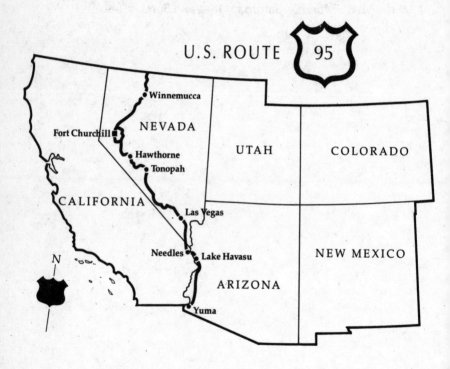

The Colorado Coastline

U.S. 95

McDermitt, Nev. to San Luis, Ariz.
945 miles

One of the few remaining Canada-to-Mexico routes, this road starts at Eastport, on the British Columbia border of the Idaho panhandle, and makes its unhurried way to San Luis, on the Sonora line, a few miles above the Gulf of California.

The road angles through much of Nevada's tumbledown past and a good portion of its booming present as it traverses the state top to bottom and misses very few corners in between. Then it becomes the Colorado River road, through some of the Southwest's newest towns along the west coast of Arizona, where water skiers frolic in the middle of the country's driest desert.

MILEPOSTS

Up on Nevada's northern border, they tried to honor a U.S. Cavalry colonel by naming a fort and a town for him. They failed. Charles McDermit came to the Quinn River Valley in the summer of 1865 when Indian attacks were reported on the stagecoach road to Oregon. Within a few days of his arrival, he was fatally wounded on a scouting patrol. A fort was immediately established in the area and named for him, and the nearby settlement, which had been known as Quinn River Station, was also changed in his honor. But a mapmaker somewhere along the line insisted on adding a second "t" to both names and poor Colonel McDermit goes through posterity being misspelled.

Fort McDermitt became a reservation for the Paiute in 1886 and the town hosts the Red Mountain Pow Wow each June, a gathering of 14 Indian nations from nine western states.

It isn't until you get 30 miles into the state on this road that you come to one of those typical border-name contrivances, Orovada.

The Quinn Valley stretches off to the west while the Santa Rosa Mountains, part of Humboldt National Forest, rise just to the east. Fur trappers coming south from the Snake River country were the first to open this road. They blazed it to the junction with the Humboldt River in the late 1820s. Its greatest activity, though, came immediately after McDermit's death, when miners trekked north to try their luck in the new gold strikes around Boise. Much later, in a far different era, gold also was discovered here. The strike was made in 1907, just to the east in the Santa Rosas by a prospector exploring the region in his automobile. The National Mine eventually produced about $8 million.

This northern corner of Nevada has one of the country's highest concentrations of Basques. They began immigrating here in the 1870s, leaving their ancestral homes in Spain after autonomous privileges were revoked by the Castilian government and their dialect was no longer given legal standing. Like all new arrivals, the Basques sought out the part of America that most closely resembled their former homes. This area was an acceptable visual stand-in for the high Pyrenees valleys and, more important, was also hospitable to sheep-raising, the occupation most of them had followed in Europe. Winnemucca is the center of the Basque community and on the second weekend of

June the town celebrates its ethnicity with traditional games, food, and dances.

The Basque dialect contains words unlike any other language in Europe. **Winnemucca**, however, is not one of them. It was the name of a Paiute chief. No one is quite sure what it means because even fewer people speak Paiute than Basque. Originally, the place was French Ford, because of the nationality of the first trader here. A bridge across the Humboldt replaced the ford by 1865 and three years later, when the Central Pacific reached here, the name was changed. Whatever the place was called, by 1900 it had a First National Bank and that was all Butch Cassidy needed to know about it. He and his gang robbed it and, reportedly, sent photographs of themselves to the bank president just to rub it in. The Humboldt Museum here features local history in its displays while the Buckaroo Hall of Fame is a celebration of Nevada's cowboy culture with mementoes from many of the area's ranches.

From here, the road rides southwest with Interstate 40 for the next 132 miles across the Black Rock Desert. This was the route of the Humboldt Trail, the primary passage to northern California during the Gold Rush years. John Bidwell is credited with leading the first party west along the Humboldt in 1841. But it wasn't until Johannes Sutter's agents started persuading Oregon-bound travelers to drop down this way (see U.S. 93) that the Humboldt Trail became a major western route. Throughout the 1850s, an unceasing parade of adventurers and families came west along the Humboldt. This was the route Mark Twain wrote about in *Roughing It*, although by the time he made the trek in 1862 some minimal semblance of comfort had been achieved. With the completion of the transcontinental railroad, which also followed this route, the trail went into the history books.

The road runs adjacent to Rye Patch Lake, the reservoir of a Humboldt River dam and a State Recreation Area prized by boaters. If you want to exit for a breather at Lovelock, named for the stagecoach station run by George Lovelock, you can take in what is reputed to be the nation's only round courthouse. Many early travelers dallied here to fatten their cattle for the crossing of the Humboldt Sink, a treacherous 40-mile stretch of desert. The remnant of a prehistoric lake that once covered this entire region, the sink's sands could trap heavily laden wagons, causing the dreams of many California-bound pioneers to end here. So many cattle grazed in the meadows at Lovelock that the topsoil eroded and the water supply dried up. The dam back at Rye Patch had to be built to replenish the fields that once fed the pioneers.

The highway allows travelers to cross the Humboldt Sink in less than an hour today and U.S. 95 turns south at its western end. But we'll continue on another 37 miles and make our turn south at Fernley, on U.S. 95A. Now an outlying suburb of Reno, this farming town was the entrance to the fertile Walker Valley. Many westward voyagers decided they'd had enough by the time they got here. Instead of going on across the Sierra, they just called it a trip and settled down to the south in the valley.

The road passes the western end of Lahontan Reservoir, named for that ancient lake that created the Humboldt Sink. The dam here was built in 1915 on the Carson River as a flood control measure and it is also an electrical power source. We pass **Silver Springs** and eight miles beyond is the turnoff to Fort Churchill. This was the chief military protection for Nevada's earliest settlers, its effective life running from the discovery of the Comstock Lode in nearby Virginia City to the completion of the transcontinental railroad, roughly from 1861 to 1869. Before the Comstock strike, Nevada was simply a space travelers passed through. But after this momentous silver find, people came to stay. This made the Paiutes, accustomed to having dominion over the land, uneasy. At one point, they attacked a party on the Humboldt Trail and killed seven men. A reprisal raid was sent north to

Pyramid Lake, which was and is the heart of Paiute country. The raiders were mauled and their commander killed. A volunteer force was hastily raised in California and, combined with a Regular Army detachment, routed the Indians. Fort Churchill was built immediately afterwards as a safeguard against any future such incident. It became a station on the Pony Express and was also the eastern end of a telegraph line to San Francisco. The bare walls of the ruined adobe barracks are now a state park, with an interpretive center explaining its history.

The Paiutes nursed their resentments of the European invasion for years, never really accommodating themselves to it. In 1890, this lingering anger suddenly burst forth in a way that would have bloody repercussions in a distant part of the West.

Jack Wilson, who was born a Paiute, had grown up with a Christian family in **Yerington**, the next town on this route, and was fascinated by the messianic teachings he heard during readings of the Bible. He became convinced that he had been chosen as the messenger of an Indian Messiah. Adopting his tribal name, Wovoka, he began preaching a religion of redemption. The white man would be swept away, the dead would rise, those who believed would be invulnerable to bullets. A ceremonial rite that became known as the Ghost Dance spread from tribe to tribe. "The name of Jesus was on every tongue," wrote a U.S. Cavalry officer at the time, "and had I been a missionary I could have led every Indian on the Plains into the church." The rites grew more hostile as they traveled east, and among the Sioux in South Dakota they erupted into open warfare. The aged chief, Sitting Bull, was killed and the massacre at Wounded Knee soon followed, all growing directly out of Jack Wilson's teaching in Yerington.

The place was originally called Pizen Switch, presumably in tribute to a poisonous blend of whiskey sold there. When the Virginia and Truckee Railroad arrived it was decided to give

Yerington a bit more dignity by renaming it for an official of the line. The Lyon County Museum recounts the old days here with several historic buildings brought to its site from various parts of the area.

The road now swings back due east to reach the Walker River and then turns south through its fertile valley. The river is named for Joseph Walker, an early trapper who is credited with leading the first party across the Sierras to California in 1833. Twelve years later, Walker was scouting for John Fremont's expedition to California. Fremont, who came to be known as The Pathfinder, decided to honor the man who had actually found most of the paths by naming the lake for him. The road runs down the lake's western shore, with 11,245-foot-high Mt. Grant dominating its southern end. This lake, eight miles across at its widest point, is another remnant of old Lake Lahontan. The waters are saline but the trout fishing is good and there is swimming at a state recreation area just off the highway.

Hawthorne is the seat of Mineral County, and it was treasure in the land that first drew people here. But its prosperity was assured by the Navy. This remote area was chosen for the sprawling U.S. Naval Ammunition Depot in the 1920s and the military remains a strong presence in the area. The Mineral County Museum, however, focuses on the old mining towns in the surrounding hills rather than on the weaponry.

The road jogs east and south in short spurts, following the contours of the mountains ranges and the Nevada state line, which makes a similar bend at this point. Failed mining towns are the only trace of settlement. The town of Luning first found silver in 1879, then copper 27 years later. Now there is very little to be found. Mina, similarly, was a processing center on the Southern Pacific for ore brought down from the nearby hills.

The road crosses Redlich Summit into Esmeralda County and on the west is the Columbus Marsh. Vast borax deposits were found here in 1864 and the town of Columbus once stood in their midst, as four companies mined the field. But by 1875 the borax was played out and everything was swallowed up by the desert.

At Coaldale, the road unites with U.S. 6 and runs east with it to the old mining town of Tonopah (discussed in the chapter on U.S. 6). If you look to the rear, though, as you make the turn onto U.S. 6, you'll see the heights of the White Mountains on the California border, dominated by 13,140-foot Boundary Peak, the highest point in Nevada.

U.S. 95 crosses Tonopah Summit and soon the first plants of the southern desert can be seen—joshua trees and cactus. Tonopah grew rich on silver, but just 25 miles to the south and three years later, Esmeralda County also revealed its gold. Tonopah was at the peak of its boom in 1903, so, at first, the new find's greatest value seemed to be its novelty. Gold was not to be sneezed at, but Nevada was silver country. Moreover, the first strike did not have an especially high assay value. But as employment started to decline in the older camp, the spillover made its way south to Goldfield. In October they hit the rich ore, and the rush was on.

Goldfield is the most spectacular example of a mine-town boom and bust in the 20th-century West. Most of Nevada's early camps already were ghosts and a part of Western lore when the Goldfield strike came in. What amounted to a modern city developed in Goldfield as a result, which made it all the more incredible when it emptied out. At first, there was no hint of such an abrupt end. This was the richest gold find in the state's history. The raw ore was so high in quality, it didn't have to be reduced. Workers could just walk off with it at the end of the shift. The mine operators introduced tough security measures and the recently unionized miners in turn charged them with price gouging in the company stores, the only places their scrip payments (used instead of U.S. currency) could be redeemed. Federal troops were brought in and for a time it appeared that fighting would break out. But there was too much money to be made to have it spoiled by violence, so the situation soon eased. Besides, lavish new hotels and saloons were opening up to provide entertainment. One tavern owner, Tex Rickard, promoted a lightweight championship fight in 1906 between Joe Gans and Battling Nelson that packed the town. It also started Rickard on his career as the most succesful fight promoter of his time, especially in the bouts he arranged for another kid from a western mining town, Jack Dempsey.

By 1910, Goldfield was the biggest city in Nevada, with 30,000 residents. By 1920, it was almost deserted. The mines gave out and even the modern superstructure could not prevent a thriving city's return to sagebrush and sand. Fire destroyed much of the old business district in 1923, but the town still presents an extraordinary sight. The Goldfield Hotel, built in 1908 at the peak of the town's prosperity, has been restored, and the former county courthouse still has many of its original fixtures, including the Tiffany lamps. On the first weekend in August the town celebrates Treasure Days with appropriately strange events such as barstool-sitting competitions.

We are still at an elevation of over 6,000 feet here and as we continue south there are occasional glimpses of the Sierra, far to the south, on the other side of Death Valley. Scotty's Junction is a primary turnoff to this area, which has the lowest elevation in the country.

Beatty grew up as a rail center for the surrounding mining camps in the Bullfrog District, which developed just a few years after Goldfield with capital invested from that town. Rhyolite, just to the west, was the largest and remains the best preserved of them. After Goldfield, however, it is a bit of an anti-climax. The ruined walls of two commercial structures do make an arresting sight when viewed across the valley. The ornate rail depot here is still in good shape and open to visitors, and so is the Bottle House, with its walls constructed of empty beer containers. This camp's cycle went even faster than Goldfield's; born in 1905, it peaked with a population of 8,000 just three years later and had died by 1912.

The road descends to the Amargosa (Spanish for "bitter") Desert, a good name for this bare, chalky, alkaline expanse. Amargosa Springs is the final turnoff for Death Valley. Shortly beyond, with a view of Mt. Charleston to the west, the highway divides for its approach to the state's most heavily populated area, Las Vegas. As the road becomes a freeway, you can see new subdivisions marching off to the foothills across the desert floor. During the late 1980s, this was the fastest-growing big city in America. The onetime gambling resort transformed itself into a high-tech, light-industrial city and retirement center. In the 1990 Census, there were more residents in metropolitan Las Vegas than there had been in the entire state in 1970.

The name Las Vegas means "The Wells," and the place grew on meadows fed by springs on the Old Spanish Trail. A fort was built by Mormon settlers in 1855 and the discovery of nearby lead deposits occasioned some excitement because it was thought lead could be smelted into bullets. The operation was unsuccesful, though, because the metal had too high a concentration of silver. So it goes in Las Vegas.

The site became a cattle ranch, and, in 1905, was part of a speculative land development when the Union Pacific Railroad sold off lots and laid out the city. It developed slowly until 1931 when the construction of Hoover Dam and introduction of legalized gambling changed the face of its life forever. Las Vegas is now among the leading tourist destinations and convention sites in the world. Its lavish shows and outlandish hotels and marriage chapels and never-closing casinos are a source of wealth and legend that has proven far more permanent than the comparatively paltry treasure mines of Goldfield.

Las Vegas is no place to tour by car on a quick pass-through. The road goes around the city by freeway and we should do the same.

We emerge from the bypass in **Henderson**, which started as a housing development for workers in a World War II magnesium plant. It is now the principal industrial center in Nevada, with several chemical and metal plants. The Clark County Heritage Museum, built around Henderson's former railroad depot, has assembled historic structures from Las Vegas, Boulder City, and several rural areas. There are indoor and outdoor exhibit areas as well as a display of rolling stock. Rail trips to run from here to Boulder City using antique equipment are currently in the planning stages.

Now the road drops straight south into even more arid country. It parallels the Colorado River, running to the east on the far side of the El Dorado Mountains. Searchlight was named, according to legend, for a brand of matches. Two prospectors building a fire as they camped one night in 1898 hit the Duplex gold strike the next day and memorialized the site with the name on their matchbox. The place reached its peak of activity in 1906 and its light has grown dimmer ever since.

Just as the town of Orovada introduced us to Nevada in the north, the roadside settlement of Cal-Nev-Ari speeds us on the way to the next two states on the route. The stay in California is very brief. About 20 miles across the border, with the Dead Mountains rising on the east, the road joins Interstate 40, heading east. It bypasses Needles, once a stopping point on vanished U.S. 66 and named for rock formations to the south on the Colorado River. The highway exits here to head south on the California side of the stream. But it's a more interesting trip to continue on the Interstate for a few miles and cross the river at Topock, Arizona, then head south on Arizona 95. (Hey, it's the same number, isn't it?) We'll meet up with U.S. 95 on this side of the border in just a little while.

Topock is the Mohave word for "bridge," by the way, and it is to a far more historic bridge, in a most improbable setting, that we are headed.

FOCUS

All Robert McCulloch wanted to do was save some money on his taxes by moving his power saw company from Los Angeles to Arizona. But things got out of hand. Now **Lake Havasu City** contains more than 25,000 people, golf courses, malls, and London Bridge—all of it sitting where there was nothing but desert in 1964.

Well, there was a lake, although not much was being done with it then. Lake Havasu was created by Parker Dam, built in 1938 as the main source of water for the City of Los Angeles. But images of the lake area were shaped by the tales of hardships the engineers went through to get that water out of the wilds and into the city. No one thought about Lake Havasu as a resort, let alone a residential community.

McCulloch, however, understood that he couldn't just move his business and plop it down on the lakeshore. He had to provide a community infrastructure. So to a skeptical and largely indifferent world he announced the building of a city in the wilderness, on the site of an abandoned landing strip. Then he bought London Bridge, and everything changed.

Lake Havasu City was the perfect symbol of the new West, made possible by the federal dam-building program on the Colorado River and summoned into being by the booster spirit. London Bridge, on the other hand, was falling down. The symbol of tradition and permanence, as familiar as a nursery rhyme, London Bridge represented the antithesis of its new home. In 1968, however, the City of London determined the bridge could no longer carry its burden of traffic and made plans to tear it down. McCulloch then stepped in and bought it for $2.4 million, dismantled it, shipped the numbered stones piece by piece, and reassembled it here.

There were reports at the time that McCulloch was under the impression that he had actually purchased Tower Bridge, the more frequently photographed Thames crossing with its decorative central towers. London Bridge was a rather plain, five-arched structure built in 1831 to replace a medieval span that had stood for 625 years. McCulloch did admit that he was "a bit shaken up" when he got his first look at because it was "a good deal dirtier than the pictures had shown it to be. Needless to say, though, I'd do it all over again. Our lot sales doubled after the dedication of the bridge."

The bridge, structurally reinforced and carrying traffic in perfect safety once again, opened in Lake Havasu City in 1971, although 53 feet were chopped from its length to fit its new location. Although still an incongruous sight, it undeniably has become the tourist centerpiece of the area. By some measures, it trails only the Grand Canyon as an attraction in Arizona. As originally conceived, the bridge stood at the neck of a peninsula, but that has since been flooded in. So the bridge does serve an actual utilitarian purpose and connects with an island.

* * *

This stretch of the Colorado has become known as the West Coast of Arizona, one of the prime water recreation areas of the Southwest. Arizona 95, recently widened and improved, bypasses several of the small communities that have sprung up along the water to serve this new trade. Cattail Cove, a unit of Lake Havasu State Park, is a major public access point. The cove is on the north shore of Bill Williams River as it empties into the lake. The river mouth is part of Havasu National Wildlife Refuge, home to the Yuma clapper rail, one of the country's rarest birds. The refuge is open daily.

The highway makes a wide swing around the cove and at the far side is Parker Dam. This is among the deepest dams in the world. Only 27 percent of its total height is visible; the rest burrows 235 feet down into the Colorado riverbed. Aqueducts that begin here cross the California desert to the west, delivering one billion gallons of water daily to the Los Angeles and San Diego areas. The dam also furnishes electric power to nearby communities in Nevada and California, as well as the major cities of Arizona. The Central Arizona Project began carrying water from Lake Havasu to Phoenix and Tucson in 1985. You can take the side road that runs across the top into California and see Parker Dam on a self-guided tour.

Just to the south is Buckskin Mountain State Park, in an area that has come to be known as the Parker Strip because of its heavy concentration of boat ramps and beaches. There is also hiking on bluffs above the river on the mountain that gives the park its name. Boat races are held on the river during the first Sunday in March, and an illuminated boat competition takes place at the start of the holiday season in late November. From all this merriment, it's difficult to imagine the bitterness this project stirred up in Arizona at its inception. The governor even sent the National Guard to the construction site to protest what Arizona regarded as a massive water grab on the part of its giant neighbor (California) to the west. The matter eventually was settled by the legal system and the U.S. Supreme Court mandated a redrawing of water rights to give Arizona a more equitable share. Now everybody's happy.

Parker is within the boundaries of the Colorado River Indian Reservation. Two peoples, the Mohave and Chemehuevi, have occupied the lands amicably since 1886. Previously, this stretch of the Colorado was regarded as the most dangerous crossing point for California-bound immigrant trains, and for military supply trains taking this road between Fort Mohave to the north and **Yuma**. The Colorado River Indian Tribes Museum, in Parker, interprets the history and culture of these tribes, as well as the Hopi and Navajo. They are noted for their work in basketry and beadwork.

The highway cuts inland from here, running through a desert valley between the Dome Rock Mountains on the west and the Plomosa to the east. U.S. 95 rejoins our route (see, I told you it would) at the town of Quartzsite. The name gives an indication of the mineral wealth of the surrounding area. On the first Thursday of February each year, rock hounds and jewelers pour into the little town for the Pow Wow Gem and Rock Show, which has grown into an international event—one of the largest in the trade. If you know your minerals, though, you will have spotted that we have another misspelling in this town's name, just as in McDermitt at the very start of this road. There is no "s" in the standard spelling of this quartz derivative. It was just tossed in by the U.S. Post Office.

Quartzsite contains a memorial to one of the more unusual experiments in American military history, supplying desert troops with camels. Edward F. Beale was the Naval officer charged with opening a wagon road from Santa Fe to southern California across the desert (see U.S. 66) in the 1850s. Beale had first seen this area during the Mexican War when he was involved in the California campaign. He was convinced that camels were the way to go here, that they would prove superior to horses in providing reliable desert transportation. He convinced Jefferson Davis, then Secretary of War, and purchasing agents were sent to the Middle East to round up some camels and experienced drivers for the trek. They started overland from Texas, but while the camels did just fine, other aspects of the scheme fell apart. The Arab drivers did not care for the hazards of the trip and quit. The horses panicked at the sight of the camels. The soldiers could not get accustomed to the camels' rolling gait and an epidemic of seasickness broke out in the desert. Most important, the start of the Civil War mandated an immediate call-up of troops in the area. The camels had been based at Fort Tyson, an outpost built in 1856 to protect travelers from Mohave raids around which the town of Quartzsite grew up. After 1861, they were turned loose to fend for themselves. For years, the camels were spotted wandering around the area and became a rich source of desert folklore. Tales of camel sightings abounded long after any of the beasts could possibly have survived.

Now the road drops down to the La Posa Plain, the floor of the desert, virtually uninhabited between here and Yuma, 83 miles to the south. The highway occupies a narrow corridor between the U.S. Army's Yuma Proving Ground, a weapons range closed to the public, on the west, and the Kofa National Wildlife Refuge on the east. The name Kofa is short for King of Arizona, the mining company that once worked this area and sent its ore out in 20-mule teams along this road.

A turnoff just south of the Yuma County line leads to Palm Canyon along a nine-mile dirt road. This is the only place in the state where wild palms grow and there is a fine viewpoint over the remote canyon in which they flourish.

Stone Cabin is named for a refuge on the old mining road. The highway then cuts across a corner of the Proving Grounds, and may be closed for short intervals during testing. On the east is Castle Dome, a landmark in this barren country, appearing much higher than its 3,793-foot elevation. There is a turnoff to Martinez Lake, formed by the Imperial Dam and adjoining Imperial Wildlife Refuge. But after Lake Havasu to the north, this side trip seems like more of the same. Instead, continue across lands that once were part of the Jose Maria Redondo Ranch, the largest colonial estate in Arizona until it was broken up by the U.S. government after the Mexican War. The road crosses the Gila River, then turns sharply west to enter Yuma.

Yuma's a name that echoes through frontier lore. A mission, a landmark on the great southern route to California, a military post and, most notoriously, a prison. How many Western movies have spun off from tales of Arizona desperados sent to Yuma's Territorial Prison, carved into solid rock bluffs above the Colorado River? For 33 years, from 1876 to 1909, the bad and the ugly, and maybe even some of the good, were tossed inside its thick adobe walls. A good many of them didn't stay long. Despite its isolation and the bounties paid to Indians who tracked down escapees, the place was famed for its frequent breakouts. The prison is a now a state park, with a museum and well-preserved cell blocks, including the Hole for Incorrigibles.

Yuma was visited by the Coronado Expedition in 1540 and a temporary mission was set up by Fr. Eusebio Kino in 1697. Fr. Francisco Garces returned on a more permanent basis in 1779, but two years later he was massacred while saying Mass, along with most of the Spanish garrison, by local Indians aggrieved at the arrogant behavior of the soldiers.

After the Mexican War, this place became the most widely used ford across the Colorado, with several ferries in competition for passengers. At that time, the crossing wasn't made to California. People were already *in* California. That state claimed the chunk of land south of the Gila River and didn't give it up until 1873, when the federal government ruled it belonged to Arizona. Residents sued for illegally collected back taxes. They are still waiting.

An estimated 60,000 people crossed here in 1850-1851. That same year a military post was established on the west bank as protection from Indians unhappy over the number of people pouring into their lands. No one settled on the east bank until 1854, when a surveying party, upset over what it regarded as exorbitant ferry rates, decided to spite the boatman and plant a town right where they stood. It was first called Colorado City and the ferryman bought one of the first lots. Yuma became a river port for surrounding mines and by 1870 was big enough to get the county seat, a rate of growth spurred by acquisition of the prison six years later. It was the second biggest city in the territory, behind Tucson, by 1880. The ferries, which were the source of its founding, continued in operation well into the 20th century. It wasn't until 1915 that a highway bridge was built here, putting the boats out of business. The river's commercial traffic had ended six years before with the construction of the Laguna Dam, but the irrigation system established by the dam and its larger successors turned Yuma into the market center of a prosperous agricultural region. Yuma also claims to have the highest percentage of winter sunshine of any city in America.

The Customhouse Museum, at historic Yuma Crossing, is the oldest American-built structure in town. Built in 1864 as a quartermaster depot for military bases in the Southwest, it continued in operation for the next 91 years. It is at the end of Second Street, a few blocks south of the Prison. The area around it is being developed as Yuma Crossing Center, a living-history outdoor museum scheduled to open in 1995. There is a self-guided walking tour set up through the area. Nearby is the handsome Southern Pacific depot, turned into the Yuma Art Center, with programs of graphic and performing arts. Right across the river, on what was once the grounds of Fort Yuma, is the Quechan Indian Museum, with displays on the history of both the Native people and Anglos in the area. It is now part of the Fort Yuma Indian Reservation.

U.S. 95 has another 25 miles to run, through an agricultural area growing citrus fruit, dates, and lettuce, in the most frost-free corner of the continental United States. The road passes just west of Desert Sun Stadium, spring training home of the San Diego

Padres. But unless you are especially fond of gazing at lettuce fields and Mexican border crossings, the trip can just as easily end in Yuma.

VISITING HOURS

NEVADA

Hawthorne: Mineral County Museum, (702) 945-5142. At 10th and D Sts. Monday, 1–3, Tuesday–Wednesday, 2–4:30, Thursday, 11–1:30, Friday, noon–3. Donation.

Henderson: Clark County Heritage Museum, (702) 455-7955. On U.S. 95, at 1830 S. Boulder Highway. Daily, 9–4:30. Admission.

Silver Springs: Fort Churchill State Park, (702) 577-2345. South on U.S. 95, then west on fort road. Daily, 8:30–4:30, Memorial Day–Labor Day. Call for schedule at other times. Free.

Winnemucca: Humboldt Museum, (702) 623-2912. Jungo Rd. and Maple Ave. Monday–Saturday, 10–4. Donation.

Buckaroo Hall of Fame, (702) 623-2225. At 48 W. Winnemucca Blvd., in the Chamber of Commerce building. Daily, 8–4. Free.

Yerington: Lyon County Museum, (702) 463-3341. At 215 S. Main. Weekends, 1–5. Donation.

ARIZONA

Lake Havasu City: Havasu National Wildlife Refuge, (619) 326-3853. South on Arizona 95. Daily, 8–4. Free.

Parker: Parker Dam, (602) 669-2174. North on Arizona 95. Monday–Friday, 8–5, free.

Colorado River Indian Tribes Museum, (602) 669-9211. South on Arizona 95, at 2nd and Mohave Sts. Monday–Friday, 8–5. Donation.

Yuma: Territorial Prison Museum, (602) 783-4771. West of U.S. 95,

·at the end of 4th St. Daily, 8–5. Admission.

Customhouse Museum, (602) 343-2500. West of U.S. 95, on 2nd Ave. behind City Hall. Thursday–Monday, 8–5. Admission.

Yuma Art Center, (602) 783-2314. West of U.S. 95, in the Southern Pacific Depot, on Gila St. Tuesday–Saturday, 10–5, and Sunday, 1–5, September–mid-July. Admission.

Fort Yuma Quechan Museum, (619) 572-0661. Across Colorado River bridge, in California. Monday–Friday, 8–noon and 1–5. Admission.

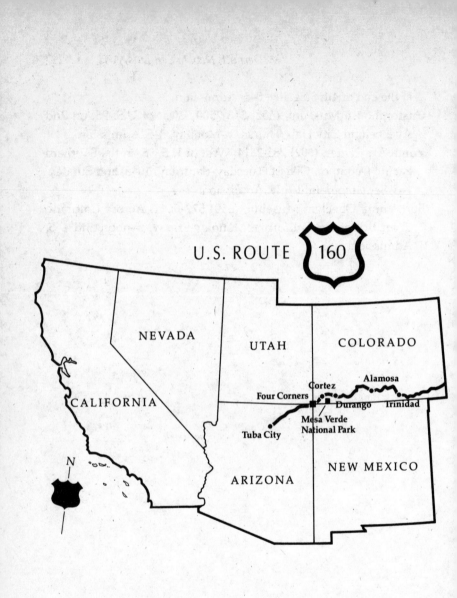

U.S. ROUTE 160

Dust Bowl to Navajo Country

⬡

U.S. 160

Bartlett, Colo. to Tuba City, Ariz.
670 miles

This is a classic old road for its entire trip across the western half of
the country. It spins off from U.S. 60 near Poplar Bluff, Missouri,
then winds far from the freeways at a tantalizing pace, through the
southern tier of that state and Kansas, before entering Colorado at
its extreme southeastern corner.

It crosses the Rockies on the edge of vast wilderness areas before
dropping into the high desert and becoming the main east-west
road through the Navajo Reservation in Arizona. There is a little
bit of everything along this road, from four-star attractions like
Mesa Verde National Park, to the only place in America where
you can do push-ups in four states at once.

MILEPOSTS

The road enters from the east and crosses a virtually empty stage
for more than 150 miles. Most of this run is through the heart of
Comanche National Grassland, a portion of the Plains preserved
as they were before the settlers came. While the Plains here present
a picture of barren solitude below endless skies, that is deceptive.

The 400,000 acres of grass teem with life, as they did when the Comanche rode here and took what they needed from its store. There is a large variety of game, fish, and birds.

Once, however, the area had another name. In the 1930s this was the Dust Bowl. During World War I, as the price of grain climbed to new records, farmers were encouraged to convert grazing land into agricultural production. But it was not a land meant for plows. When prices fell and the cycle of drought returned, the land started to blow away. Stripped of the grass that protected it from the wind, the soil wound up blackening the skies of the Midwest and turned this part of Colorado into desolation row. Now the farms have disappeared and the land has healed.

The road follows the Santa Fe Railroad as far as Springfield, Colorado. The town was named by settlers from the Missouri city, which lies a few hundred miles to the east along this same highway. Carrizo Mountain rises to the south and, occasionally, you can glimpse distant mesas across the border in the Oklahoma panhandle and New Mexico. Rudyard Kipling was an enormously strong influence in the naming of American towns in the late 19th century. There are, in fact, places named both Rudyard and Kipling in Michigan's Upper Peninsula. A bit north of this road, along U.S. 24, one passes through Simla and Ramah, named by a rail executive's wife for places she had read about in Kipling's novels. On this road we have Kim, named for the title character in another of Kipling's books when the town was founded in 1918.

We cross the canyon cut by Chacuaco Creek and run alongside the Purgatoire River. The stream's name is an example of the intermingling of cultures in this area. It originally was part of a much longer Spanish name which meant "Souls Lost in Purgatory." The first part of that name has been retained by the town of Las Animas, several miles downstream (see U.S. 50). It commemorates the Indian massacre of a Spanish expedition of 1596. Its leader had murdered his rival several days before and the accompanying priests, horrified at this act of brutality, returned home. So no last rites were given to the Spaniards who died in the subsequent attack. Their souls were assumed to be lodged in purgatory and the river named for them. French trappers who worked the upper reaches of the river heard the name and kept only the second half, translating it as Purgatoire. That's how it came down to the first Anglo settlers, who decided to stick with it.

The Purgatoire runs through the center of **Trinidad**, named for another Spanish religious reference, this time to the Holy Trinity. This is soft coal country. Coke (fuel made from soft coal) produced here was sent up to the smelters in Pueblo, where much of Colorado's mineral wealth was refined. Just west of the city, in Cokedale, you'll still find rows of brick ovens that once converted the coal. A National Historic District, the onetime gritty manufacturing town is now an artists' colony.

Trinidad grew up as a rendezvous point on the Santa Fe Trail, at the base of Fisher's Peak and Raton Pass to the south. It was the meeting place of the Hispanic and Anglo Southwest. The city still reflects that today in its mixture of styles that causes it to resemble a New England village plopped down on top of a town in Mexico. The melting pot didn't always work well. In 1867, a four-day riot that took place between the two groups of settlers had to be put down by the U.S. Cavalry. But Main Street today is designated "Corazon de Trinidad"—Heart of Trinidad—and along its length you can see the rich jumble of styles that gives the town its character. There is the Baca House, the residence of a wealthy Hispanic ranching family in the 1870s. Adjacent to it is the Bloom House, a Victorian chateau built in 1882 by the operator of the first coal mine in the area. Across from these residences is the Pioneer Museum, with artifacts from the town's beginnings on the Santa Fe Trail and its development as a thriving industrial city. Another important place in the Corazon is the Arthur Roy Mitchell Museum, featuring a collection of work by the Western artist and his contemporaries, as well as first-rate examples of Hispanic religious folk art. The whole area, with its brick streets and old-time atmosphere, makes a delightful place for browsing and strolling.

The highway swings north with Interstate 25, along the route of the old Goodnight Cattle Trail from Texas, with the Sangre de Cristo Range to the west. Dominating the horizon are the Spanish Peaks, which we are in the process of swinging around.

The highway cuts away from the Interstate at **Walsenburg**. An old Spanish settlement, originally called Plaza de Los Leones, it was renamed for German-born merchant Fred Walsen when it was built up as a coal-mining town in 1873. The courthouse and jail on Main Street are both listed in the National Historic Register and the row of shops nearby, including several antique stores, are also evocative of bygone times.

Now the highway turns west, and after passing Lathrop State Park, a water sports center on Walsenburg's western outskirts, it starts to climb towards La Veta Pass and the Cuchara Valley. The two Spanish Peaks, which top out at 13,623 feet, now lie to the south. There is an air of mystery about these isolated mountains, which form a unit of the San Isabel National Forest. Indian legends cautioned travelers against approaching them and the Utes believed that the thick clouds that often cluster near their summits were the source of all rain. Spanish settlers repeated tales of a priest with the Coronado expedition who ventured there and found gold on their slopes, but vanished on his way back to Mexico before he could reveal the location.

La Veta, the name of a town on the slopes of the Spanish Peaks, means "the vein" in Spanish. This village, five miles south of the highway, was settled by families from New Mexico's Rio Grande Valley in 1761 and retained a strong Hispanic character well into this century. Fort Francisco was built here in 1862. One of the oldest buildings in Colorado, it is now a museum of area culture, containing several restored businesses and a schoolhouse. Look for Goemmer Butte, just outside of town, a landmark formed by volcanic activity in the area.

Back on Highway 160, the road crosses La Veta Pass at 9,413 feet. One of the more navigable passes through the Rockies, this was the route of the Denver and Rio Grande Railroad in 1877. Fur trader James Percell made the first recorded crossing of the pass in 1803 and he was followed by both the Pike and Fremont exploring expeditions. This is the gateway to the vast San Luis Valley, a 60-by-125-mile tract running between the Sangre de Cristo and San Juan ranges of the Rockies. Much of it was part of the Trinchera Ranch, a one-million acre grant from the Mexican government in 1843 that was the largest private holding in Colorado. In recent years, several land companies acquired title to remnants of the grant and sold it off in individual parcels. As late as the 1980s, the ranch was billed as the largest undeveloped private tract in the contiguous 48 states.

The town of **Fort Garland** sits on the location of a military post, built here in 1858 to control the Utes. It was garrisoned for 25 years and one of its commandants in the 1860s was Kit Carson. His residence is now part of the fort museum. The adobe buildings have been completely restored, and exhibits relating the history of the region and post also contain displays of folk art from the San Luis Valley.

Just to the north is Mt. Blanca, the southern edge of the Sangre de Cristo. At 14,317 feet it is the highest peak in this portion of the state.

The Rio Grande runs through the center of the big valley. It was the avenue of settlement from New Mexico, accounting for much of the area's Hispanic character. The river town of **Alamosa**, the commercial center of the area, is also the home of Adams State College. Alamosa means "cottonwood grove" and during its first lively days as a railroad camp on the Denver and Rio Grande the trees were used primarily as departure platforms for the town's plentiful supply of bad guys who required hanging. The town was brought in on flatcars from the old terminal in Fort Garland, with all the wooden structures that once stood there simply loaded up and re-erected among the cottonwoods. One of the old engines and depots of the rail line are exhibited in Cole Park, at 4th Street and the river. Just east of town and south of the road is the Alamosa/Monte Vista National Wildlife Refuge, which offers fine views of bald eagles, whooping cranes, and many species of migratory fowl. There are two walking tours through the area as well as a viewing tower.

The surrounding area is rich in lettuce and potato farms, the red McClure variety of the latter crop being the top shipment out of Monte Vista. The state's oldest professional rodeo, the Sky-Hi Stampede, is held during the last week of July and the bringing in of the crops in October is the occasion for a Harvest Festival.

The highway follows the Rio Grande towards the valley's western extremity. In **Del Norte**, the Rio Grande County Museum has displays on life in the area. A few blocks away, on Spruce Street, the old Barlow–Sanderson Stage station has been preserved.

At South Fork, U.S. 160 turns away from the river and into the Rio Grande National Forest, beginning its ascent to Wolf Creek Pass. This is the most scenic portion of the drive, a dazzling crossing of the Continental Divide at the 10,850-foot level. The area is known for the length of its winter season and Wolf Creek ski area averages more snowfall than any other resort in Colorado: 465 inches each season. It is also known as one of the state's top fall foliage drives, with memorable views of September aspens. The road was built in 1916 and was one of the great early highway-building achievements in the state. Wolf Creek Pass is another of those places associated with legendary treasures, just as the Spanish Peaks are to the east. Treasure Mountain, to the east of the summit, got its name through tales of a buried trove of gold bullion, hidden by Spanish miners in the 18th century. Like 99 percent of such caches, it has never been found.

The Divide marks the eastern boundary of San Juan National Forest. Soon the highway picks up the river of the same name and runs alongside it into **Pagosa Springs**. The springs are still issuing their 153-degree waters, believed to be the hottest in the world, and their geothermal energy is now used to heat many of the town's buildings. They were so prized for their healing qualities that the place became a source of conflict between the Utes and Navajo. According to one account, leaders agreed to avoid bloodshed by having the matter settled by a clash of two tribal champions, much like a medieval tournament. The Utes picked an aide to Kit Carson, Lieutenant Colonel Albert Pfeiffer, who brought down his opponent with a throw of his Bowie knife. Those were tough men, but then you had to be able to withstand the local springs' 153-degree temperatures.

Some of our earliest childhood images of the West were shaped by one of this area's longtime residents, Fred Harman. He drew the nationally syndicated comic strip, "Red Ryder," and its brilliantly colored landscape panels spread the beauty of southwestern Colorado across the pages of hundreds of Sunday newspapers. Many of his original paintings are displayed at the Fred Harman Art Museum, just west of town, along with a collection of personal mementos.

To the north of Pagosa Springs are the wilderness areas of San Juan National Forest, almost untouched and accessible only by foot or on horseback. Outfitters in town have information on trips into these remote areas, but they are a bit beyond the scope of this book. We'll be content to gaze at them from a distance on the highway.

At Chimney Rock is a turnoff to ruins of the Anasazi People. The canyon setting, with sheer 1,200-foot-high walls, make this a unique place, but as far as historic importance goes, the big attraction is just a few more miles ahead at Mesa Verde.

The road crosses the Piedra River, Spanish for "rock," and emerges from the National Forest to bustle into Durango. This town is a gateway to some of the greatest sightseeing and ski country in the Southwest, with scenic drives and railroad trips branching off in every direction. More than that, Durango is an especially flavorful place with two distinct historic districts that preserve its wealth of Victorian buildings. The place grew up after 1880 as a Denver and Rio Grande Railroad town and as you walk through its core you'll think that time came to a halt here shortly after that date. Many of Colorado's mining towns have managed to retain that sort of ambience, but Durango is a good-sized community of about 13,000 residents. Main Avenue here offers one of the most delightful promenades in the state. The Strater and General Palmer Hotels, built between 1887 and 1890, are among Colorado's oldest inns and both have been restored to the full glow of their prime years. The Strater also offers summer theater in its atmospheric Diamond Circle Theatre.

The town is the point of departure for narrow-gauge rail trips along the Durango and Silverton line (which will be discussed more fully in the chapter on U.S. 550). The depot on Main Avenue is an attraction in itself and the Palace Grill, next door, is another of the town's Victorian gems. Walking maps of the historic districts can be picked up at the Chamber of Commerce, at 111 South Camino Del Rio.

The La Plata Mountains, with their lodes of silver, rise to the north as the road continues west. We have now entered the high desert, and sage country stretches away to the northwest. Jog north for a few miles to the Jackson Reservoir, on the Mancos River, with its lovely backdrop centered by Hesperus Mountain (13,225 feet high) to the east.

FOCUS

The great Philadelphia Centennial Exposition of 1876 was a show-case for America's advancing technology. Steam engines, telephones, and electrical marvels captivated the public and sent a thrill of achievement across the country. But for a few days, a group of photographs and clay models stole the show. They were the work of Western photographer William Henry Jackson and they showed recently discovered Indian cave dwellings in Colorado.

That was the American public's introduction to Mesa Verde, which has since become the symbol of all such cliff dwellings in the Southwest, and one of the signature sights of this part of the country. But most people were getting their first astonished look at them through Jackson's photos, and even then just a tiny percentage of the mesa's treasures were known.

They were discovered in 1859 by Captain J. N. Macomb, who was conducting a geologic survey of the area (although subsequent historical research indicates that a Spanish priest may have written an account of the ruins as far back as 1776). Jackson visited the cliff ruins two years before the Exposition and made his studies and models of Two Story House, which he concluded had been built in the 12th century.

He was probably very close to the mark. More sophisticated research indicates that the first crude habitations were built on the mesa about 2,000 years ago. The inhabitants reached their peak of complexity and skill in the 13th century, building whole communities out of the rock walls. The fantastic monuments, which have been described as "hanging cities," were being built just as the occupants were abandoning the site. It must have been an incredible chapter in the history of these people, almost as if they were determined to leave as much as possible of themselves behind before they departed Mesa Verde forever.

It is only dimly understood why this place, as well as so many other pueblo communities in the Southwest, was abandoned around 1300. There was widespread drought at the time, but not as severe as others that have turned up in tree ring studies of previous eras. There was also pressure from hostile raiders, new and less settled peoples moving into the area. But that had also occurred before. Apparently, the combination was too much to overcome and entire pueblo communities decided to pick up and leave, seeking safer and more fertile territory to the south. Eventually, there must have become something of a panic. We are left with the image of builders feverishly erecting ever more elaborate edifices for people who were making their way out through the back door.

The in-depth exploration of Mesa Verde didn't really get started until 1886. The elevated tableland on which the dwellings are located rises to the south of U.S. 160, with a turnoff eight miles west of Mancos. As the Spanish name indicates, Mesa Verde is green, being covered with vegetation. The area was used as grazing country on a ranch owned by the Wetherhill family, five brothers of Quaker background. They had come upon many of the ruins on roundups and that excited the curiousity of Richard Wetherhill, who had a lively amateur interest in archeology. On an exploring trip to the more remote canyons, he discovered Balcony House, the most impressive ruin yet found. And in 1888, with his cousin, Charles Mason, he came upon the Cliff Palace, tucked into its cave-mouth hideaway. With more than 200 rooms, it is the largest of the structures in Mesa Verde. Its size and setting make it one of the most powerful and enduring images in North America, a place where people speak in whispers and feel the unseen presence of the past.

Wetherhill continued his explorations for years and was the first man in this century to see most of the major ruins. Writer C.W. Ceram tells the story of two scientists who came upon a ruin in

one of the mesa's more inaccessible canyons. Congratulating themselves on an important find, they scrambled to reach it, only to
find a slab of stone on which was written: "'What fools these mor-
tals be.' R. Wetherhill." Wetherhill later assisted Baron Gustavus
Nordenskiold, a Swedish archeologist who conducted the first systematic investigation of the area. The most recently opened archeological area in the park, to which the public was first admitted in
1972, is called Wetherhill Mesa.

Other ranchers were not as scrupulous about protecting the
ruins, however, and many scavenged them for articles to sell. Since
much of the land was on the Ute Reservation, it was up to
Congress to protect it, but mining interests managed to block any
legislation for 15 years. Finally, in 1906, Mesa Verde became a
national park, with the Utes trading their rights here for other
lands. The boundaries have been changed five times since in an
effort to bring more recently discovered ruins into the park.

Roads loop around to the more familiar ruins, including Cliff
Palace and Balcony House, the fortress-like structure that can only
be entered by ladders. These are the two can't-miss sights in the
park. There is a visitor center 16 miles south of the park entrance
and a museum five miles beyond that. Both should be seen for a
fuller understanding of what lies ahead. Most of the major ruins
can be entered only when rangers are on duty, generally from
early June through September. Spruce Tree, the best preserved of
the major ruins in the park, and Far View, near the visitor center,
are open for self-guided trips all year. Access to Wetherhill Mesa is
only by bus tours leaving from the visitor center.

＊ ＊ ＊

Back on Highway 160, the road follows the Dolores River Valley
into the town of **Cortez**. This is the center for tours to the wealth of
archeological sites in this area, including Hovenweep National

Monument and the Lowry Ruins (see U.S. 666) to the north. The University of Colorado operates an information center in town, with displays of Indian crafts, as well as storytellers and traditional dancers. Check locally for the schedule of events. Cortez has also become a bustling oil town, with development of the Aneth fields to the west.

The road swings sharply to the south, running with U.S. 666, and enters the Ute Mountain Reservation. Tours to lesser-known and exceptionally well-preserved Anasazi ruins leave from reservation headquarters, at **Towaoc**, just west of the highway. This is also the site of Ute Mountain Pottery, where tribal artisans craft ceramics using the patterns and methods of their ancestors of a millenium ago.

Turning west once more, the road leaves Highway 666 and parallels the Mancos River across the reservation to the border. Which border? A fair question, and the answer is unique in the entire country. We're now at Four Corners, the only place in America at which four states meet. Most travelers stop here and perform a little ritual. Climbing four steps to a concrete platform, they contrive to place parts of their body in each of the four corners marked off on the dais. Some crouch in crablike poses, others appear to be playing some variation of Twister. Others simply run around each quadrant of the little circle as fast as they can go, passing through four states in less than a second. The cream of the jest, however, is that this is not really the Four Corners. As an adjacent sign indicates, the actual place of meeting is off the road, about a quarter mile away.

Arguments about the location have been going on since 1868, when E.M. Darling brought a survey team here to mark the 103rd meridian, the border between Colorado and Utah. In this open desert country, there are no natural boundaries to separate state from state as in other parts of America, so borders were designated by lines on maps. Seven years later, however, when another survey team arrived on the site to fix the Arizona–New Mexico border, they found that Darling had missed by a few hundred feet. Later surveyors claimed that this team was off, too, and the border kept shifting every few years with each new survey. Finally, in 1931, the U.S. General Land Office built the little platform here and said: "That's it."

Further complicating the concept is that these are really not the borders of four states, at all. The entire property is on Indian land, with the Navajos having title to the Utah, Arizona and New Mexico portions, while the Utes own the Colorado corner. The two tribes don't agree on the boundaries of their lands, either—the Utes claim that they are being gypped out of about 100 yards of New Mexico that should rightfully be theirs. Oh, never mind.

U.S. 160 enters Arizona and for the rest of its course will cross the sprawling Navajo Reservation, a 25,000-square mile tract that runs across three states. Between this point and the junction with U.S. 163, near Kayenta, no paved road existed until after World War II. This is mesa country, with only an occasional small settlement or a Navajo shepherd breaking the quiet immensity of the land. The Carrizo Mountains, dominated by 9,412-foot-high Pastora Peak, are just south of Teec Nos Pos, the first settlement in Arizona. Past the intersection with U.S. 191, at Mexican Water, the road parallels Comb Ridge, running to the north, almost to Kayenta. U.S. 163 is the road to Monument Valley and is covered in the next chapter.

Black Mesa now rises to the south, as the road crosses Marsh Pass. A turnoff north leads to **Navajo National Monument**. The 13th-century Anasazi ruins here are in magnificent, rugged country. But the hike to Betatakin, a 130-room dwelling that is the most accessible of them, involves a fairly strenuous climb and can only accommodate 24 visitors at a time. Unless you are in fairly good physical condition, you should probably be content with viewing them from Betatakin Point, which involves only a half-mile walk.

The visitors center also does a fine job of explaining the area's significance and displaying artifacts from the ruins.

Highway 160 enters the Kletha Valley, passing the tan sandstone formation known as Elephant Feet. Just past Red Lake, the road clips a tiny corner of the Hopi Reservation, which is entirely surrounded by the Navajo lands. The bulk of Hopi territory, which contains mesa-top villages that are among the oldest continuously inhabited places on the continent, lie to the southeast, a bit beyond the scope of the old roads. Moenkopi was originally a Hopi settlement, and was once the largest of their towns. But a religious split in 1907 broke it apart, and eventually, it came to be dominated by its larger neighbor to the north, Tuba City, and became part of the Navajo lands.

The town is not named for the musical instrument, but rather was the result of the Anglo mispronunciation of the name of a local tribal leader, Tuve. Jacob Hamblin, a Mormon trader, established a post here in 1877, and several of the stone structures he put up still stand. It is also the western headquarters of the reservation. There are many crafts shops in town and the Western Navajo Fair takes place here in September.

Just west of Tuba City you can make out dinosaur tracks in the sandstone along the road. It's only a few more miles to the highway's end, at the junction with U.S. 89, so these prehistoric footprints make a good place to end our track.

VISITING HOURS

COLORADO

Alamosa: Alamosa National Wildlife Refuge, (719) 589-4021. East of town, south of U.S. 160. Daily, daylight hours. Free.

Cortez: University of Colorado Information Center, (303) 565-1151.

Call for schedule of Native Peoples events in the area.

Del Norte: Rio Grande County Museum, (719) 697-2847. One block south of U.S. 160, at 580 Oak St. Daily, 10–5, June–August; 11–4 at other times. Closed January. Admission.

Fort Garland: Museum, (719) 379-3512. On U.S. 160 at Colorado 159. Monday–Saturday, 10–5 and Sunday, 1–5, Memorial Day–Labor Day. Admission.

La Veta: Fort Francisco, (719) 742-3474. South of U.S. 160, on Colorado 12. Daily, 9–5, Memorial Day–mid-September. Admission.

Mesa Verde National Park: (303) 529-4465. South of U.S. 160 on park road. Many of the largest ruins are closed during the winter months. Chapin Mesa Visitor Center: Daily, 8–6:30, April–October; 8–5 at other times. Far View Visitor Center: Daily, 8–5, Memorial Day–Labor Day. Admission.

Pagosa Springs: Fred Harman Art Museum, (303) 731-5785. West, on U.S. 160. Daily, 10–4, Memorial Day–early October. Donation.

Towaoc: Ute Mountain reservation, (303) 565-8548. South of Cortez, on U.S. 160. Call for schedule of tours and events.

Trinidad: Pioneer Museum and Baca House, (719) 846-7217. Center, on Main St. Monday–Saturday, 10–4, and Sunday, 1–4, Memorial Day–Labor Day, Admission.

Arthur Roy Mitchell Museum, (719) 846-4224. At 150 W. Main St. Monday–Saturday, 10–4, mid-April–September. Donation.

Walsenburg: Old Courthouse and Jail, (719) 738-1740. At 400 Main St. Monday–Friday, 8–4. Free.

ARIZONA

Navajo National Monument: (602) 672-2366. North of U.S. 160, on Arizona 564. Call for information on tours. Free.

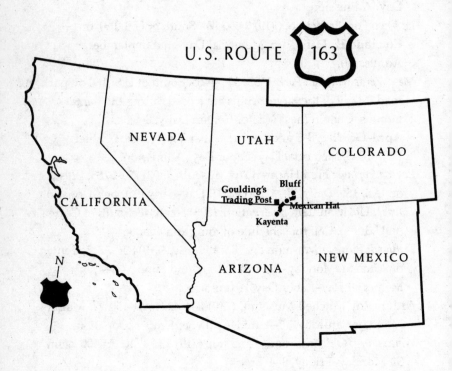

U.S. ROUTE 163

NEVADA

UTAH

COLORADO

CALIFORNIA

Goulding's
Trading Post   Bluff

Mexican Hat

Kayenta

ARIZONA

NEW MEXICO

N

John Ford Country

⬡

U.S. 163

Bluff, Utah to Kayenta, Ariz.
71 miles

This road is over almost before it starts. But it is the main route through Monument Valley and that alone assures it a place among the great highways of the Southwest.

It didn't become part of the federal highway system until well after World War II and even today there are only three places that could roughly be described as towns lying along its path. It remains a road to some of America's loneliest and most majestic landscapes, through scenery that defines our mental image of the Southwest.

MILEPOSTS

The road begins at the junction with U.S. 191 in Bluff. While the number changes, U.S. 163 is, in reality, a continuation of that highway. The topography along its length is a fulfillment of the magnificent Utah landscape that preceded it along Route 191. So why did the feds think it was necessary to make a number switch? Well, Highway 191 runs more-or-less north-south, while this road angles sharply to the southwest. So it was felt that a new numerical designation was required. It makes about as much sense as most decisions made in Washington.

Bluff is a testament to the power of faith over geography. The Mormon Church, enthused over the explorations of Jacob Hamblin along the San Juan River in 1879, directed that this remote region, in the furthest corner of Utah, be settled. So pioneer parties set out from Panguitch in December and headed directly west to reach this area. That can't be done. Or, at least, it is extraordinarily difficult. Even today, with all our engineering skill, no road runs directly across this country. A party of 200 set out and after four months of incredible hardship and a crossing of the Colorado River at Glen Canyon they reached this site on the San Juan. Too exhausted to go any further, they founded their settlement here, in the shadow of the rock formation known as the Navajo Twins.

For the next 20 years, this was the end of the road. Not even a trail was cut through south of this point until 1900. Paiute raiders were a threat to cattle ranchers as late as 1923, when the tribal leader, Old Posey, died of wounds after a jailbreak. Bluff's current population of 120 is less than the original party of settlers, but it functions as a tourist stop and the northern gateway to Monument Valley. There is a fascinating Pioneer Cemetery here and the Pioneer House, built in 1898, is one of the oldest residences along the San Juan. Watch also for St. Christopher's Episcopal Mission, perched amid the red sandstone rocks, with a great view across the river valley.

The road climbs Comb Ridge, named for its serrated edges. Look for the turnoff to Goosenecks State Park. This is an overlook across an incredibly convoluted stretch of the San Juan. The river twists around for almost six miles to advance one mile ahead in a straight line. The lookout point atop the cliffs enables you to survey the river's progress, as it thrashes back on itself like a snake in torment. The first exploration of this area was done by boat and the view over the Goosenecks gives you some idea of what a slow proposition that must have been.

Back on the main highway, you can see the rock formation after which the town of Mexican Hat is named. It looks like an upside-down sombrero, about 400 feet high, with the brim 62 feet across. The village was the center of both oil and uranium booms, but tourism is the economic staple now. There is a very sad story about the San Juan crossing at this point. A prospector named James Douglas found gold on a sand bar here in 1909. Almost immediately afterwards, the river rose and the bar was flooded. Douglas staked the place out year after year as he waited for the water to recede. Finally, after 20 years of frustration, he jumped to his death from the bridge here. In 1934 the river did go down, but no one knew where Douglas's claim was located. Douglas Mesa, to the west, was named for him, as a gesture of sympathy.

The Navajo Reservation begins on the far side of the river. No road came through here until 1921. There is a turnoff at Redlands for a view into the area ahead, which is the beginning of Monument Valley.

This was one of the most isolated corners of the United States when movie director John Ford came here in 1938 to film his classic Western, *Stagecoach*. He returned time after time, captivated by the dramatic backdrops of these towering mesas and fantastically sculpted rocks. They were almost a silent chorus is his movies, commenting on the puny efforts of the human beings who lived out their small dramas in their shadows. One commentator wrote that "Monument Valley is to the Hollywood Western what Yankee Stadium is to baseball." The images in Ford's classic films shaped the American concept of how the West should look. Monument Valley is still an out-of-the-way sort of place, but most people experience a sense of déjà vu when they first come here, so deeply are its landscapes ingrained in their imaginations.

Goulding's is the site of a trading post, just on the Utah side of Monument Pass, and the entry station to Monument Valley Navajo Tribal Park. Guided tours of some of the less accessible parts of the Valley in four-wheel drive vehicles may be arranged here. There is a visitor center in the park itself, with information on self-guided tours, particularly to the Mystery Valley section, with its red buttes that tower 1,000 feet above the desert floor. This area is simply unforgettable at sunset or sunrise and every effort should be made to get there at either time to watch the colors change on the rocks. It may be the closest thing we can experience to the dawn of creation.

The Mittens stand athwart Monument Pass, with one of the rocks in Utah and the other in Arizona. Just to the west, across the state line, is Boot Mesa and a little further along you'll pass Owl Rock. To the east is Agathla Peak, the 6,098-foot high volcanic formation around which much of *Stagecoach* was shot. This is also where Hoskinini escaped with his followers in 1864 when Kit Carson rounded up the Navajo at Canyon de Chelly (see U.S. 191) and transported them to New Mexico. His band went on tending their sheep here in isolation until his death in 1909, long after the rest of the tribe was allowed to return to their homes.

The highway runs through Kayenta, by far the largest town on the route with a population of over 3,000 and the commercial center for the Monument Valley area. The road ends just a mile past the town, at the junction with U.S. 160. Not much of a drive, but the most memorable 71 miles you're ever likely to travel.

VISITING HOURS

UTAH

Goulding's: Monument Valley Navajo Tribal Park, (801) 727-3287.
East from U.S. 163 on reservation road. Daily, 7 A.M.–8 P.M.,
mid-March–September; 8–5 at other times. Admission.

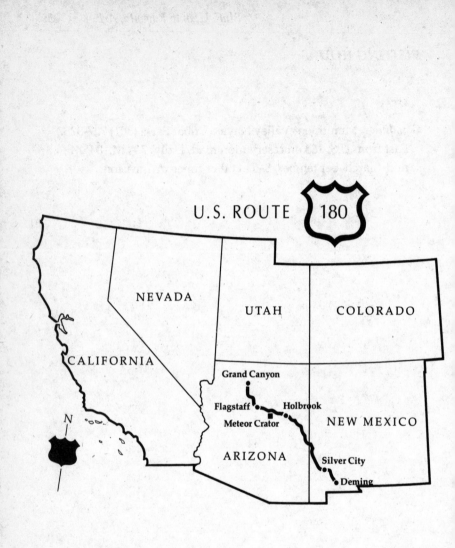

U.S. ROUTE 180

NEVADA

UTAH

COLORADO

CALIFORNIA

Grand Canyon

Flagstaff   Holbrook

Meteor Crator

NEW MEXICO

ARIZONA

Silver City

Deming

N

To the Edge of Creation

◯

U.S. 180

Deming, N.M. to Grand Canyon, Ariz.
455 miles

This old road bobs and weaves through the Southwest like an after-hours reveler trying to figure out the shortest way home. It starts just west of Fort Worth, Texas and first enters our turf in the southeastern corner of New Mexico as a four-lane highway. Then it ducks back into Texas and heads for El Paso before reappearing in New Mexico as part of northbound Interstate 10.

It finally leaves the fast lane at **Deming.** That's where we pick up U.S. 180 for the last leg of its run; due northwest, through some breathtaking high mountain scenery in New Mexico and Arizona, on a dead course for the country's most celebrated hole in the ground.

MILEPOSTS

The highway wriggles free from the Interstate at Deming for the first time since re-entering New Mexico and heads north into the Mimbres Valley. The Mimbres People occupied this area for about 450 years, disappearing sometime in the 12th century. The pottery they left behind, with its exquisitely painted geometric designs, is ranked among the highest artistic achievements of the Southwest. (The chapter on U.S. 70 has information on Deming's Luna Mimbres Museum, which displays a good sampling of this work. If you don't care to stop there, an even better opportunity lies a few miles ahead of us, in **Silver City**.)

Off to the east is Cook's Peak, standing in isolation at 8,408 feet. The mountain was a famous landmark on the old Butterfield Stage Road, now paralleled by Interstate 10. The Spanish called it the Peak of the Mimbres and it was a familiar landmark for them, too. Over this road, the output of the copper mines for which we are headed was hauled back to Mexico 200 years ago. There is a fine viewpoint of the peak and surrounding territory near the intersection with eastbound New Mexico 61.

Follow this state road past the old resort of Faywood Hot Springs, once the spring training home of baseball's Chicago White Stockings in the late 19th century. Just beyond the resort is City of Rocks State Park. Volcanic ash has been twisted into fantastic shapes here by the wind, forming what appears to be the outline of an urban skyline when viewed from a distance. No one has been able to fix the location of the prehistoric volcano that threw off such an impressive display. According to some theories, it was located near Albuquerque, almost 200 miles to the northeast. The reddish rocks tumble across the desert floor as if placed by an urban planner seeking an advanced degree in arranging mass.

Double back to U.S. 180 and head north. Near the marked turnoff to the airport, south of Hurley, was the site of Fort McLane, established in 1861 during the campaign against the Apaches led by Mangas Coloradas. The mentor of Cochise, this leader raided the district constantly during the Civil War years. Finally captured and brought to the fort, he was killed on January 17, 1863. The official report said he was trying to escape; other witnesses said he was goaded into resistance by being poked with bayonets, then shot down.

Hurley is the mill town for the **Santa Rita** copper mines just ahead of us. The oxygen-fired smelter was installed here in 1984 and is connected by pipeline to the open pit mine, 14 miles to the northeast. It is one of the most advanced set-ups in the industry. The mine itself is reached by turning right on New Mexico 356 and following it through Bayard to New Mexico 152.

The Santa Rita was discovered by Lieutenant Colonel Manuel Carrisco, commander of the Spanish military posts in the area, and has been worked since 1800, making it the oldest active mine in the Southwest. In the whole country, only some mines in Michigan's Upper Peninsula have been worked longer.

The Santa Rita became a penal colony and copper was sent back to Mexico along the road we have just traveled, there to be made into the national coinage. The mine later passed into private hands and by the time of the first American exploration into this country it was already famous for its production. But its remote location and the constant threat of raids by Mangas Coloradas and Cochise prevented any expansion until 1873. Martin B. Hayes then acquired the site, centered around the Chino mine, which proved to be the richest. By 1904, it had passed through several owners, including the Hearst family estate, and was thought to be played out. But surveys indicated that operation as an open pit mine could extend its productive life and in 1909 the Chino Copper Co. began to dig. The pit is now the third largest in the world, 1,000 feet deep and almost two miles across. The mining town of Santa Rita, which once occupied the adjacent area, has been almost completely consumed. There is a viewpoint at the edge of the pit, with the rock formation of the Kneeling Nun in the background. The name comes from an old story about a nun in love with a Spanish soldier who was turned to stone as she prayed. That was her story and she's sticking to it. An adjacent museum shows off exhibits on the history of the Santa Rita area and antique mining equipment.

Now head west on Highway 152. You'll pass Fort Bayard, an outpost of the 9th U.S. Cavalry, the all-black unit that was known as the "Buffalo Soldiers." The fort was decommissioned in 1899 and used as an Army tuberculosis sanitarium and a hospital for elderly handicapped patients, but many of the old fort buildings still stand.

We rejoin U.S. 180 and continue into Silver City, one of the west's great mining camps, and also one that made the transition to permanent community better than most of the others. Although surrounded by mining activity, the future site of Silver City was still a marshy meadow in 1870. When silver was found near the town of Shakespeare (see U.S. 70) a bunch of locals went down to investigate. "Boys," said one of them, "if that's what silver looks like, we better get back home. Because we've got lots of it." So they did. Within a year, Silver City had become a boomtown. Despite constant Apache raids, which were especially heavy along what is now U.S. 180 between Fort Bayard and the town, the lure of riches was stronger than the fear of Cochise. Unlike other mining camps, though, the early residents of Silver City had visions of permanence. They set up a brick plant, incorporated under the first town charter in the territory, established a model school system, and brought in electricity only two years after New York City. So when the silver boom died in 1893, Silver City was in position to survive—as a ranching town, health resort, and educational center.

One of its more spectacular transformations occurred in 1895 when a massive flood struck the town and turned the chief business artery, Main Street, with all its homes and stores, into a 35-foot-deep ditch. The Civilian Conservations Corps turned it into a park in 1935 and the Big Ditch is now a civic asset near the heart of town, just south of the highway.

A few blocks west, on Broadway, is the Silver City Museum. Once the mansion of Henry B. Ailman, who turned a silver strike into a banking fortune, the museum has excellent displays on local history and the nearby company town of Tyrone. This was a Mediterranean-style model village, created by Phelps Dodge to house miners in 1915, which closed only six years later when the mines gave out. It later operated as a dude ranch, but when an open pit mine was dug on the site in the 1960s, Tyrone disappeared. Another town of the same name now stands a few miles away.

On the western edge of downtown is Western New Mexico University, established in 1893 as the first teacher's college in the state and a foundation of Silver City's ongoing existence. Fleming

Hall houses the school museum, with the world's largest collection of Mimbres pottery and other artifacts of Southwestern cultures.

Silver City was also the boyhood home of Billy the Kid and it is here that he acquired many of his endearing habits. He pulled his first robbery here and escaped from his first jail, although local historians indignantly deny that he also killed his first man. That happened across the border in Arizona and Silver City could hardly be held responsible for that. The site of the cabin in which he lived is marked on the eastern edge of the Big Ditch. So is the former jail, on North Hudson, which he fled by climbing up the chimney.

The road turns north as it leaves town and heads into the wild country of the Mogollon Mountains and Gila National Forest. It was to this area that a young naturalist named Aldo Leopold came early in this century as a federal forest administrator. Conservation theory then held that wise maintenance of resources could enhance commercial use of the land while protecting the public's recreational interests as well. Based on what he observed here, though, Leopold began to campaign for the establishment of wilderness areas, in which there would be no manmade intrusion whatsoever. The Gila Wilderness Area, created in 1924, was the first in the country and a turning point in federal conservation policies. Leopold's *Sand County Almanac*, published in 1949 (one year after his death), has become one of the basic texts in the cause of wilderness protection. As the road enters the national forest, just past the town of Buckhorn, the Leopold Vista overlooks the wilderness he championed.

When you reach Glenwood, watch for the unnumbered road heading east to Whitewater Canyon. It ends five miles in, at The Catwalk. This metal pipeline was once used to supply gravity-propelled water to nearby mining camps but in the 1930s it was turned into a walkway through the canyon. It now is a safe and spectacular foot trail above the churning waters of the canyon, which is only 20 feet wide at some points. The walk leads to several grassy slopes where you can relax and take in the view.

Double back to U.S. 180 and continue on to Alma. You'll pass the tomb of James C. Cooney, who discovered gold in this area while on patrol as a sergeant based at Fort Bayard. He kept his secret until his enlistment expired and he could return as a civilian. He staked several claims in the area, which became known as the Cooney Mining District, but was killed by Apaches in 1880 while working one of his strikes. Butch Cassidy and some of his associates reputedly hid out from the law here by working as cowhands under assumed names at the WS Ranch, which is still in operation on the land adjacent to the road.

Now watch for eastbound New Mexico 159, the road to **Mogollon**. Once the richest mining town in the Cooney District, Mogollon is spectacularly situated within a canyon. The location is one reason why it didn't crumble to ruin after the gold gave out during World War I. While it is almost deserted in winter, it is a lively art colony during the summer months, with galleries and theater groups occupying its picturesque weathered buildings. There are also tours of the abandoned Little Fanney Mine. The town is nine miles in from U.S. 180 on narrow, winding road, a moderately difficult drive but not dangerous in good weather.

Back on U.S. 180, we continue into Saliz Pass, through increasingly rugged country, above the San Francisco River. While not as remote as the moon, we do pass through Luna. The town was named, however, for Solomon Luna, an early sheep rancher in the area.

The highway crosses into Arizona, with Luna Lake, part of Apache–Sitgreaves National Forest, on the north. This is an area that plays against type on the Arizona travel posters. High in the White Mountains, surrounded by forests of aspen and pine, the landscape here looks more like Colorado and is developing as a summer resort for Arizonians escaping the heat of the desert. Alpine, perched at an altitude of 8,030 feet, was originally called Bush Valley, after the first settler, who showed up in 1876. But later inhabitants felt the unusual Arizona ambience demanded a more descriptive name. It still observes Bush Valley Pioneer Days, though, with a Memorial Day weekend bash.

The road joins U.S. 666 here for the northern portion of the Coronado Trail (see the chapter on that road for a more detailed discussion). We turn due north, with the wilderness area surrounding 10,955-foot-high Escudilla Mountain on the east. The formation resembling a bowl near its top gave the peak its Spanish name. Nutrioso, in turn, was named for the profusion of beavers explorers found in the area.

The highway passes through Springerville (see U.S. 60) and, still heading north, runs parallel to the Little Colorado River. The route carved by this stream is followed by U.S. 180 for much of the remainder of the trip. Lyman Lake is formed by a dam on the Little Colorado, the third one on the site. The first two, built by Mormon pioneers, were washed away by floods in 1903 and 1915. A state park surrounds the reservoir, which has been developed as a major recreational facility.

St. Johns grew up as a Mexican community at a ford on the Little Colorado and was first called *El Vadito*, or "little river crossing." But when pioneer Sol Barth established a sheep ranch here with winnings from a card game, he magnanimously changed the name to honor the family of the first woman resident. Well, actually, her name was San Juan, but it's close. This was great country for high-stakes card games, by the way. The nearby town of Show Low (see U.S. 60) got its name from a game in which the winner of a ranch pulled the low card.

St. Johns shows the influence of its Mormon roots, with wide, poplar-lined streets. It grew up after 1880 with settlers from Utah brought here by the Udall family, who went on to prominence in Arizona politics. A small local facility, the Apache County Museum, recounts the stories of its pioneer days and early residents.

Now we take our leave of U.S. 666 and strike out to the northwest, crossing the Little Colorado once more and then the Milky

Wash. Just across the Navajo County line is the turnoff to **Petrified Forest National Park.**

Many felled forests of stone had been discovered by trappers and explorers in the west by the time Lieutenant A. W. Whipple reached this area in 1853 and reported in astonishment that "trees have been converted to jasper." Tales of petrified lands had become a staple of mountain man lore. As early as 1830, Jim Bridger reported on his trip to the Yellowstone area, saying that he had found birds petrified in mid-flight and "the sun and the moon shine with petrified light." In one variation of the story, a horse and rider wander off the side of the cliff, only to reach the far side safely because gravity had been petrified, too.

Geologists, much later, surmised that these mysterious areas had been valleys some 200 million years ago and logs carried there by mountain streams were buried by silt. Slowly, minerals in the ground water seeped into the trunks and replaced the wood cells with silica. Stains of iron oxide provided the colors. When the Rocky Mountains were formed, this entire region was uplifted, and the ancient logs rose to the surface.

The Arizona forest is the largest in the West and the national park preserves five separate tracts. They have been protected since 1906, after a half-century of steady pilferage by souvenir hunters. Rainbow Forest Museum just inside the south entrance, off U.S. 180, has excellent displays on the varieties of wood found in the park and a lucid explanation of how the wood formed. The park road then runs north for 21 miles, through most of the park's main attractions, including the Agate Bridge, the petroglyphs on Newspaper Rock, and the ruined pueblos of the Anasazi people who lived in this stone land for almost 1,000 years. The road also loops up for an overview of the Painted Desert, an area of brilliantly colored rock formations permeated by minerals, each giving a distinctive hue, which change constantly depending upon the angle of the sunlight.

From here, get on westbound Interstate 40. At **Holbrook,** 25 miles away, U.S. 180 joins this Interstate and runs with it all the way to **Flagstaff**. This is the route of old U.S. 66, the chief casualty of the Interstate system. Before that, it was the route of the Santa Fe Railroad. Holbrook was, in fact, named for the chief engineer of the company when the line came through in 1881. And before that it was part of the Beale Wagon Road, the pioneer route from Santa Fe to California.

Holbrook became the chief supply point for the vast Navajo and Apache reservations. It also was the shipping point for the Aztec Cattle Co., usually referred to as the Hashknife outfit because of the shape of its brand. It was the third largest cattle ranch in the country in the 1880s and when its cowboys rode into town, most of Holbrook stayed indoors. Holbrook itself was reputed to be the toughest cattle town in the Southwest and the old Bucket of Blood Saloon, on the far side of the tracks on Southeast Central Avenue, is regarded as a proud reminder of those times. Another sanguine souvenir is the Blevins House, on the far side of the tracks, at 216 Northeast Central. On September 9, 1888, Sheriff Commodore Perry Owens paid a call to apprehend one of the Blevins brothers, who was wanted for murder in Texas. In the ensuing gunfight, the offending Blevins and three allies were shot. Owens, who had gone to the house alone, was hailed for restoring the rule of law to Holbrook. A more sedate piece of history is the Navajo County Courthouse, built in 1898, which now contains exhibits of local history and an especially well preserved jail cell. So it isn't entirely sedate. The Hashknife Sheriff's Posse still rides on special events, such as the Pony Express ride to Scottsdale each January and the Bucket of Blood Races in May.

The road runs with the Interstate for the next 87 miles. It's a pleasant enough drive. On clear days, the snowy heights of Humphreys Peak, tallest in the state at 12,643 feet, guards the western horizon. You dash past Joseph City, an old Mormon town named for the religion's founder, Joseph Smith. Next comes **Winslow**, another old Santa Fe rail town, founded one year after

Holbrook and named after the line's president.

Twenty miles past Winslow look for the turnoff to the south to Meteor Crater. One mile wide and 600 feet deep, it just shows what can happen when heavenly bodies pay a call. More properly, this should be called meteorite crater. It earns an extra three letters at the end of its name for surviving the blaze of friction when it entered the Earth's atmosphere and actually reached the surface. This does not happen very often with meteors and when you look at this massive hole you will be very grateful for that. Usually, they are observed in the summer months from a safe distance as shooting stars. This one made its breakthrough about 50,000 years ago and wiped out every living thing in a radius of 100 miles. It is such a well preserved and other-worldly place that astronauts were trained here for lunar landings. There is also a museum at the site.

Back on the Interstate, you'll note the turnoff to Canyon Diablo. Now just a name on a highway sign, the place was cursed by pioneers who had all kinds of problems crossing its 500-foot wide expanse on the old wagon road. It was also the site of a famous train robbery in 1889. The Santa Fe was especially vulnerable at this point because its trains had to slow for the canyon passage. Bucky O'Neill, one of the legendary lawmen on the Arizona frontier, picked up the bandits' trail and followed it 300 miles north to Canyonville, Utah, where he found them engaged in a gun battle with the local gentry. O'Neill's arrival turned the tide and he returned to Arizona with four prisoners.

Another turnoff worth making is **Walnut Canyon**, on the eastern edge of Flagstaff. This national monument preserves the cliff dwellings of Sinagua Indians, who inhabited the place for about 200 years, leaving because of drought in the mid-13th century. Built on ledges above the gorge, the ancient homes occupy a protected and scenic spot. Paved trails lead to the dwellings and along the canyon rim.

Backtracking to the Interstate, you can just continue right on into

Flagstaff on the surface road. It turns into Santa Fe Avenue, the city's main street, in a few miles, and heads through the middle of the business district, laid out opposite the railroad tracks. (The history of Flagstaff is discussed more fully in the U.S. 89 chapter.) Just past the center of town, U.S. 180 cuts away to the north as Humphreys St. and then becomes Fort Valley Road.

This highway passes Thorpe Park and enters the city's museum district. The Arizona Historical Society Pioneer Museum adjoins the Coconino Center for the Arts, and the two facilities put on a variety of exhibits during the year relating to local history and the performing and graphic arts. The Pioneer Museum also preserves several buildings important to Flagstaff's history. One mile beyond these two institutions is the Museum of Northern Arizona, with outstanding displays on the natural sciences of the region and the crafts of the Hopi and Navajo people. Its Indian crafts exhibits in July and August are among the best of their kind in the country.

Now the road enters its final leg, running towards the towering San Francisco Mountains, with Humphreys Peak straight ahead. This is Arizona's top skiing area and the Fairfield Snow Bowl operates its lifts during the summer months, too, so visitors can take in a remarkable vista of the surrounding peaks and the Grand Canyon. The mountain range was named by the Franciscans, who had established a mission in the 17th century at Oraibi, to the northeast, in what is now the Hopi Reservation. The Humphreys for whom the tallest point is named was the chief surveyor for the U.S. Army and came through this area seeking a transcontinental railroad route.

The highway winds on through Coconino National Forest, opening up on views of massive red buttes to the northeast. It clips a corner of the Kaibab National Forest and at the crossroads town of Valle turns due north for its final approach to one of the continent's truly awesome places.

FOCUS

Get up before dawn. Don't argue, it's for your own good. Your hotel can tell you where to go. Drive there, park your car and wait.

There are a few places on this globe where people huddle in the first faint glow of day to await the rising sun. They are places so charged with wonder that to witness the birth of the day there seems almost a recapitulation of the birth of time. The Grand Canyon is such a place. When the first rays of light strike the canyon wall, sending the dark stone shimmering into bands of vibrant color, it is like witnessing a reawakening of the world.

The Canyon is about time. The eons it took for a river to carve a miracle. Each layer of rock, each band of color tells the story of ages that have vanished, worlds that have flown. How old is it? The oldest rock, geologists say, is 2 billion years old. But what does that mean? The mind can't grasp it. And when you hear that the most recent stratum of rock represents 250 million years, how can it be comprehended? You stand at its edge and feel as if you're peering into the well of eternity.

Officially, U.S. 180 ends at the entrance to the national park. Beyond that point, it is simply a park road. But it is still the highway that runs to the rim.

There really is no warning, no indication of what lies ahead. You continue to drive along through pine forest and suddenly through a break in the trees, the world opens up in a burst of incandescence. What did the first explorers who came upon this vista make of it? Well, for the most part they were unimpressed. A party sent here by the Coronado expedition in 1540 reached the rim. Its leader, Garcia Lopez de Cardenas, looked the place over and returned to the main expedition to report that it held no interest.

More than 300 years later, attitudes had not changed much. Lieutenant Joseph Ives explored the area in 1857 for the U.S. Government and issued this much quoted summary of the

Canyon: "...After entering it there is nothing to do but leave. Ours has been the first and will doubtless be the last party of whites to visit this profitless locality."

It could not be farmed or mined. It was an obstacle rather than an opportunity. The only early visitor who felt any different was Fr. Francisco Tomas Garces who descended into the gorge in 1776 to minister to the souls of the Havasupai who lived there.

But in 1869 John Wesley Powell led one of the epic voyages of Western exploration down the Green and Colorado Rivers. His nine-man party became the first known travelers to pass through the length of the Canyon. A one-armed Civil War veteran who later became head of the U.S. Geological Survey, Powell made a second trip in 1871 and published his findings, complete with the first maps of the area.

The book brought the Canyon to the attention of Americans. Previously an obscure, dimly known, impossibly inaccessible place, the Canyon now became a goal of visitors to the West. The first known settlers arrived as prospectors and remained to open the tourist trade. By the 1880s, travelers on the Santa Fe line were boarding stagecoaches in Flagstaff and other nearby points for a half-day trek to the rim. The railroad extended a branch here in 1901 and four years later the El Tovar Hotel opened on the south rim. Reopened after a major renovation in 1991, the hotel, with its soaring beamed lobby, is a monument to a more leisurely era of tourism.

The area first came under federal protection as a national forest preserve in 1893 and was made a national park in 1919. It has become one of America's distinctive sights. Arizona is nicknamed for it. Ferde Grofe celebrated it in music and his "On the Trail" segment of *The Grand Canyon Suite*, simulating a mule ride to the Canyon floor, is one of the most quoted pieces in American music. But nothing will have prepared you for the actual sight of it.

For one thing, it keeps changing. You can stand in one point for an entire day and watch a kaleidoscopic panorama that blends color and shadow depending on the angle of the sun. There is an almost infinite number of ways to see the Canyon, too. Since we are dealing with car-based traveling, we'll stick to those that do not require a vigorous body. While the mule trips and hikes to the Canyon floor are wonderful, rangers do not recommend them for those whose most strenuous activity has been turning the ignition switch.

But, by all means, take a walk along the South Rim Nature Trail. This is a flat, three and a half mile walk that leads to excellent viewpoints and explains many of the Canyon's natural features. Also visit the Yavapai Museum near Grand Canyon Village for the best geological overview of the region. If you visit in the off season, between Labor Day and Memorial Day, you can take your car to the scenic places on the West Rim Drive, where you get the best views of the river. In season, however, only shuttle buses are allowed on this road because of heavy traffic. The East Rim Drive, however, is open all year and just as worthwhile. Drive out to the Tusayan Ruin, a small prehistoric pueblo and museum; and the Watchtower at Desert View, a splendid vantage point that extends back across the Canyon and into Navajo country to the east.

There is probably no more impressive ending to any old road than this.

* * *

VISITING HOURS

NEW MEXICO

Deming: City of Rocks State Park, (505) 536-2800. North of town and east of U.S. 180 on New Mexico 61. Daily, 7:30–dusk. Admission.

Mogollon: Tours of Little Fanny Mine, (505) 539-2481. East of U.S.

180, on New Mexico 159. Call for schedule.

Santa Rita: Mining Museum, (505) 537-3381. East of U.S. 180, on New Mexico 152. Tuesday–Sunday, 10–4, Memorial Day–Labor Day. Free.

Silver City: Museum, (505) 538-5921. At 312 W. Broadway. Tuesday–Friday, 9–4:30 and weekends, 10–4. Free.

Fleming Hall Museum, (505) 538-6386. On the campus of Western New Mexico University. Monday–Friday, 8–4:30 and Sunday, 1–4. Free.

ARIZONA

Flagstaff: Arizona Historical Society Pioneers Museum, (602) 774-6272. North on U.S. 180. Daily, 10–4. Free.

Museum of Northern Arizona, (602) 774-5211. North on U.S. 180. Daily, 9–5. Admission.

Fairfield Snow Bowl Chair Lift, (602) 779-6127. North, on U.S. 180. Daily, 10–4, Memorial Day–Labor Day; weekends, 10–4, through October. Fare.

Holbrook: Navajo County Courthouse, (602) 524-6558. At 100 E. Arizona St. Monday–Saturday, 9–4, May–September; closed Saturday at other times. Free.

Petrified Forest National Park: (602) 524-6228. North of U.S. 180 on park road. Daily, 7 A.M.–8 P.M., June–August; 8–6, May and September; 8–5 at other times. Admission.

St. Johns: Apache County Museum, (602) 337-4737. West, on U.S. 180. Monday–Friday, 1–5. Free.

Walnut Canyon National Monument: (602) 526-3367. Eastern edge of Flagstaff, south on park road from U.S. 180. Daily, 7–6, Memorial Day–Labor Day; 8–5 at other times. Admission.

Winslow: Meteor Crater and Museum, (602) 774-8350. West on U.S. 180, then south on county road. Daily, 6–6, mid-May–mid-September; 7–5 at other times. Closed mid-November–mid-March. Admission.

U.S. ROUTE 191

Vernal • Flaming Gorge Dam
Price •
Green River
Moab •
Blanding •
■ Canyon de Chelly
Ganado •

NEVADA

UTAH

COLORADO

CALIFORNIA

ARIZONA

NEW MEXICO

N

Arches, Canyons, and Awe

⬡

U.S. 191

Dutch John, Utah to Chambers, Ariz.
550 miles

A monumentally scenic old road, U.S. 191 originates up in Jackson, Wyoming, near the Grand Tetons, one of the most spectacular corners of the country. We pick U.S. 191 up at Flaming Gorge Reservoir and follow it through the heart of Utah's canyonlands, wild and remote country that was closed to automotive exploration for much of this century. The southeastern part of Utah is one of the least-known places in any state. For travelers who like to dodge crowds, the challenge here is to find one.

When it passes into Arizona, the highway becomes the main north-south artery through the vast Navajo Reservation.

MILEPOSTS

The best-known residents of Brown's Hole were probably Butch Cassidy and the Wild Bunch. They used this valley in extreme northeastern Utah as the base for their tours of the western banking system in the 1890s. In later years, however, rancher John Honslinger wintered his cattle herds here and it is for him that the town of **Dutch John** was named. There was no town here, however, until 1957 when it was built as the construction base for Flaming Gorge Dam on the Green River. This 502-foot-high concrete structure in the Flaming Gorge National Recreation Area formed a reservoir that runs for 91 miles and reaches across the Utah–Wyoming line. The dam itself is just south of town and there are several access points to the reservoir all around the Dutch John area. Maps and information on fishing and boating can be picked up at the visitors center, which is adjacent to the dam. This area is known for trophy trout and first-rate rafting trips on the Green below the dam. The Firefighters Memorial, dedicated to those who battle forest fires, is just south of town. The best view of the gorge is from an overlook just west on Utah 44 at Red Canyon, where some of the most intensely colored of the red rocks that gave the place its name can be seen. The overlook is situated 1,360 feet above the river.

Between the junction with Utah 44 and Vernal, Utah, U.S. 191 has been officially designated a Scenic Byway. Along this stretch, the road passes through Ashley National Forest on the eastern edge of the Uinta Mountains. The views of aspen in the autumn are particularly lovely on this drive. The Uinta is the only major range in the United States that runs east–west, one of the facts about this area that seems to fascinate geologists. Actually, this part of the country is virtually a textbook in geology. Some of the most significant landforms and fossil finds in all of North America can be found within a few miles. The road to Vernal is labeled "The Drive Through the Ages" and there are several stopping points at which levels of strata, billions of years old in some instances, are pointed out and explained with interpretive displays.

Vernal, which is Dinosaur Central, U.S.A., is discussed more fully in the chapter on U.S. 40. The two highways run west together for 57 miles, until Highway 191 breaks to the south at Duchesne. Here it becomes a Scenic Byway again, running through Indian Canyon on its way through the Uintah and Ouray Indian Reservation and crossing Castle Gate Pass in the Ashley National Forest, at 9,100 feet. The pass is generally closed by heavy snows in the winter months. Near the summit is the Avintaquin recreation area, with picnicking facilities.

Castle Gate, for which the pass is named, is a towering rock formation that stands at the head of the Price Valley, where this road joins U.S. 6. A coal mining town grew up at its base, but when Highway 191 was cut through in the 1940s, part of the big rock went with it. The town didn't fare too well, either. Butch Cassidy and his gang rode down this way from Brown's Hole and stuck up the mail train in 1897. A massive flood almost wiped the place out in 1917. Finally, in 1924, a horrific mine explosion killed 173 men. Castle Gate is barely a wide spot in the road today.

The highway enters Castle Valley and arrives in **Helper**, another coal town, which gets its name from the original "little engines that could." To haul the coal out of this area, loaded trains had to ascend Soldier Summit to the northwest of town (see U.S. 6). Extra engines were attached to help them make the grade. In railroad parlance these extra engines were known as "helpers." Many of the helpers were stored in the yards here and soon the entire community was known by that name. The Western Mining and Railroad Museum brings together artifacts from the era when Helper won its name.

Price is the commercial center of the coal region, with about 20 mines still operating in the immediate vicinity. But while coal rings the cash registers, the fossil of choice around here is the dinosaur. The Prehistoric Museum of the College of Eastern Utah is one of the best of its kind in the west, with exhibits of the eggs, tracks, and skeletons of the great lizards. Many of them were found at the Cleveland-Lloyd Dinosaur Quarry, 35 miles south of Price on an unpaved road. More complete skeletons have been removed from this area than any other site on the globe; since 1928, more than 12,000 bones have been uncovered here where animals were trapped in the muddy bottom of a prehistoric lake when they had come to drink. The museum also has an outstanding display of unbaked clay figurines of the Anasazi Indians, believed to be up to 900 years old.

The workers drawn to Price's mines give it a more multi-ethnic flavor than most small Utah cities. It was, especially, a center for Greek immigration. The Hellenic Orthodox Church, built in 1916, is a local landmark and one of the oldest of that denomination in the West. The town celebrates its Greek Festival Days on the second weekend in July.

Butch Cassidy was also attracted to the place, especially when he heard that he had been killed there. The outlaw turned up himself to view the remains that were mistakenly identified as his, and had the rare opportunity of attending his own funeral. A visiting marshal who knew Cassidy showed up to make the final identification, however, and the error was discovered before interment.

One of the best preserved murals of the WPA Art Program is also in Price. It was painted in the Municipal Building between 1938 and 1941 and depicts the history of Carbon County.

The road runs through Wellington, last mining town in the valley, and then heads out into open country. Past Cedar you can see the Book Cliffs, looking like a library shelf in stone, rising on the east. The road crosses the Price River, and to the west are the rugged pinnacles of the San Rafael Swell, an area of spectacular geological formations. There are magnificent views over the Swell from Cedar Mountain Recreation Area, west of the highway on a dirt road. But more of that sort of scenery lies ahead, much closer to our route.

Highway 191 joins Interstate 70 and runs east with it for 23 miles. On the way it passes Green River, one of the premier melon-growing centers in the country. The Melon Days festivities on the weekend after Labor Day are a big end-of-summer ritual. Summer gets off to a rolicking start, too, with the annual Friendship Cruise to Moab, Utah. A flotilla of craft makes the journey along the Green and Colorado Rivers each Memorial Day weekend through some of the finest rafting waters in the West. Green River is now a center for raft trips throughout the summer months; rafting was, in fact, the reason for the settlement of this town. The last community on the Green before its junction with the Colorado, Moab was known as the point of embarkation for the first explorations of the Grand Canyon by John Wesley Powell, in 1869 and 1871. His voyages came this way, after putting in miles to the north in Green River, Wyoming. The Powell River History Museum, overlooking the Green, tells the story of these voyages of exploration and the role they played in Utah's growth.

This would be a good time to regard your road map. As Highway 191 breaks away from the Interstate and heads south, look across southern Utah. Not another road in almost 200 miles parallels the route south to the Arizona border. U.S. 191 runs virtually alone through one of America's most magnificent corridors, a land of soaring red rock arches, yawning canyons, snow-capped peaks, and racing rivers. For the next 137 miles, between the Interstate and the town of Bluff, this is a drive to savor.

The La Sal Mountains, named by Spanish explorers for salt deposits in the area, rise to the southeast, their 12,000-foot-high elevation accentuated by the flatness of the surrounding plain. We are on the western edge of Arches National Park, and soon there is a viewpoint that looks across to the Devil's Garden section. We'll soon see the arches close-up, but first take a short side trip west along Utah 313 to Dead Horse Point. This is one of the most famous viewpoints in the Southwest and it is easily accessible by paved road, which is why it is recommended. Two thousand feet below you the Colorado River makes a huge bend at the base of sheer sandstone cliffs. The view looks right into the mouth of the gorge. The walls aren't as high nor as brilliantly colored as the Grand Canyon, but this area gives you a far clearer river view. The hues alter subtly with the changing angle of the sun. We are still north of the junction with the Green here, at the edge of Canyonlands National Park. The name Dead Horse Point comes from the time a herd of wild mustangs were trapped on this promontory and died of thirst. There is a visitor center on the site, which is a state park.

Now return to U.S. 191, and in just six miles you'll come to the entrance to Arches. This was once the floor of a prehistoric sea. Sediment deposited here 150 million years ago was exposed when the water receded and then shaped by eons of wind. The hundreds of arches in this park are Entrada sandstone, which is especially susceptible to the forces of erosion. There are also countless pinnacles, balanced rocks, and natural windows; the park is a museum of mineral grace, a collection of monolithic delicacy.

Park roads lead to several of the most interesting areas, including The Windows, a grouping of eight massive arches. There are also turnoffs to viewpoints that offer vistas of the La Sal Mountains and the Colorado River. The park's signature sight is Delicate Arch, which is seemingly balanced by the flimsiest of supports. There are views of this arch from the road, but to see it close up you must take a three-mile round trip hike over a moderately strenuous trail. If you can manage it, by all means do it. It is picture postcard material.

The area was used as rangeland after 1885 (there are remnants of an old ranch within the park) and very few outsiders ever reached the remote area. A campaign to win National Park Service protection was succesful in 1929 but the first road to the arches wasn't cut through for another eight years, when the county took a bulldozer and graded an old pony trail. That's how recent tourist access to this area is. It became a national park in 1971.

Moab used to be known as the only town in Utah to which admission was charged. It was at the far side of the perilous Colorado River crossing, on the Mormon immigrant route to the new settlements in Arizona. Ferry service began in 1881 and charged a hefty fee of $2.50 a wagon, the only access to the town of Moab. But that toll was paid almost cheerfully. When the pioneering Elk Mountain Mission party came through in 1855 it took them four days to get across the river. A bridge was finally completed in 1912. At the time, it was the last westward crossing of the river until the far side of Grand Canyon at Needles, California. Moab truly was a "jumping-off place," which was what the settlers called the crossing here.

Although the Mormons were very fond of Biblical references in naming their towns, Moab was not chosen to honor the land that was constantly at war with the ancient Israelites. The origin is traced back to a Paiute word, *moapa*, meaning "mosquito water." All things considered, even the Biblical Moab has better connotations.

Moab was the goal of the Elk Mountain Mission party, mentioned above. But after their difficult journey here, the Utes ran them out in only three months. Constant raids kept all settlers at bay for another generation and it wasn't until 1880 that they returned on a permanent basis. It was a placid sheep-raising center for many years, but several 20th-century developments changed all that. Immediately after World War II, the discovery of uranium nearby touched off a modern mining boom. The mining activity is pretty much played out now, but Moab remains an important potash-producing area. Moviemakers also discovered the area after World War II and dozens of westerns were filmed in the nearby canyon country, as well as part of the *Indiana Jones* series. That, in turn, established the town as a center of tourism, and it serves as the base of exploration for adjacent Arches and Canyonlands National Parks. Moab has also become the four-wheel drive capital of the west, as owners of off-highway vehicles flock in to explore the rugged back country. A Jeep Safari is held each Easter weekend to kick off the season.

The Dan O'Laurie Memorial Museum, on East Center Street, has displays about the town's history, with several exhibits on uranium. There is also a Hollywood Stuntmen's Hall of Fame, which pays tribute to the riders who took the falls and made the leaps that thrilled audiences through decades of western movies. The Hall has memorabilia from several films made in the area, and stages live stunt shows as well. If you didn't sign up for a rafting trip back at Green River, this is your second chance. Moab is right on the Colorado and trips into Canyonlands, which is best explored by water, originate here.

We are now right at the base of the La Sal Range, with 12,721-foot Mt. Peale looming to the east. Past La Sal Junction, the sage plain of the Lisbon Valley stretches boundless and bare all the way into Colorado. Rock formations, some of them fantastically shaped and named, speckle the roadside. Among the most prominent are Looking Glass Rock, with a hole in its center that seems to be a mirror, and Wilson Arch. If you want a good rock to read, turn west on Utah 211. This is the paved side road to Newspaper Rock, a huge formation covered with Indian petroglyphs. The news is a few hundred years old and there are no baseball scores, but the comics in the pictographs still hold your attention.

The mountains that rise to the west are part of the Abajo Range, also known locally as the Blue Mountains. At the base of the highest of them, Abajo Peak (11,345 feet) is the town of Monticello.

The place is named for Thomas Jefferson's Virginia estate, but the similarities end there. It is the seat of San Juan County and at an altitude of 7,000 feet it is one of the highest towns in the state. This part of Utah was so sparsely populated in the 1890s that Colorado tried to use it as a dumping ground for its Ute population, in one of the less glorious chapters in Western development. Colorado had greater influence in Washington, because it was a state and Utah was still a territory so it managed to get a bill passed declaring this area "deserted." The residents objected to that, however, and sent the Utes right back to Colorado. The Indians claimed an ancestral attachment to the land, though, and a militia was called out from Monticello to persuade them to leave. The Ute reservation was eventually established in southwestern Colorado.

The road passes Devil's Canyon, named for sudden floods that would smash wagons against the rock walls, in Manti-La Sal National Forest. It then enters **Blanding**, the urban center of San Juan County. Settled in 1905 as Grayson, the town changed its name in order to obtain a library from philanthrophist Thomas Bicknell. He offered one to any town in Utah that would name itself for him. The people of Grayson eagerly complied, only to find that another town had beaten them to it and already claimed Bicknell. Ever the good sport, Bicknell made the offer good when the name was changed to that of his wife's family. Blanding it has been ever since.

As late as 1940, the place had only 600 people and was still the biggest town in the county. But with the coming of the road, growth has spurted and it now has more than 3,000 residents.

Blanding had been occupied a good 1,000 years before the present town was founded. Edge of The Cedars State Park preserves the remains of an Anasazi Indian Village in the northern part of town that was inhabited from about 750 A.D. to 1200 A.D. The houses and ceremonial chambers occupy a ridge overlooking a canyon. The museum on the site has one of the area's largest collections of Anasazi pottery and it examines how this ancient culture influenced the shape of life in this region. There are several Indian trading posts near town and the Naatsilid Pottery enables you to observe traditional Navajo crafstmen at work.

The road to the south runs alongside Recapture Creek, named by an early settler who was convinced that the Aztec leader, Montezuma, had escaped his Spanish captors and made his way to this area before being recaptured. Just to the southeast, there is a town called Montezuma Creek, and if that doesn't clinch it I don't know what does.

The road reaches the San Juan River at Bluff, which is also the starting point of U.S. 163, the scenic road to Monument Valley. That route is designated as the continuation of the Scenic Byway we have been following and you may want to continue the drive on that highway. The Bluff area is described in the chapter on U.S. 163.

If you're staying on Highway 191, the road breaks south again and crosses the San Juan, entering the Utah portion of the Navajo Reservation. This enormous tract of land is the largest reservation in the United States, covering 25,000 square miles in three states. The highway will run through it for all but a few miles of the rest of its course. It crosses into Arizona in 20 miles and follows Chinle Wash through several small settlements. Watch for the two Round Rocks which give that community its name. They are just to the west as the highway enters town. Chinle is one of the largest Navajo communities, with just under 3,000 residents. The name means "canyon mouth," and true to its word it sits at the entrance of **Canyon de Chelly**.

This area is a National Monument within the reservation, but it is still occupied by the Navajo and access to the canyon floor is allowed only with an Indian guide. The two roads that run along the rim and a short trail to the White House ruin may be entered anytime. During five distinct periods, different cultures occupied this deep, hidden canyon. The oldest habitations have been dated all the way back to 350 A.D., and various Pueblo peoples lived here for the next 1,000 years. The Navajos moved in on the remains of the earlier people and regarded it as their homeland when Kit Carson forcibly removed them to New Mexico in 1864 (see U.S. 60). They returned four years later and have used the canyon floor for grazing and farming ever since. Most of the ruins can only be seen from overlooks on the rim, but White House is reached by a short trail. This was the culminating structure of the Pueblo period in the canyon, a five-story building occupied from about 1050 to 1300. After it was abandoned, no new pueblos were built here. Set into a nook in the canyon wall, the place was almost impregnable and accessible only by ladders that could be drawn up in an attack. White House is reached by way of the south rim drive. The other road leads to the adjoining Canyon del Muerto and the overlooks of Antelope House and Mummy Cave, where well-preserved human remains were found. Besides their historical interest, the canyons are exceptionally beautiful, with red sandstone walls rising almost vertically from the floor.

From Chinle, the highway contines south through the evocatively named Beautiful Valley, with tall mesas rising in the background, then turns sharply east to **Ganado**.

FOCUS

When John Lorenzo Hubbell arrived in Navajo country in 1876, the legends of the West were still being made. Geronimo and Tombstone were as yet unknown, names that would figure in the future. The memory of the Navajo Long Walk to forced exile in New Mexico was still a fresh wound and a wall of distrust separated the tribe from the few whites who came to their lands. A small trading post had been opened near the town of Pueblo six years before Hubbell showed up, operated by "Old Man" Leonard. Hubbell took it over in 1878 and ran it until his death 52 years later. By that time, he had become a legend.

Hubbell was among the first to recognize the artistry of the Navajo craftsmen and understand that a market was developing for them in the big cities of America. A change in artistic sensibility was coming over the United States in the late 19th century. The sense of inferiority to European art was ending and a new generation, secure in their identity as Americans and proud of their emerging national heritage, were looking inward to find inspiration. Native Americans within the space of a generation underwent a change, from hated adversary and barrier to progress, to the inheritors of an ancient tradition that was an intrinsic part of what it meant to be an American. Hubbell, a native of the Southwest, comprehended that and determined to build on it.

As he won the trust of his Navajo customers, a sense of obligation developed in him. He wanted to bring attention to their artistry and help improve their lives. His trading post became the focal point of these efforts. The commercial structure and residence that stand here today were built in 1883. While administered as a National Historic Site by the National Park Service, every effort is made to operate the post commercially just as it was when Hubbell ran it. It is a functioning store, but it is also a window into the past.

Hubbell was a savvy politician and suggested that the name of the town in which his post was located be changed. Pueblo, he argued, could easily be confused with the name of the city in Colorado. Why not Ganado, the Spanish word for herds. Since the local tribal leader was named Mucho Ganado, this suggestion was not an unpopular one. Hubbell eventually became a sheriff, a member of the Territorial Council, and a state Senator, while building his business into a commercial empire of 24 trading posts and stores. His home became a stop for visiting celebrities, including politicians, writers, and artists. From the politicians and writers he asked help in winning public support for the Navajo; from the artists he asked a picture. The collection of paintings and drawings they gave him make his old ranch house one of the most valuable repositories of Western art in Arizona.

Hubbell encouraged his Indian customers to concentrate on silversmithing and rug weaving. He demanded high standards and those who sold to him knew they would be rewarded with a national market for their products. In the visitor center today, adjacent to the trading post, a room is set aside for the weavers, so you can watch them at the traditional craft, working in the red and black colors that define Navajo rugs. Many of them are women from remote parts of the reservation who speak no English, or don't care to in the presence of outsiders. Tours of the Hubbell home are given only at stipulated times, and it is best to check in advance because the schedule changes with the season. (It is also good to know that while the rest of Arizona does not observe Daylight Savings Time between April and October, the Navajo Reservation does.

The best part of a trip to this place, though, is still a walk through the old trading post. This is the way it was here in the days when the legends were made and it is the way it has remained.

* * *

The highway resumes its run through the mesa lands of the reservation. Near Wide Ruin are the remains of 13th-century pueblos that have been identified as antecedents of early Hopi culture. The Hopi Reservation is just to the west here, but no U.S. highways penetrate its interior. The road ends at Chambers, just outside the limits of the Navajo Reservation, at the junction of Interstate 40 (formerly Route 66).

VISITING HOURS

UTAH

Arches National Park: (801) 259-8161. North of Moab, off U.S. 191. Daily, 8–6, summer; 8–4:30 at other times. Admission.

Blanding: Edge of Cedars State Park, (801) 678-2238. Off U.S. 191, at 660 W. 400 North St. Daily, 9–6, mid-May–mid-September; 9–5 at other times. Admission.

Dutch John: Flaming Gorge Dam, (801) 889-3713. On U.S. 191. Daily, 8–4, May–September. Free.

Green River: Powell River History Museum, (801) 564-3426. Overlooking the Green River, across the bridge from the town center. Daily, 8–8, summer months; 8–4 at other times. Admission.

Helper: Western Mining and Railroad Museum, (801) 472-3009. At 296 S. Main St. Daily, 9–5, mid-May–September. Donation.

Moab: Dan O'Laurie Museum, (801) 259-7585. At 118 Center St. Daily, 1–5 and 7–9, in summer; 3–5 and 7–9 at other times. Donation.

Hollywood Stuntman's Hall of Fame, (801) 259-6100. At 111 E. 100 North St. Tuesday–Sunday, 10–4, March–October. Admission.

Price: Prehistoric Museum, (801) 637-5060. In City Hall, Main at 2nd Sts. Monday–Saturday, 10–5. Free.

ARIZONA

Canyon de Chelly National Monument: (602) 674-5436. East from U.S.
191 at Chinle on reservation road. Daily, 8–6, May–September;
8–5 at other times. Charge for guides.

Ganado: Hubbell Trading Post, (602) 755-3254. On U.S. 191. Daily,
8–6, June–September; 8–5 at other times. Free.

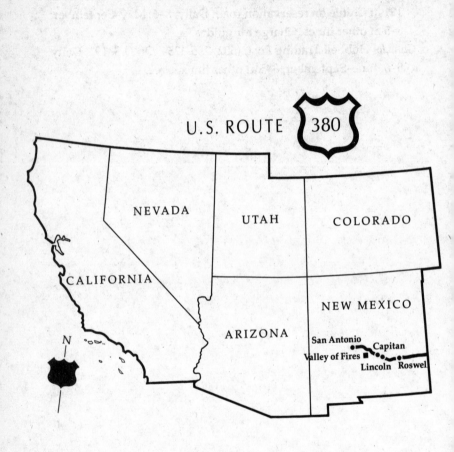

U.S. ROUTE 380

NEVADA

UTAH

COLORADO

CALIFORNIA

ARIZONA

NEW MEXICO

San Antonio
Valley of Fires
Capitan
Lincoln
Roswel

N

The Kid's Country

⬡

U.S. 380

Tatum, N.M. to San Antonio, N.M.
242 miles

This is one of the roads that seem intended primarily to fill in the blank spaces on the Western map. It begins north of Dallas and embarks on a straight and lonely journey through Texas. The highway passes through no town of any size. It is just a ribbon of pavement that connects one cluster of life to another across a wide and empty land.

In New Mexico, U.S. 380 runs from the west Texas border to the Rio Grande. In its most interesting stretch, between Hondo and Carrizozo, the road links the legend of a bad man, a celebrated bear cub, and a burnt-out valley of lava.

MILEPOSTS

According to geologists, there is almost no surface that occurs so perfectly level in nature as the Llano Estacado, the Staked Plains of eastern New Mexico. These southern flatlands, east of the Pecos River, have been called a sea of grass. And to the early settlers, they presented all the wide and trackless mystery of the sea, devoid of landmarks or marked paths to guide one home. (See other descriptions of the Staked Plains under U.S. 54, 60, and 70.)

This central portion of the Staked Plains was a great hunting ground for three Indian nations. Evidence of Comanche, Apache, and Kiowa have turned up on the territory crossed by U.S. 380 and there are indications that the three tribes met to trade in the area. But what brought them here to begin with was the buffalo. Enormous herds of the animals came here to graze, and to be hunted. Mounds in parts of western Lea County are believed to be remnants of buffalo traps that were set before the Indians had access to horses.

Tatum, the first town on the route, is a crossroads with a population of less than 1,000, named for the owner of the general store that was the nucleus of the first settlement in 1909. This was a dry farming area for many years, but after World War II it began to develop as an oil production center, as well.

U.S. 380 climbs towards the Mescalero Ridge, named after the Apache band which, in turn, drew its name from the mescal plant. This small cactus was found throughout the entire range of the Apache. Writes one chronicler of that nation: "The mescal gave the Apache a quasi-bread, two intoxicants, thread and even clothing, and countless minor staples. Roasted mescal was very nutritious and it could be stored for six months." Small wonder this New Mexican manna would give its name to an entire band of the tribe.

At Caprock, the terrain changes markedly. Rimrock formations, the surface outcroppings of the plateau, can be seen, and the land begins to rise towards the Rockies. Sardine Mountain (3,973 feet), becomes visible in a few miles to the north. The origin of the name is lost in obscurity but it probably is a corruption of a Spanish surname, possibly *Sarvinia*. There is no connection between this sardine and the aforementioned sea of grass.

State Highway 409 leads south to a state park with an evocative name: Bottomless Lakes. The unusual patches of blue on the plains here were caused when surface rock caved in to expose the underground water that runs below this entire area. They were given their names when cowboys tried to gauge the depth with weighted lariats and found that they never touched bottom. But geologists say that a strong underwater flow carried the lines away. The parks feature well-equipped recreational facilities, including fishing and swimming.

The highway passes through the heart of Roswell, the state's fourth-largest city (described in the U.S. 70 chapter). Then, for the next 47 miles, U.S. 380 parallels U.S. 70 before branching off to the northwest at Hondo.

The road then follows the Bonito River into a peaceful valley filled with apple orchards. In the early fall, fruit and cider stands are plentiful along the road between Hondo and **Lincoln.**

FOCUS

To students of western lore, the name Lincoln rings like an alarm. The range war fought here is a fabled part of the region's history. Countless movies have dramatized the events surrounding this frontier brawl in the late 1870s; in its bloody tracks the name of Billy the Kid entered the realm of American folklore.

Shot dead more than a century ago, The Kid remains a major tourist industry in New Mexico. Towns all over the state trade on their association, no matter how remote, with this gunman. There is a thick romantic patina over a character who has been portrayed on film by the likes of Robert Taylor and Paul Newman. The evidence is clear, however, that Billy the Kid's character corresponded more closely to that of an enforcer in an urban drug gang.

No one really knows who he was or where he came from. The most widely accepted version is that he was born in New York City as William H. Bonney and came to New Mexico with his mother after his father died. Other sources claim that he was really named Henry McCarty, and he was recorded under that name as a witness at the marriage of his mother to a man named Antrim in Santa Fe in 1873.

The family moved to Silver City, but after his mother's death the following year, things fell apart. The family became, as they would say today, dysfunctional, and the youngster soon picked up his nickname and many bad habits. Within three years, The Kid had also picked up the first notch on his gun, killing a man named Cahill in Arizona. A coroner's jury ruled the shooting criminal, but the killer was already out of the territory.

By 1878 he was back in New Mexico, with tales of many dead men behind him, working for John Tunstall, an English-born rancher and merchant. He had adopted the name of Bonney, which may have been his mother's maiden name. The alias was an understandable precaution for a man wanted by the law, but one newspaper account also referred to him as Kid Antrim.

Apparently, Tunstall took a liking to the young man and gave him a new horse, a saddle, and a job as a range hand. Unfortunately, The Kid had returned to the middle of a deadly feud. Tunstall was allied with cattle baron John Chisum, who accused many smaller operators of running off his stock. Chisum's opponents were politically powerful in Lincoln County and one of them, William Brady, was sheriff. The situation attracted hired killers from all over the territory. Many of them rode in the sheriff's posse.

One such loose collection of lawmen arrested Tunstall on a trumped-up charge. After he had given up his arms and placed himself in their custody, they shot him. No one was prosecuted for the crime. Some weeks later, Brady and a deputy were gunned down in the middle of Lincoln and Billy the Kid was accused of the crime.

On April 18, 1878 The Kid pleaded not guilty at his arraignment. Before the trial could begin, the election of a new sheriff to replace the one recently dispatched to the choir invisible resulted in one of the Tunstall group winning the office. But the governor set the election aside and appointed a member of the opposing faction, which quickly hired every available gunslinger around for reinforcement.

In July, the inevitable showdown came. The new sheriff and his posse trapped The Kid and 18 of his allies in the Alexander McSween House and then entrenched themselves across the street in the courthouse. After a gunfight that lasted two days, the deputies finally succeeded in setting a wing of the house on fire. According to witnesses, the men in the house sent repeated volleys of rifle fire at their attackers, while the flames crept closer, and Mrs. McSween played the piano. One can only wonder what selections she might have chosen under the circumstances.

The new sheriff and four members of the opposition, including McSween, were killed. The Kid escaped after dark and the McSween house was looted by a mob. The territorial governor, General Lew Wallace (who was in the midst of writing *Ben Hur*), offered The Kid amnesty if he turned himself in. But two men sworn to kill The Kid were set free from the Lincoln jail and Billy chose to go on the run instead.

Finally arrested in December 1880, he was tried, convicted of murder, and returned to Lincoln to be hanged. But two weeks before the sentence was to be carried out, he slipped his handcuffs in his cell, killed two guards, and escaped. The next Lincoln County sheriff, Pat Garrett, was of a different caliber from his predecessors. He set out to track The Kid and end the cycle of vendetta. Three months later, he caught up with him near Fort Sumner with fatal results (see U.S. 60).

The entire town of Lincoln is now preserved as a state monument. When the county seat was removed to Carrizozo in 1910, Lincoln went into suspended animation, preserved through neglect. So the town that exists today does not look that much different from the Lincoln known by Billy the Kid.

The Old Courthouse has been restored to its appearance on the day of the famous gun battle and contains several rooms of exhibits on the range war. Many of the homes and commercial structures on the adjacent streets, including the original Tunstall store, date from the 19th century, as does the Wortley Hotel, built in 1862 and restored in 1960 still accommodates overnight guests. A museum operated by the Lincoln County Heritage Trust has displays on regional history and the colorful people who passed through this little town.

Events are held here all through the summer months, highlighted by the re-enactment of The Kid's escape from the courthouse jail. That is quite spectacular, but it probably couldn't compare with just one more encore on the piano by the redoubtable Mrs. McSween.

* * *

Eight miles beyond Lincoln is the turnoff to **Fort Stanton**. Built as a cavalry outpost in 1855, the fort was most active during the campaigns against the Mescalero Apaches. It was while stationed here as an officer with the all-black 9th Cavalry, that the future leader of the American Expeditionary Force in World War I was given his nickname, Black Jack Pershing. There is now a small museum on the grounds.

Capitan grew up on a spur of the El Paso and Northeastern Railroad in 1897, when coal deposits were discovered in the area. First called Gray, after a local homesteader, the name was changed in recognition of 10,083-foot mountain El Capitan, on the eastern horizon. But neither fuel nor scenery brought the town its greatest recognition. That came through the furry survivor of a 1950 forest fire, a little cub who became the living Smokey the Bear.

Already a cartoon favorite for several years, Smokey was a lovably gruff bear in a ranger hat who admonished us with the words "Only you can prevent forest fires." Smokey appeared on t-shirts, lunch boxes, television commercials, and comic books; all of the licensing fees, by a 1952 act of Congress, went to the U.S. Forest Service. Even the police who patrol highways in many states became known as "Smokies" because their hats resembled the model favored by the famous bear.

Smokey was created by a Los Angeles advertising agency in 1945 to replace Walt Disney's Bambi as a campaigner against forest fires. Through the 1940s, the image was refined from a playful cub to the more dignified, although slightly paunchy, bear whose image is known around the world.

But in 1950, when the orphaned cub was found clinging to a charred tree by a game warden after a fire in Lincoln National Forest, Smokey became a living being. He took up residence in the National Zoo in Washington, D.C. and became one of its most popular exhibits. From time to time, he appeared in events such as the Tournament of Roses parade. Most important, Smokey sold his product. There was an absolute drop in the number of human-caused forest fires despite increases in population and forest use after he was adopted as a symbol.

The original Smokey died in 1976 and his remains were carried back to Capitan. The Smokey Bear Historical State Park contains memorabilia of the bear's public career, as well as exhibits on fire-fighting and the forestlands of New Mexico.

U.S. 380 emerges from the mountains at Carrizozo (see U.S. 54) and within a few miles enters the Malpais ("bad country" in Spanish) and the Valley of Fires.

Something spectacular happened here just a little while ago, geologically speaking. A volcano to the north, Little Black Peak, erupted and sent rivers of lava flowing down into this valley. It happened somewhere between 1,500 and 2,000 years ago, making this one of the youngest lava fields in the country.

Since the days of the Spanish explorers, the area has been shunned by settlers. The black land cannot be grazed or cultivated, and even miners come away empty. So it has simply remained an empty, barren land.

But not altogether barren. The lava field is home to a surprising variety of plants and wildlife, who have adapted to this unique environment. For example, the squirrels and lizards who make their home here have much darker coats than their nearby relatives, which enable them to blend in with the lava and escape predators.

A nature trail crosses part of the Malpais in Valley of Fires State Park. It stops at well-marked points to explain the significance of the lava formation and the plants growing there, and also leads to spectacular viewpoints across this dark valley. It is not especially strenuous, although thick-soled shoes are recommended because you will be walking across the sharp lava at several points.

The road crosses the Oscura Mountains and at Bingham, on the mountains' western edge, it passes just north of the Trinity Site, where America's first nuclear device was succesfully tested on July 16, 1945. (New Mexico's relationship with the nuclear age is described more fully in the U.S. 54 chapter.) The town itself grew up along coal deposits that were developed in the 1880s but are now abandoned.

The area south of here is known as the Jornada del Muerto, "Journey of Death," which gives you some idea of what the Spanish thought of the neighborhood. The most feared stretch of the El Camino Real, the road from Mexico to Santa Fe, it crosses 90 miles of desert and lava flows between water holes.

At the Rio Grande, the highway comes to its end at the village of San Antonio, named for a mission built here in 1629. One of its founders, Fr. Garcia de Francisco de Zuniga, is buried in the area, according to old chronicles. The village today is known for cotton and alfalfa production, as well as for being the birthplace of hotelier Conrad Hilton. The only San Antonio Hilton, however, is the one located in Texas.

VISITING HOURS

NEW MEXICO

Capitan: Smokey the Bear Museum, (505) 354-2748. In town, on
  U.S. 380. Daily, 9–5, summer; 9–4 at other times. Admission.
Fort Stanton: Museum, (505) 354-2211. South of U.S. 380, on New
  Mexico 214. On grounds of State Hospital. Call for times.
Lincoln: National Historic Landmark, (505) 653-4372. On U.S. 380.
  Daily, 9–6, March–mid-November. Admission to buildings.

U.S. ROUTE 395

Alturas
Susanville
NEVADA
Reno
Carson City
UTAH
COLORADO
Mammoth
Mountain
Manzanar
Independence
Mt. Whitney
CALIFORNIA
Victorville
ARIZONA
NEW MEXICO
N
Ronan

California's Back Door

◯

U.S. 395

New Pine Creek, Calif. to Victorville, Calif.
652 miles

This is the road through California's back door. It follows the eastern slope of the Sierra to parts of the Golden State that are altogether different from the familiar images of beaches, Nob Hill, and Hollywood that define California for the rest of the world.

U.S. 395 begins up on the Washington border with British Columbia and then tracks a course across the eastern edge of Washington and Oregon. In California, it is a most unusual road in that it is hardly ever interrupted by freeways. Especially on its run through the Owens Valley, with the highest peak in the continental United States rising in all its majesty just to the west, it is one of America's most magnificent old roads.

MILEPOSTS

We start off in fairly spectacular fashion—in California's extreme northeastern corner, on the Oregon border, with the Warner Mountains rising on the east and Modoc National Forest on the far side of Goose Lake to the west. At this point, we are more than 700 miles from Los Angeles by the most direct route. The scenery and texture of life here are much more like the Pacific Northwest than anything that should be in a book about the Southwest. But California is a very big place and even most natives of the state never get way up here.

Many of the 49ers making their way south from Oregon and Idaho came this way and they used Goose Lake as a shortcut. The lake goes through dry cycles and when the bed was exposed in the 1920s, residents were astonished to find wagon ruts. They could only have been made by emigrant trains during the last recorded dry spell in the 1850s. At its fullest, the lake extends as far south as Davis Creek.

You'll notice a side road heading into the Warner range marked Fandango Pass. Thereby hangs a cautionary tale. A wagon train came through this pass and its members were so overjoyed at arriving in California's green and pleasant land that they held a dance. *Fandango*, the Mexican term for such a celebration, had entered the language during the Mexican War and was in current usage on the frontier. Modoc warriors, observing the dance in progress, moved in on the unguarded merrymakers and slaughtered them. The site of the Fandango Massacre is marked on this side road. The route was one of many cut-offs from the Oregon Trail to California. This one, opened in 1846, was named for scout Lindsey Applegate. It is only coincidental that it is also the entrance to apple orchard country around Davis Creek.

After a run alongside the Pit River, the road arrives in the first town of any size on the way, **Alturas.** This was an early example of a typically California phenomenon—Anglo boosters using the Spanish language for dramatic effect. The town was first called Dorris Bridge, for a pioneer family, but settlers renamed it in 1876. Although the mellifluous Spanish word means "heights," Alturas is actually located in a valley. But it sounded better, and who's counting? Land promoters around the state soon learned that the most barren desert outpost sounds much more appealing when it was given a Spanish name.

A local museum contains exhibits on Modoc County history, with special emphasis on the area's native people, for whom the county was named. That was not done by choice. This area was originally part of Siskiyou County to the west. But it withdrew in a snit when Siskiyou refused to pick up the tab for a new road to Cedarville, across the Warner range to the east. The Alturas bunch defiantly formed their own county and named it Canby, in honor of Brigadier General Edward S. Canby. He had been killed under a flag of truce during the Modoc War of 1873, the highest-ranking American officer to fall during the Indian wars in the West. But as a slap at their rebellious attitude, the State Legislature renamed the new county Modoc, after Canby's killers. Alturas also holds a Fandango celebration each July, commemorating the unfortunate pioneer incident back up the road. It seems unlikely that they would play "Save the Last Dance for Me."

The road continues running south with the Pit, named for sharp-staked animal traps the Indians set along its banks. U.S. 395 passes through Modoc National Wildlife Refuge. Watch for the Great Basin Canada goose, sandhill cranes, and other migratory fowl. Beyond the refuge, this is a vast stock-raising area, so remote that the valleys just across the mountains to the east are named Secret and Surprise. You'll also find the town of Likely along the road. According to local legend, the place had grown tired of the U.S. Post Office rejecting its suggestions for a name. One fun-lover suggested that since it didn't seem likely that they'd ever come up with a suitable name, they may as well try that one. And they did.

This is open sagebrush country, with Tule Lake Reservoir just to the east. But as we continue south, the landscape changes and we enter the invitingly named Honey Lake Valley. Small insects left their secretions, known as honey dew, on the leaves of trees in the area and the Indians used it for molasses. The valley was one of the first areas settled in this part of California, although its early residents did not regard themselves as Californians. They felt more of an affinity for their neighbors in Utah Territory, in what is now Nevada. So in 1856 they voted to unify with them and form the new Territory of Nataqua, with its capital in **Susanville**. Isaac Roop, a landowner in this area, was named provisional governor. Nataqua claimed 50,000 square miles of land north of the point at which the current state boundary bends sharply east, so the event was hard for the California Legislature to ignore. In 1861, Nevada was awarded territorial status by the federal government and a new survey determined that Roop's holdings were definitely within California. This did not impress the Nataquans, who organized themselves as Roop County, Nevada. When the sheriff of neighboring Plumas County, California arrived in Susanville to arrest his Roop counterpart, he was confronted by armed resistance and forced to retreat. This brought on the Sagebrush War of 1863, a five-hour gun battle between posses of the two counties at Roop's Fort, in Susanville. At its conclusion, Roop accepted his fate as a California resident and Nataqua went off the maps. Roop's Fort, built in 1854, still stands in Susanville with an adjoining museum of the Nataqua adventure.

Susanville is a five-mile jog west from where the highway turns abruptly east, at Johnstonville. Return to this point after the short side trip and pick up the route. Susanville, by the way, was named for Roop's oldest daughter, and Janesville, along this stretch of road, was named for the wife of the area's first settler, Malcolm Bankhead. The dry bed of Honey Lake, which gives the valley its name, is just east of the road here. The road skirts the eastern edge of the Sierra here, with Dixie Mountain rising to a height of 8,323 feet within Plumas National Forest.

Hallelujah Junction stands at the entrance to Beckwourth Pass, the route over the Sierra just to the west discovered by a black frontiersman, Jim Beckwourth. The highway becomes a freeway here and speeds into Nevada, over the route of Beckwourth Road, which opened in 1852. Beckwourth was one of the more active mountain men and also played an instrumental role in the founding of Pueblo, Colorado (see U.S. 50). His biography was an early frontier best-seller and set the standard for colorful exaggeration in pursuit of a higher truth. In other words, his respect for fact was minimal. But there is no dispute about his claim on Beckwourth Pass.

The highway bypasses **Reno** as a freeway, but if you want to get a look at The Biggest Little in City in the World, the old route, now marked U.S. 395 Business, runs right through its heart as Virginia Street. The first Nevada city to gain national notoriety for its gambling and liberal divorce laws, Reno has been outpaced by fast-growing Las Vegas since the 1950s. "Reno-vating," the Walter Winchell line for a celebrity divorce, has now passed out of the language. But its downtown is still a glittering nest of neon. The place grew up on the Truckee River as the final rest stop before the Sierra crossing. This is the route through Donner Pass and it was here that the unlucky party made its final, fatal mistake in 1846; lingering too long into October before tackling the mountains. The Comstock Lode brought a town into being here as the Central Pacific railhead for Virginia City. A lot auction conducted by the railroad in 1868 transformed it into a city.

The highway runs alongside the University of Nevada campus, on a ridge north of town. This was the second school in the nation established under the Morrill Act, which granted public lands for new universities and widened educational opportunities after the Civil War. It was started in Elko in 1874 and moved here 12 years later. The Nevada Historical Society Museum and Mackay School of Mines Museum are both located on campus. The first facility, which shows off Indian and pioneer artifacts as well as displays from the old Carson City Mint and historic gambling paraphenalia, is right on the highway. The mining museum has exhibits on the state's considerable mineralogical activity.

The newest facility in Reno is the National Automobile Museum of the William F. Harrah Foundation. This is among the finest collection of vintage cars in existence. It places the automobile in its historical setting in the development of America. Included in the exhibits is an examination of the growth of the highway culture along the old roads. Displaying the fruits of a lifelong hobby by casino-owner Harrah, the museum opened in 1989 in a striking new facility on Lake Street, overlooking the Truckee, just a few blocks east of U.S. 395 on its course through downtown.

After rejoining the main section of Highway 395, we swing south into the Washoe Valley, with the peaks of the Carson Range rising on our west. The hot springs at Steamboat once fed a Victorian resort, of which nothing remains. Not much is left, either, of the racing stables that once flourished in this valley, produced two Kentucky Derby winners, and shipped its prized hay east in the 1890s. But the Bowers Mansion still stands, on a side road just west of the highway. This was the first Great House in Nevada, built with the first fortune made from the Comstock Lode. Until its construction in 1864, the state was generally regarded as one big mining camp that would empty out once the metal was gone. This mansion symbolized permanence. Lemuel Bowers was a resident of a **Carson City** boarding house, run by Ella Cowan, which served prospectors working the nearby hills. A Mormon convert from Scotland, Ella had come to the area with her husband. She refused, however, to accompany him back to Salt Lake City when Brigham Young recalled settlers from across the West to help defend it from an anticipated federal assault. To pay his board, Bowers gave his landlady the rights to a strip claim adjoining his own. She held on to it and in a few years found herself owning the heart of the Comstock.

She and Bowers joined their claims and their destinies, and then set out to spend as much of their new fortune as they could on this house and its furnishings. But four years after its completion,

Bowers died and left no clear title to his claims. When they were legally challenged, his wife went broke trying to defend them in court. She tried running the mansion as a hotel, turned to spiritualism, and eventually ended her days as a poverty-stricken fortune teller advising clients how they might acquire such wealth as she had lost. The mansion is now the centerpiece of a county park and there are tours of its restored interior, which features many original items.

Washoe Lake is just to the east as the road becomes freeway once more on its approach to Carson City (described in the chapter on U.S. 50).

Nine miles south of the point of separation with Highway 50, a side road to the west leads to **Genoa**, the oldest community in Nevada. Mormon Station was settled by traders sent out from Salt Lake City in 1849 when this area was still part of Utah Territory. A stockade was erected, a log cabin built, and by 1851 a government had been formed. It became the first seat of the first county in Nevada and was renamed Genoa by a local man who claimed to have seen the Mediterranean Sea near that Italian port and described it as looking a lot like Lake Tahoe. In 1859, the first territorial legislature met here but voted to move the state government to the more centrally located Carson City. The place is now a Historic State Monument, featuring a replica of the original Mormon Station stockade and cabin, and the old county courthouse. Among the exhibits in the courthouse are the belongings of Snowshoe Thompson, a Swedish-born pioneer who carried mail from Genoa across the wintry Sierra passes to the California mining camps in the 1850s and became a legendary figure in Nevada's early years.

Another resident of Genoa in those years was George Ferris, who would go on to invent the amusement park wheel named for him. His sister, Margaret, stayed close to home and became the wife of Nevada's alfalfa king, Henry Dangberg. Arriving in 1864 from Germany, Dangberg quickly understood that all those miners in the Comstock needed to eat and that the cattle ranches that were developing in the area would require feed. His foresight enabled him to charge premium prices for his hay, which he reinvested in his land and irrigation works. At the time of his death in 1904 he controlled 36,000 acres. His company built the town of Minden and modeled it after a German village recalled from Dangberg's youth. It has remained primarily an agricultural town, but the prevailing ethnic group is now Basque, as it is in the neighboring community of Gardnerville. The Basque restaurants in the area are highly regarded.

Skirting the edge of Toiyabe National Forest, the highway passes Topaz Lake, a reservoir formed by dams on the West Branch of the Walker River, and re-enters California. The river is named for Joseph Walker, who made the first westward crossing of the Sierra in 1833. He followed this stream south through the Antelope Valley, along the route of U.S. 395. Then he swung west, at the current junction of California 108, to Sonora Pass. Walker was on a reconnaissance mission to California directed by Captain Benjamin Bonneville. This officer had been granted a leave from the U.S. Army, ostensibly to head a fur-trapping expedition into the West. But documents that came to light a century later indicated that this was a cover story. His real mission was to obtain information on Western lands claimed by Great Britain and owned by Mexico. Walker was the first European to enter the Yosemite Valley and he also discovered Walker Pass, through which he would lead the first overland emigrant train to California in 1843. But the practical information he obtained was minimal.

Even the road through Sonora Pass had been found six years earlier by Jedediah Smith. He also came this way on the return leg of the first recorded overland trip to California and the first crossing of the Sierra.

The road crosses Devil's Gate at an elevation of 7,519 feet and descends into the Bridgeport Valley. The uncertainties of the

California–Nevada border, which resulted in the Sagebrush War back in the Susanville area, also led to some problems around here. When a new survey was made in 1864, the residents of Mono County were informed that they had located their county seat in the wrong state. So **Bridgeport** was laid out and all the records transferred here. The town's first school building, dating from 1880, now houses an historical museum of this error-prone area.

At the southern end of the valley is Mono Lake, three times saltier than the sea. There is no natural outlet, although five major streams empty into the lake. Over the centuries, the salinity content has built up to such a degree that no fish can live in its waters. The lake teems with tiny shrimp, though, and brine flies, and because of their presence it is also attractive to birds. Migratory species come in the hundreds of thousands; during the late spring nesting season the lake is estimated to contain 20 percent of the world's population of California gulls. The lake has also been the source of litigation in recent years. The Los Angeles Department of Power and Water has diverted its water since 1941 and the Sierra Club contends that the practice is doing irreparable environmental damage. The suit, with severe implications for the city's long-term water supply, is wending its way through the state's courts.

The road runs along Mono Lake's western edge and a county park gives access to its shore along a boardwalk, with views of Paoha Island at its center. Lee Vining, the town nearest the lakeshore, is named for the leader of a party that struck gold nearby in 1852. Other sources indicate that Vining later ran a sawmill here, which gives you some idea of how fast the gold ran out. This is also the intersection with westbound California 120— the Tioga Pass Highway through Tuolumne Meadows to Yosemite National Park—one of the West's great scenic highways. Our route, however, continues into the Pumice Valley, on the lake's southern shore.

When Mono Lake's waters were diverted by Los Angeles, tufa towers were exposed. These rock forests, made of calcium carbonate, formed when fresh water emerging from springs beneath the lake mixed with the alkaline content of the lake water. The towers stand in groves along the shoreline and are part of the Mono Lake Tufa State Reserve. Access is along eastbound California 120.

Just to the south on this road you can see the Mono Craters, evidence of the volcanic activity that shaped this entire area.

Heading south once more, the Aeolian Buttes rise to the east, while off to the west is Grant Lake, the northernmost reservoir formed by the Los Angeles water system project. The road enters Inyo National Forest to Mammoth Lakes, one of the state's primary ski resorts and an area of extraordinary scenic beauty. The gondola up **Mammoth Mountain** operates for sightseers during the summer months and the trip is worth the view. There is a visitors' center just west of U.S. 395 on California 203, which has information on the range of activities available in this recreation area. The top scenic attraction nearby is **Devils Postpile National Monument**, a group of 60-foot-high, symmetrically shaped basalt columns, formed by volcanic activity about 100,000 years ago. A trail leads to the top of one column, so highly polished by glaciers that it resembles a mosaic tile.

Back on Highway 395, the road becomes a freeway briefly as it rushes past Crowley Lake, largest reservoir in the water system, and crosses Sherwin Summit at 7,000 feet before starting its descent into the Owens Valley. This area has been described as America's Deepest Valley, because it is walled-in between the sheer uplift of the state's highest ranges—the Sierra to the west and the White Mountains to the east. The Sierra, especially, bursting straight up from the valley floor, are absolutely spectacular through this area, with the elevation of one peak after another exceeding 13,000 feet. Bishop, named for an early cattleman in the valley, is its largest town and commercial center, although it has a population of only about 3,500.

The highway parallels the Owens River to the east. Just north of Big Pine, you can make out a cluster of radio telescopes, put up by California Institute of Technology in 1959 for deep-space research. The location was chosen because of the valley's low population and because the surrounding mountains act as a shield from earth-bound radio interference. South of Big Pine, there is a turnout overlooking the Tinemaha Reservoir to the east. Watch for the herd of dwarf Tule Elk that roams here. Almost extinct in their native San Joaquin Valley, about 50 of the animals were transplanted in 1934 and have increased tenfold. Seven miles south of the reservoir is the original Owens Valley intake for Los Angeles. This project, completed in 1913 at a cost of $23 million, fed the city's explosive growth in the early decades of the 20th century and still supplies the bulk of its water, although enlarged many times and enhanced by other projects on the Colorado and Feather Rivers.

Independence grew up near an Army post, established here during Inyo Indian uprisings in the 1860s and wiped out by an earthquake in 1872. The Commander's House was part of the rebuilding, and when the fort shut down five years later this Victorian residence was moved into town. It has been restored and filled with antique furniture, some of it made by soldiers at the fort. Just a few blocks west of Highway 395 is the Eastern California Museum. There you'll find some exhibits that give the name of this town a poignantly ironic ring.

FOCUS

On an early autumn morning in 1990, Mamoru Eto sat in the office of the Attorney General of the United States. The country's top legal officer knelt beside Eto's wheelchair and handed him a check for $20,000. This ceremony was the final act of a tragedy that started 48-years earlier, when 120,000 Japanese-Americans were taken from their homes on the West Coast and placed in ten internment camps for no other reason but their race. Eto, who was 107 years old, joined eight other former internees in accepting reparations from a government that had finally admitted it was wrong.

The camps were scattered over six western states and Arkansas. But the biggest was Manzanar, located just south of Independence, California, in a beautiful meadow at the base of the state's highest mountains. More than 10,000 at a time were housed there in what some still refer to as a relocation center, but more properly should be called a concentration camp. The internees remained there for almost the entire war, from the spring of 1942 to the end of 1944. Seventy percent of them were American citizens.

In the months that followed the bombing of Pearl Harbor, anti-Japanese hysteria swept the West Coast. Much of this was ostensibly based on a fear of sabotage. But a good portion was also a function of racism, and, in a few documented instances, the motivating factor was greed, with patriotism masking a grab of the assets owned by relocated residents.

This policy came to be regarded as a nadir in the history of civil liberties and treatment of minorities by the U.S. government. In 1944, the U.S. Supreme Court upheld the policy by declaring that it was justified under wartime exigencies, although no case of a Japanese-American aiding the enemy was ever documented. Justice Frank Murphy, in his dissent, wrote that the exclusion order "goes over the very brink of constitutional power and falls into the ugly abyss of racism." It took 39 years for the government to agree with him. A congressional commission finally concluded in 1983 that the internment had been "a grave injustice" motivated by hysteria and made possible by a failure of political leadership. Congress waited five more years, however, before finally passing the law approving the payouts to the survivors of the camps and their heirs. Even after so many years, there was still bitter opposition to reviewing the past and admitting the wrong.

The exhibits at the Eastern California Museum focus on Manzanar, Spanish for "apple orchard." Through old newspaper clippings, personal recollections, and mementos, the story of what happened there emerges from decades of silence, which persisted in part by the choice of those who were interned and wished to forget the humiliation and anger; and in part by residents who hoped it would all just go away. Certainly, this camp cannot begin to compare in brutality and inhumanity with those run by the Axis powers. But the barbed wire and guard towers and sense of racial victimization were just as real. Many of the exhibits dwell on the community that was formed in the camps; the bands and ball-games and shows and publications. Some depict the pride the internees felt in returning the old orchards to productivity and feeding the residents with the fruit. But what comes through most clearly is the hurt felt by the Japanese-Americans that their own country could have turned on them like this.

The Manzanar exhibits take up only one corner of the museum. The camp itself is a short drive away, on the west side of the road. A state historical marker gives notice of its proximity. The guard tower still stands at the entrance, affixed now with plaques put there by the state and Japanese–American groups. Just to the north is the one remaining structure, the camp auditorium, which is used as an equipment garage by the county road department. At the westernmost end of the property is the camp cemetery, hold-ing those who did not survive to see the apology for Manzanar. Nothing else remains. Just the memories of how fragile freedom can be, even in the most open of countries.

* * *

Just south of Manzanar are the rugged contours of the Alabama Hills, which you may have seen dozens of times before because they have been a favorite outdoor movie set for decades. Not only have they provided the backdrop for more than 100 Westerns, but they even posed as India in the classic films, *Gunga Din* and *Lives of a Bengal Lancer*. The town of Lone Pine celebrates an annual Sierra Film Festival, honoring stars who shot pictures in the hills. The first such award went to Roy Rogers (who we will meet again at the close of this old road). The marker is just west of the highway, on Whitney Portal Road and Movie Road. Free maps at the chamber of commerce pinpoint where many major films were made.

Whitney Portal goes on to the shoulder of the highest peak in the 48 contiguous states, Mt. Whitney, towering regally above at 14,495 feet. It was named for J.D. Whitney, head of the state geological survey that determined in 1864 that it was the highest peak yet discovered in the country. Seven years later, Clarence King became the first man to climb it. At least, he thought he did. He wrote a book about his adventure and accepted several accolades, but in 1873 the marker he left at the summit was discovered, instead, on nearby Mt. Langley. Apparently, confused by low-hanging clouds, King had climbed the wrong mountain. Since Langley was a good 400 feet lower than Whitney, not much glory was attached to the feat. Rushing back to put things right, King again made a dash at Whitney. This time he got it straight, but found that three other climbers had preceded him to the top by a month.

Owens Lake is another of the saline lakes that formed here when retreating glaciers left them lower than the level of their outlets. The area was once rich in borax mining and Cartago is what's left of a company town named for one of the mines. In the 1870s, steamships operated on the lake but evaporation and diversion has shrunk it to about half of its former size.

We pass another of the Los Angeles reservoirs, Haiwee, on the east. The road then veers east into the Indian Wells Valley, with the twin El Paso peaks to the west, south of Inyokern. This was one of the last gold areas discovered in California. It was called the Rand, after the district in South Africa which was very much on prospectors' minds in 1893. Johannesburg, California and its neighbor **Randsburg** both grew up along this strike. The Yellow Aster mine proved to be mostly tungsten, although gold was recovered as late as 1925. Many of the old homes and buildings have been restored and reoccupied in recent years and the Desert Museum in Randsburg contains some antique mining equipment. Red Mountain, just down the road, was a silver strike found in 1919 in a pit that had formerly been given up for lack of gold. This town of metal shacks is a good deal less atmospheric, however, than its neighbors up the hill.

At Kramer Junction, we reach a crossroads in the high desert of the Mojave. Empty lands stretch off to the east and the peaks of the San Bernardino Mountains, walling off the green fields of the eastern Los Angeles suburbs, rise in front of us. The road never makes it that far, though. It ends just short of Cajon Pass, where it is absorbed by Interstate 15 and the sprawl of the Los Angeles area comes out to meet us. New housing spreads back from the road near Adelanto (Spanish for "progress"), as developers build on the desert in an effort to provide affordable housing for the prohibitively expensive Los Angeles market. Watch for Palmdale Road here and follow it east. Just short of Interstate 15, you'll find the Roy Rogers-Dale Evans Museum. It contains memorabilia of the Western movie team, who live near the adjacent town of **Victorville**. It's a suitable make-believe ending to this journey through an authentic chunk of the old West.

VISITING HOURS

CALIFORNIA

Alturas: Modoc County Museum, (916) 233-2944. At 600 S. Main St. Monday–Friday, 9–4 and weekends, 10–4:30, May–October. Donation.

Bridgeport: Mono County Historical Museum, (619) 932-7911. In City Park. Daily, 10–4, May–September. Admission.

Devils Postpile National Monument: (619) 934-2289. West from U.S. 395, on California 203. Daylight hours, mid-June–October. Admission.

Independence: Commander's House, (619) 878-2411. Center, on U.S. 395. Sunday, 1–4, April–October.

Eastern California Museum (Manzanar Exhibit), (619) 878-2411. West of U.S. 395 on Center St. Thursday–Monday, noon–4; Saturday opening at 10. Donation.

Mammoth Mountain: Chair Lift, (619) 934-6611. West from U.S. 395 on California 203. Daily, 9–3:30, June–September. Fare.

Randsburg: Desert Museum, (619) 374-2111. At 161 Butte Ave. Weekends, 10–5. Admission.

Susanville: Roop's Fort, (916) 257-2757. West of U.S. 395, on California 36, at 110 N. Weatherlow St. Friday–Tuesday, 10–4, May–September. Free.

Victorville: Roy Rogers-Dale Evans Museum, (619) 243-4547. East from U.S. 395 on California 18; follow signs from Interstate 15. At 15650 Seneca. Daily, 9–5. Admission.

NEVADA

Carson City: Bowers Mansion, (702) 849-0644. North on U.S. 395. Daily, 11–1 and 1:30–4:30, mid-May–October. Admission.

Genoa: Museum, (702) 782-4325. West of U.S. 395 on Nevada 57, on Main St. Daily, 10–4:30, mid-May–mid-October. Donation.

Mormon Station, (702) 782-2590. West of U.S. 395, on Nevada 57. Daily, 9–5, May–mid-October. Donation.

Reno: Nevada Historical Society Museum, (702) 789-0190. On U.S. 395, at 1650 N. Virginia St. Monday–Saturday, 10–5. Free.

Mackay Mineral Museum, (702) 784-6987. On the University of Nevada campus, on N. Center St. Monday–Friday, 8–5. Free.

Harrah's Automobile Museum, (702) 333-9300. Center, at 10 Lake St. S. Daily, 9:30–6. Admission.

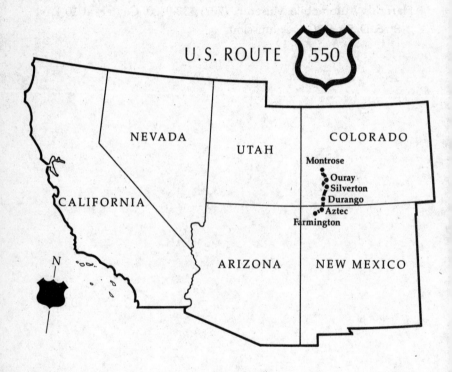

U.S. ROUTE 550

NEVADA

UTAH

COLORADO

Montrose
Ouray
Silverton
Durango
Aztec
Farmington

CALIFORNIA

N

ARIZONA

NEW MEXICO

Million Dollar Highway

◌

U.S. 550

Montrose, Colo. to Farmington, N.M.
158 miles

One of the shortest of the old roads, U.S. 550 is also definitely one of the most scenic. It is known as the Million Dollar Highway, one of the West's storied drives, through the rugged San Juan country of western Colorado.

On this route we'll see colorful old mining towns, incomparable Rockies scenery and some of New Mexico's most important prehistoric finds. So fasten your seat belt for the mountain curves ahead on this short but eventful ride.

MILEPOSTS

The road heads south from **Montrose**, getting its start at the junction with U.S. 50., then following the route of the Uncompahgre River through the hills. Uncompahgre is Ute and means...well, no one is really quite sure what it means. Read one source and it will state that the meaning is "red water canyon." But another will say, just as assuredly, that the word means "natural hot water springs." It seems "water" is in there someplace, but beyond that you can take your pick.

The Ute Indian Museum, just south of town, is dedicated to the great tribal leader, Ouray, whose last residence was a farm on these grounds. Understanding from the start that his band could not hope to stand up to the military force of the Americans, Ouray took a conciliatory position. He urged compromise, pacifism, and negotiation. Still, the tribe was slowly forced off the most desirable land by miners and settlers. The rich agricultural area around Montrose was once their homeland, but after 1881 they were pushed into the barren lands of southwestern Colorado and eastern Utah. At one time, in fact, Colorado tried to force the entire tribe into Utah, which was only a territory at the time and thus carried less influence in Washington. It was not one of the more glowing chapters in U.S. history.

Ouray's widow, Chipeta, lived here until 1924. Shortly before her death she broke a vow made to Ouray and revealed his burial place so he could be reinterred beside her at this place. The museum, the only one in Colorado dedicated to a single tribe, carries displays on Ute history. It also pays tribute to the two Spanish priests, Dominguez and Escalante, who came through here in 1776, looking for a short cut from Santa Fe to southern California. They were the first to map much of western Colorado and Utah (see U.S. 6).

The Uncompahgre is dammed just north of Ridgway, and a recreation area opened along the reservoir there in 1989. Watch for the turnoff to the overlook, near the visitor center, for a spectacular view across the lake to the jagged ridges of the San Juan. The Sneffels Range, to the south, has been used as a backdrop in several movies, including *How the West Was Won* and *True Grit*. These mountains, by the way, were named for the subterranean peak in Jules Verne's science fiction classic *Journey to the Center of the Earth*. Verne, himself, got the name from an Icelandic mountain, Snaefals.

Ridgway is the entrance to the San Juan Skyway, a National

Forest loop through these mountains, with U.S. 550 comprising the eastern leg. Between here and Durango, a distance of 83 miles, you will be in some of the most glorious mountain scenery on the planet, with every curve in the road presenting a picture postcard view.

Ouray, the first stop, may be the best of all. The entire town is a National Historic District, a piece of Victorian confection set down amid 14,000-foot-high peaks. The place grew up as a silver camp in 1875 and for the next 20 years enjoyed a fair rate of prosperity. The major mine in the area was called the Mineral Farm, because the metal was so near the surface that it could almost be harvested. A toll road from the south was built here by Otto Mears in 1883 (about which we will hear more shortly) and four years later Mears's railroad, the Denver and Rio Grande, arrived from the north.

By 1890, Ouray had a population of 2,000, but the collapse of silver in the Panic of 1893 seemed to prepare the town for the sort of fate that was so common in the mining boom-and-bust cycle. In 1896, however, Tom Walsh, who had taken a chance on a supposedly played-out mine, struck gold at the Camp Bird. His initial investment of $10,000 brought him back $24 million in the next six years, the greatest return of any mine in Colorado history. His daughter, Evalyn Walsh McLean, went on to become a Washington hostess, owner of the Hope diamond, and the author of a book succinctly titled, *Father Struck It Rich*. Most mining production shut down after 1911, and from that time on Ouray went into a decline so picturesque that it seems to have been purposely planned.

Walk along Main Street (which is U.S. 550) and Fourth Street, one block to the east. Every building is a delight. Private homes, hotels, an opera house, the Elks Lodge, churches—all of them look as if they'd been lifted from an old tintype and plopped down in this spectacular setting. There is a Museum, at 5th Street and 6th

Avenue, originally a hospital from 1887 to 1958, which contains a good collection of old photos and memorabilia, allowing you to trace Ouray's development.

At the north end of town is the hot springs and bath house, which is also on the National Historic Register. The 102-degree springs are a possible source of the Uncompahgre River's name.

Just north of town is the Bachelor Syracuse Mine, from which silver and gold have been taken continuously since 1884. A train runs 3,350 feet into a horizontal shaft drilled into Gold Hill and guides explain how metal was removed from the mine with some of the original equipment. There is also the chance to pan for gold on the premises.

The area is dotted with waterfalls. Cascade Falls, visible from most parts of town, is a short walk from the eastern end of Eighth Avenue. Box Canyon Falls drops 285 feet within a beautiful city park in the southwestern corner of town. The Amphitheater is a natural rock formation that towers to the east of Ouray and is popular for hiking and camping. There is a fine overlook back across the entire town from here.

Ouray is the beginning of the portion of U.S. 550 known as the Million Dollar Highway. This segment follows the path originally carved into sheer cliffs that was run as a toll road by Otto Mears. The road made Ouray's mines profitable by lowering transport costs. The Million Dollar Highway then follows a route between Ouray and **Silverton**. You'll see even more theories for the derivation of this name than you will for the Uncompahgre. One version says that the original road cost $1 million to build. Another, that the road was paved with tailings, or refuse from the area's mines, that contained $1 million in gold-bearing gravel. Apparently, though, the name originated in the 1920s when the road was widened for automobile travel. In one planning session, someone remarked that the cost of the project would turn it into a "million dollar highway," and the label stuck. Of course, these days that amount would barely cover the cost of running the bulldozers to build a mile of urban freeway. But when this road opened in 1924, people still respected numbers like $1 million.

The road passes Bear Creek Falls, with an observation point across the surrounding countryside, and then ascends Red Mountain Pass. The distinctive color comes from the iron pyrite that the rocks contain. The road makes the crossing at 11,008 feet and then drops down to Silverton.

Although the center of town, like Ouray, is a National Historic District, Silverton prides itself on being a working mining town. "The mining town that never quit," is its motto. It also sits about 1,500 feet higher in the San Juans than Ouray, at a breathtaking 9,305 feet. Silverton observes Hardrockers Holidays each August. No, it's not a music festival, but a competition that tests skills used in the mines, such as drilling and hand-mucking. Yukkh. The town's name indicates the metal of preference. According to one story, the boast of the first camp was that "We've got no gold, but there's silver by the ton." Between that first strike, in 1871, and 1918, about $65 million was taken from the mines here. The false-front structures on Blair Street still give visitors the sense of that earlier era, and vintage buildings, such as the San Juan County Courthouse and Grand Imperial Hotel, heighten the feeling that you're walking through a whole different era in the West. The San Juan County Museum, in the former jail, has excellent mining and railroad displays, as well as the original jail cells.

Silverton may be best known as the northern terminal of the Durango and Silverton narrow-gauge line, one of the West's great scenic rail tours. The run between here and Durango (see U.S. 160) parallels the highway, although staying closer to the Animas River, to the east. The railroad was built in 1882 to get the output of Silverton's mines to the outside and was the last regularly scheduled narrow gauge passenger train in the country. The Silverton depot is the original. In May, the Iron Horse Classic pits bikers against the train in one of the more unique racing events in the country.

San Juan County doesn't have a single farm within its borders. There's not enough level ground to support one—not an acre of tillable soil. It's all cliffs and crags and canyons, with Highway 550 running through the heart of it.

There are two different rivers in the state bearing the name Animas, which means "souls" in Spanish (see U.S. 160). In both cases, the name is the shortened form of "in memory of souls lost in Purgatory." The name Purgatory, meanwhile, became attached to geographical features nearby. In eastern Colorado, it was the Purgatoire River, which English usage transformed into the Picketwire. In this part of the state it is **Purgatory** Ski Resort, a name that has probably frightened off its share of novices over the years. Chair lifts operate to the top of the mountain during the summer for remarkable views across the surrounding area.

The highway passes Electra Lake, formed by a dam on the Animas, and named not for the character in Greek tragedy but for its function as a source of electric power.

The highway sticks close to the Animas as it passes through Durango (see U.S. 160) and enters the Southern Ute Reservation before crossing the line into New Mexico. The Animas is a wider river here, close to its junction with the San Juan, and the surrounding land more fertile than anything we've encountered since leaving Montrose at the start of this trip.

It was farmers in this area who first explored the pueblo that became **Aztec Ruins National Monument**. A local schoolteacher, wishing to instill a sense of curiousity about the world in his pupils, organized a Saturday dig here during the winter of 1883. The ruins had been known since 1777 when a Spanish explorer mapped them. Anglo settlers of the area automatically attributed them to the Aztecs. William Prescott's *Conquest of Mexico* was a 19th-century classic of popular history and almost every literate

American encountered the book's description of the great Aztec civilization at one point in their education. It was simply assumed that most ruins found in the West were the work of that people. But the Aztecs never came anywhere near this area. Moreover, these ruins are far older than anything the Aztecs built in Mexico City.

The first schoolboy exploring party found itself in an underground burial chamber, with a skeleton propped up in a corner. They alerted the entire town and soon it became a regular weekend pastime to burrow into the rooms and collect artifacts found there. Fortunately, when archeologists finally got around to making a systematic investigation of the ruins 33 years later, they realized that the locals had entered just a tiny portion of the buried complex. By 1923, the site was determined to be of such importance that it was declared a National Monument.

There were two separate communities that lived here about a century apart. The original group was related to other peoples found in northwestern New Mexico who were part of the Chaco Culture. Their residential complex, a quadrangle containing 500 rooms and careful construction of sandstone and timber, dates from the early 12th century. The Chaco builders only occupied this home for about 30 years before they left, possibly because of drought, and the site stood abandoned for the next century. Then another people, related to those who lived just to the northwest at Mesa Verde, moved in on the empty structures and restored them. But by 1250 A.D. they, too, had gone, and 600 years would pass before anyone entered the site again.

The most important segment of these ruins is the Great Kiva, 48 feet in diameter and, at some points, eight feet underground. This is not the largest kiva ever uncovered, but it was fully restored in the 1930s and gives the most complete picture available of what one of these religious chambers looked like at the time of their use. A self-guiding walk circles most of the major sites and a visitors' center displays some of the artifacts found here.

In the town of **Aztec** itself, the local museum on Main Street contains more exhibits of Indian antiquities, some of them possibly originating at the Aztec Ruins. The greater part of this museum's displays, however, concern pioneer life and the oil and natural gas industry that now dominates the economy of this part of the state.

From here, the road speeds as a four-lane highway into Farmington, the commercial center of northwestern New Mexico and the nursery of the region's fruit industry.

The highway ends here, in the fruit belt, at its junction with U.S. 64, after its brief but beautiful journey.

VISITING HOURS

COLORADO

Montrose: Ute Indian Museum, (303) 249-3098. South, on U.S. 500. Monday–Saturday, 10–5 and Sunday, 1–5, mid-May–mid October. Admission.

Ouray: Museum, (303) 325-4576. On 6th Ave. Monday–Saturday, 9–5 and Sunday, 1–5. Admission.

Bachelor Syracuse Mine, (303) 325-4500. North of town on U.S. 500 and east on a county road. Daily, 9–5, mid-May–mid-September. Admission.

Purgatory: Ski Lift, (303) 247-9000. On U.S. 500. Daily, 10–5, June–Labor Day. Fare.

Silverton: Durango and Silverton Narrow Gauge Railroad, (303) 247-2733. Depot, at 479 Main. Daily, 6 A.M.–9 P.M., early May–late August; 7–7, to mid-October; 7–5:30, through October; 8–5 at other times. Call for reservations. Fare.

San Juan County Museum, (303) 387-5838. In the former jail, on Green St. Daily, 9–5, Memorial Day–September; 10–3, first two weeks in October. Admission.

NEW MEXICO

Aztec: Museum, (505) 334-9829. At 125 N. Main St.
Monday–Saturday, 9–5, June–September; 10–4 at other times.
Aztec Ruins National Monument: (505) 334-6174. North of Aztec on
U.S. 550. Daily, 8–5. Admission.

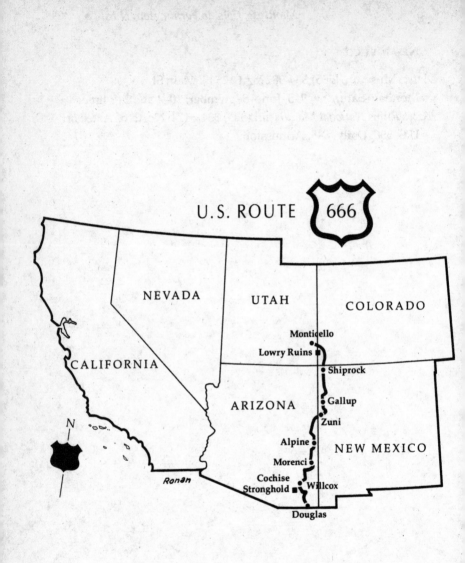

U.S. ROUTE 666

NEVADA

UTAH

COLORADO

CALIFORNIA

ARIZONA

Monticello
Lowry Ruins

Shiprock

Gallup

Zuni

Alpine

NEW MEXICO

Morenci

Cochise
Stronghold   Willcox

Ronan

Douglas

N

Coronado Trail

$\bigcirc$

U.S. 666

Monticello, Utah to Douglas, Ariz.
596 miles

This is another old road that we can track start to finish within the territory covered by this book. It makes brief visits to Utah and extreme southwestern Colorado before cutting through the heart of New Mexico's Navajo and Zuni country. After veering west into Arizona it becomes a spectacular mountain highway known as the Coronado Trail, retracing the route of the first European explorer to lift the veil of the Southwest.

The highway got its number because it flits in and out with old Route 66, covering areas just off that main road. Some time ago, when I appeared on a radio talk show while publicizing the first volume of *Where the Old Roads Go*, a listener demanded to know why this highway had been given the numerical symbol for the Devil, as expressed in the *Book of Revelations*. Well, this may not be the Devil's Road, but it makes a hell of a trip.

MILEPOSTS

The starting point of the journey is named for Thomas Jefferson's estate, but the landscape around Monticello, Utah looks nothing like Virginia. At the base of the Blue Mountains, with 11,345-foot Abajo Peak in the rear view mirror, we head east into the purple sage country and cross the border into Colorado after just 17 miles.

Zane Grey lived near the town of Dove Creek for a time and after his *Riders of the Purple Sage* became one of the first best-selling Western novels in 1912, folks around these parts were quick to identify themselves in the book. Grey traveled through much of the Southwest, however and his settings were by and large composites of many areas. The sage is undeniably purple here, though, and if you want to call this the setting for the famous novel, it's as good a choice as any.

The road bends south to run along the western edge of San Juan National Forest. At the aptly named **Pleasant View**, there is a dirt turnoff to the west, which leads to the Lowry ruins after a nine-mile trip. This was an outlying portion of the same community whose ancient structures are part of Hovenweep National Monument. Lowry, however, is more accessible. Hovenweep means "deserted canyon" in the Ute language—a fair description. The Lowry area, apparently, had religious significance to the people who lived here in the 11th century. There are ten kivas, the circular and partially subterannean ceremonial shelters that were an important part of the Pueblo culture. The largest at Lowry is the best-preserved painted kiva found in the area.

Back on Highway 666, the road passes through Yellow Jacket, named for the number of hornets' nests found in a nearby canyon. At Cortez, it joins with U.S. 160. (The stretch between here and Chimney Rock, in the Ute Tribal Mountain Park, is described in that chapter.)

The road crosses the Mancos River and immediately afterwards passes into its third state within 100 miles—New Mexico, and the Navajo Reservation. This highway is the north-south axis of that portion of the 25,000-square-mile reservation, largest in the country, lying in this state. The Navajo lands also extend across the border into Arizona, where U.S. 191 parallels the course of this road.

Shiprock is the largest town and administrative center for the New Mexico area. There is a visitors' center, which offers information about the surrounding tribal lands, in town.

These are lands that have grown rich on mineral reserves. The Four Corners Power Plant is just east of Shiprock on Navajo land, and so is Navajo Mine, the largest open-pit coal operation in the West. But the rock formation that gives the town its name is from an earlier age. Shiprock rises about 1,500 feet above the valley floor to the southwest. Oddly enough, the Navajo word for it means "winged rock," and with its outcroppings it certainly looks more like a fantastic bird out of a legend than it does a ship. One Indian story tells of the rock sprouting wings and carrying Navajos to safety from a hostile party of Utes. There is some conjecture that early settlers referred to it as "Sheep Rock," then, as the Navajo legends spread, the name somehow came to be "Ship." The formation is sacred and off limits to climbers.

The road heads south into mesa land, with the Chuska Mountains angling ever closer from the west. Newcomb was named for the operator of a trading post that opened here in 1914. Tohatchi, at the base of haunting Chuska Peak, has been a medical and educational center for the reservation since 1895, when a boarding school and hospital were established here. The 8,795-foot Chuska ("white spruce") Peak is another place of veneration for the Navajo.

The road leaves the reservation boundary and runs past the mining town of Gamerco, built in 1921 and named for the Gallup American Coal Company. The coal deposits in the area were first uncovered by the Santa Fe Railroad construction crews as they came through the area in 1879. Mining activity gave **Gallup**, the larger town to the north, a more ethnically diverse population than most Western communities of its size, though it is the Native

American population that flavors its life. Gallup is the major trading center for the adjacent Navajo and Zuni reservations and the Inter-Tribal Indian Ceremonial held here is the best-attended festival of its kind in North America. Started by local businessmen in 1922 as a tourism booster, the ceremonial now draws more than 50 tribes from the United States and Canada each August for an annual celebration of native cultures. There are dances, rodeos, crafts shows, and parades. If you can't make it for that, though, you can still visit Red Rock State Park, where the ceremonial is held. It is eight miles east of town along Interstate 40 (the old route of U.S. 66). Red Rock Museum has permanent exhibits of Southwestern Indian artwork and a gift shop featuring the crafts of Navajo, Zuni, and Hopi artisans. The setting in itself, surrounded by red sandstone bluffs, is worth the side trip.

One of the offbeat stories of World War II is also commemorated in Gallup; the achievements of the Navajo Code Talkers. Phillip Johnston, who grew up on the reservation as a missionary's son, devised the idea of having Navajos make up a radio-transmitted spoken code for the U.S. Marines based on the tribe's unwritten language. Since much of it depended on vocal inflection, Johnston was convinced it would defeat any efforts to decipher it. He was right. At the peak of its use, 400 Navajo were enlisted as Code Talkers and Marine officers said it was invaluable for securely relaying advance plans for the battle of Iwo Jima. A special room in the Gallup-McKinley County Chamber of Commerce Building is set aside to salute the Code Talkers.

At Gallup, Highway 666 runs west with the interstate into Arizona before branching south again. A far more interesting way to get to the same place is to continue south from Gallup on New Mexico 602, into the Zuni Reservation. Then head west on Highways 604 and 53 to **Zuni**, the largest inhabited pueblo in New Mexico and the source of one of American history's most destructive legends.

FOCUS

You have to look a little to find the old church. It is south of the main highway, into the Zuni pueblo. Take one of the narrow streets near the center of the town and wind along with it until you come to the plaza. At its western end is the Mission Nuestra Senorita de Guadalupe.

The historical roots of this mission go back to 1629, when Franciscan priests were sent out from Santa Fe to spread the faith through the pueblos of the West. The mission was known then as Halona. But before that it was called Cibola, and to the Spanish who first came into this land it was mistakenly believed to be the treasure house of the Seven Cities of Gold.

The legend had its start in the 16th century. A party of Spanish seamen, shipwrecked on the Texas Gulf coast, had arduously made their way across the broad plains of northern Mexico and what would later become the state of Texas to reach the Spanish settlements. They encountered several Apache bands on the way who told them of fabulous treasure cities to the north. *Cibola*, they were called.

When the colonial authorities in Mexico City heard the report, they quickly organized an expedition to find them. A priest, Fr. Marcos de Niza, was placed in charge of a preliminary scouting party that left in 1539. Sent to assist him was Estavenico, a black sailor who had been part of the original band of castaways. When Niza stopped to celebrate Easter Mass, Estavenico forged ahead, the first person who was not a Native American to enter the American Southwest. Ignoring Niza's instructions to wait for him, Estavenico arrived in what is now New Mexico at the Zuni pueblo of Hawikiuh. What happened afterwards was never fully explained. Estavenico, apparently, tried to bluff his way into the confidence of the village leaders; he failed, and was put to death. Niza arrived a few days later and when he heard what had happened decided not to press his luck. Instead, he turned back to Mexico with wildly exaggerated reports of the riches he had almost found.

Mexico City was in a frenzy of excitement. The great expedition of Francisco Vasquez de Coronado, one of the epic journeys of discovery in world history, was sent out to claim Cibola. Historians differ on Coronado's exact route but most feel that he entered what is now Arizona through the Huachuca Mountains and came north along the route followed by U.S. 666. He defeated the Zuni in a pitched battle at Hawikiuh and then proceeded to Halona to claim the treasure. There was none. While his soldiers cursed the name of Fr. Niza, they found nothing but an Indian village, already hundreds of years old, upon their arrival. Coronado pushed on, full of hope, for another two years, getting all the way into southwestern Kansas before returning to Mexico empty-handed.

A Spanish presence was established here, eventually, and the original mission built in 1629. Three years later, however, the priest at the time was killed by villagers irate over the religion being imposed on them. The Zuni, fearing reprisals, fled to a mesa-top stronghold. They eventually returned, but the mission was destroyed during the Pueblo Rebellion of 1680, which drove the Spanish out of New Mexico for 12 years. Upon their second return, the Zuni took up residence in the present pueblo and construction of a new mission began in 1699.

That is essentially the building that stands here today. After the American takeover of New Mexico, the church was abandoned and began falling into ruin. The Franciscans built a new church, north of the main road, in 1922. But in 1966, excavation and restoration of the old mission began and six years later it was rededicated as a church.

That's when Alex Seowtewa entered the picture. He was a bus driver for the church school, but came from a family with an artistic background. His father had painted murals for the new church. According to tradition, there also had been murals along the walls of the old mission, and Seowtewa received permission to return them to their place. Using images drawn from both Christianity and Zuni beliefs, Seowtewa set about to illustrate the cycle of the seasons and the accompanying religious rites. Assisted by his son, Kenneth, he received a grant from the National Endowment of the Arts in 1989. One of them is always on hand at the church to explain the symbolism in the murals and demonstrate the techniques of their work.

The key figures in the murals, and in the tribal system of religion are the *kachinas*: supernatural beings given form by men of the pueblo at annual rites. Many of the posts are hereditary and performed by the same clan for generations. The rites correspond to the needs of the season, from rain to crops to game. The most important is the Shalako Dance of late fall, when supplication is made for the well-being of the pueblo. In 1990, however, the Tribal Council voted to bar all outsiders from these rites because of violations of rules forbidding photography or recording. The ban is described as temporary, but it is best to check with the Council at the telephone number at the end of this chapter.

The Zuni are celebrated for their skill in crafting turquoise and silver jewelry. Several stores on the main road offer good buys in this, along with kachina dolls. But the greatest treasure in Zuni, surpassing even the legendary prize of Cibola, is taking form along the walls of the old church.

* * *

The ruins of Hawikiuh, where Estavenico met his fate and Coronado vanquished the Zuni, are 9 miles southwest of the pueblo by a dirt road. If you want to push directly on, however, leave town heading west on New Mexico 53. This turns into

Arizona 61 across the state line, and 26 miles from Zuni, it reunites with U.S. 666.

The highway heads south through the empty mesa lands of Apache County and crosses the Little Colorado River at St. Johns. Between here and Alpine, a stretch of 57 miles, it combines with U.S. 180 (see that chapter for a description of that road).

The Coronado Trail climbs to its most scenic heights after U.S. 666 resumes its solo run and crosses into Greenlee County. It winds through Apache-Sitgreaves National Forest, and along the way passes the Hannagan Meadow recreation area, which is covered with blue gentians during the summer months. At the K.P. Cienega area the road reaches the crest of the Mogollon Rim at 9,200 feet, and then descends towards Stray Horse Canyon. Then it climbs once more, up 8,550-foot Rose Peak. A lookout tower stands at the crest. This is an especially steep and winding road and U.S. Forest Service officials do not recommend it for trailers. Even with a standard car, it's best to drive slowly, taking in the spectacular scenery at an unhurried pace.

Like many other Arizona copper towns, **Morenci** balances precariously on a steep hillside. Until 1912, the streets were so narrow and precipitous that no wheeled vehicles could negotiate them and all deliveries were handled by burros. Burro Alley is still the name of the street that climbs to the highest point in town, Longfellow Hill. The Phelps-Dodge open pit mine is just outside of town and an overlook enables you to peer into its maw.

Clifton lies at the foot of the hill, after a 1,300-foot descent from Morenci. This was the commercial center for the mines in this district, and where there were miners there was usually trouble. So in 1881 Clifton built a handsome new jail, blasted right out of the face of the adjoining cliff. It was such a difficult job that the jail's first occupant was its builder, who celebrated its completion by getting drunk and disorderly.

The road runs west with U.S. 70 (see that chapter for a description), through a row of farm towns, made prosperous by the irrigation projects along the Gila River. At Safford it turns sharply south. Mt. Graham looms on the western horizon and if you haven't already had your fill of mountain driving, the Swift Trail branches off on a 35-mile run to its 10,717-foot summit. The climb takes you through five ecological zones and the view from the top extends all the way to Mexico, both New and old. This is part of Coronado National Forest and several recreation areas lie along the route.

Back on Highway 666, you can make out the outline of Dos Cabezas Mountain, straight ahead. This peak, with twin rock outcroppings that resemble two heads, was a landmark on the old military road through Apache Pass, which ran on its far side. This was one of the most dangerous passages in the West and in the 1860s, when Cochise was raiding this area, stagecoach drivers had to be given triple pay to make the trip. Even 11 companies of Union troops, heading east to New Mexico to counter the Confederate advance in 1862, were not safe from attack here. They managed to fight their way out of the Pass only by opening fire with howitzers. The Southern Pacific Railroad finally opened a new route across the much wider and safer Dragoon Pass in 1879, relegating the perils of Apache Pass to the history books.

The highway turns west along the rail route, now occupied by Interstate 10. **Willcox** was a town created by the rails, becoming the major cattle shipping point for this part of the Southwest. Its economy is still dominated by the vast ranches that surround it. There is a fine little museum, the Cochise Visitor Center, at the Interstate exit to the town, outlining the history of the region and the struggle between the settlers and the Apaches defending these lands. Go into town for a look at Railroad Avenue, an especially well-preserved block of 19th-century commercial structures facing the tracks from across a park.

Among the old buildings is the Rex Allen Arizona Cowboy

Museum. Allen, one of the top movie cowboy stars of the 1940s, was raised in Willcox. His career memorabilia and collection of Western material is housed in the former Schwertner Saloon and the adjacent Willcox Theatre, where his hometown friends went to see his movies. The depot at the end of the block is the original. Built in 1881, it is the oldest remaining station on the Southern Pacific line.

U.S. 666 turns south from the Interstate 9 miles west of Willcox. But push on for another 13 miles instead and get off at the **Dragoon** exit. This town and the nearby mountains were given the original name for U.S. mounted troops, before the term "cavalry" was adopted in the 1860s.

Follow the signs to the Amerind Foundation. This outstanding museum of Indian archeology and ethnic studies is situated in Texas Canyon, where William S. Fulton came in the 1930s to explore the remains of a prehistoric village. Fulton was dedicated to working out an understanding of contemporary Indian cultures by excavating the ruins of their predecessors and interpreting his findings. He roamed Arizona in territorial days and came to Texas Canyon to live when he saw its archeological possibilities. The foundation and museum were established in 1937, then expanded in 1959 to house the impressive collection of materials. The scope of the foundation has widened to take in all of North America's native cultures. It also includes works by 19th-century artists who observed and recorded the rites and appearance of Indians of that time.

Continue east from the Interstate exit along this road. Mt Glenn, the highest point in the Dragoons at 7,512 feet, is to the south. You'll pass through Dragoon, an old copper town, and after a 14-mile drive, rejoin U.S. 666. The highway runs down the length of Sulphur Springs Valley, a rich agricultural and ranching area. Once it was the favored hunting grounds of the Apache; then, when white settlement threatened it, the favored raiding grounds of Cochise and Geronimo.

A turnoff to the west leads to the Cochise Stronghold in the Coronado National Forest. Here lies the burial place of that famous warrior, considered the most gifted of all the Apache leaders in the years of warfare with the United States. "All men of prominence who met him and had dealings with him testify to a certain poise and dignity of character that marked his behavior," wrote historian Frank C. Lockwood about Cochise. "It is sufficient evidence of his superior intelligence and great force of character that for ten years he coped with the best brains and the strongest wills that the United States Government could array against him."

Recognizing the overpowering force that could be brought to bear against him, Cochise first advocated a policy of non-interference with traffic across the Overland Trail. But early in 1861 he was falsely accused of leading a raid on a white settlement and kidnaping a young boy. Detained under a flag of truce, he escaped by slashing a hole through a tent. When six members of his band were executed in retaliation, he declared open war. Within 60 days, about 150 men were killed on the Overland Trail and Cochise had, in effect, closed it and isolated the Tucson settlement. For the next decade, this corner of southeastern Arizona was the most perilous piece of property in the West. Cochise defeated or eluded every force sent against him (although for a good part of the period the government was somewhat distracted by the Civil War). Military careers were shattered in this unsuccesful campaign. Finally, the Grant Administration sent out veteran General O.O. Howard with instructions to conclude a peace treaty.

Howard was the former head of the Freedmens Bureau, the agency responsible for liberated black slaves, and it was for him that Howard University in Washington, D.C. was named. He brought the same missionary zeal to the Southwest, but also exhibited a practical side by turning to Tom Jeffords for assistance. Jeffords ran a stage line that somehow managed to avoid attacks from Cochise. Some say the Apache leader trusted him as an honest man; others claim he was supplying weapons to the Indians. Tiring of the endless war, Cochise agreed to the terms relayed by Jeffords, trusting Howard on his say-so, and in 1872 he made his peace. Two years later he died and Jeffords arranged for his burial in a canyon deep in the Dragoons. After the interment, Cochise's warriors rode their horses back and forth across the site to obscure all evidence of the location. Jeffords was reportedly the only white man who knew the secret but he never revealed it. The vicinity is now part of a National Forest recreation area, with trails and a picnic area, accessible by gravel road.

Back on the main highway, you'll pass through Sunsites, a modern retirement community, and just beyond that is Pearce. About $30 million was taken from this gold camp between 1894 and 1904. The Commonwealth Mine lured many prospectors from the played out mines of Tombstone (see U.S. 80) and they brought with them some of their unruly habits. Pearce was headquarters of the notorious Alvord-Stiles Gang, a group that was especially difficult to apprehend because Alvord was the constable of Willcox and Stiles held the same job in Pearce. These bad apples twice escaped from the Tombstone jail. Stiles was eventually gunned down in Nevada in 1908 and Alvord simply disappeared.

The rest of the highway's run is a rush through the scattered farm towns of Sulphur Springs Valley, and into the old copper smelting community of Douglas, on the Mexican border.

VISITING HOURS

COLORADO

Pleasant View: Lowry Ruins, (303) 882-4811. West on County Road. Daily, 8–6. Free.

NEW MEXICO

Gallup: Red Rock Museum, (505) 722-3839. East on Interstate 40 and New Mexico 566. Daily 8 A.M.–9 P.M., Memorial Day–Labor Day; Monday–Friday, 8–4:30 at other times. Donation.

Navajo Code Talkers Museum, (505) 722-2228. In Gallup-McKinley County Chamber of Commerce, 103 W. 66th Ave. Monday–Friday, business hours. Free.

Zuni: Mission Church, no phone. South of New Mexico 53, in center of pueblo. Monday–Friday, 8–noon and 1–4:30. Donation. For information on ceremonial regulations call (505) 782-5581.

ARIZONA

Dragoon: Amerind Foundation, (602) 586-3666. West of U.S. 666, on Interstate 10, at Dragoon exit. Daily, 10–4, September–May. Admission.

Morenci: Phelps-Dodge Copper Mine, (602) 865-4521. On U.S. 666. Monday–Friday. Call for tour schedule. Free.

Willcox: Cochise County Visitor Center, (602) 384-2272. On U.S. 666, at Willcox exit. Monday–Saturday, 9–5 and Sunday, 1–5. Free.

Rex Allen Museum, (602) 384-4583. Center, on Railroad Ave. Daily, 10–4. Admission.

Index